AN EXODUS FROM TURKEY

To our Perin:
'Spread your wings and let the winds of freedom
carry you to new heights'

AN EXODUS FROM TURKEY

Tales of Migration and Exile

**Ahmet Erdi Öztürk and
Bahar Baser**

EDINBURGH
University Press

Edinburgh University Press is one of the leading university presses in the UK. We publish academic books and journals in our selected subject areas across the humanities and social sciences, combining cutting-edge scholarship with high editorial and production values to produce academic works of lasting importance. For more information visit our website: edinburghuniversitypress.com

Edinburgh University Press Ltd
The Tun – Holyrood Road
12 (2f) Jackson's Entry
Edinburgh EH8 8PJ

Typeset in 11/15 EB Garamond by
IDSUK (DataConnection) Ltd, and
printed and bound in Great Britain

A CIP record for this book is available from the British Library

ISBN 978 1 3995 1965 6 (hardback)
ISBN 978 1 3995 1966 3 (paperback)
ISBN 978 1 3995 1967 0 (webready PDF)
ISBN 978 1 3995 1968 7 (epub)

CONTENTS

FOREWORD

DIASPORA OR EXILE? TURKISH INTELLECTUALS IN TERRITORIAL CONTINUITY

SAMİM AKGÖNÜL

One of the interviewees of this book told me once that this group of exiled intellectuals, especially after 2016, was becoming the new 'Young Turks' against the oppressive regime. I hope the new Young Turks won't imitate the old ones when/if they return to Turkey.

First things first: let's start with some conceptual discussion. Several scholars think that the term 'diaspora' does not suit to explain the Turkish case because according to the classic definition, a diaspora needs a traumatic event as the starting point of the dispersal, mythicised and transmitted as a legendary moment.[1] Indeed, Turks living abroad do not have singular but plural traumatic *momenta*, often in contradiction. Those who settled in Germany in the 1960s did not follow the same push and pull factors than those who settled in the 1990s in Sweden. The wave of migration due to the political refugee movement of Kurds is not the same trauma as the leftists of the 1980s who found asylum in France. But this plurality is more related to the moment than *momentum*. In other words, whether people leave Turkey for economic, political or familial reasons, they still *leave* it.

---

[1] See for example Safran (1991); Cohen (1997). Apart from the traumatic dispersal, both of them require a collective commitment to the homeland's prosperity in order to qualify a group of minorities as 'diaspora'.

Yet, to become a diaspora, one needs time. Diaspora transmits its wounded collective memory to generations born, raised, educated, socialised *in* diaspora and therefore who never *left* physically the mythical homeland. Thus, if there are without any doubt several diasporas from Turkey settled everywhere in the world such as Armenian, Kurdish, Alevi, Sunni or leftist diasporas, it's still difficult to assert that there is an 'intellectual diaspora' for several reasons.

Above all, the other diasporas related to Turkey managed somehow to build a 'local life', if I may say, in diasporic host lands. These host lands are not hosting them anymore, they are permanent, even if sometimes – not always – this immutability has cost the construction of a 'territorial continuity'. This concept, developed by Emmanuel Ma Mung for the Chinese diaspora (Mung 2004), is particularly (but partially) operational for diasporas from Turkey except maybe for the last one analysed in this book. Several interviewees, such as Engin Sustam or Eser Karakaş, declare that they don't belong to diaspora and they don't live in the 'territorial continuity'. It's true on the other hand that if these intellectuals form a 'new diaspora' as Yavuz Baydar states, they have not yet been able to cut the umbilical ties with what happens in Turkey. Maybe when generations are born from this particular type of exile, who will cultivate cautiously their 'difference' from other diasporas, we will be able to see a specific diaspora which structures a specific dynamism based on a togetherness of ancestors: they had to leave Turkey because they were intellectuals, and the regime, like all authoritarian regimes, was by definition anti-knowledge, anti-neurons, anti-freedom: 'War is peace. Freedom is slavery. Ignorance is strength.' Isn't it?

The second concept that this book interrogates wisely is *exile*. What does it mean exactly? Are these people in exile? Here too, we can perhaps recall another notion very present in Turkey, difficult to translate: *gurbet*.[2] This word is derived from *garib* ('poor', 'pitiful'

---

[2] Often, and wrongly in my opinion, translated as, precisely, 'exile'; see Schiffauer (2008).

but also 'weird') in Turkish, itself derived from the Arabic root *g-r-b*, which gives the infinitive of the verb *garaba* ('to move away'), including strongly the idea of bitterness, frustration. Tears also? Maybe. *Gurbet* is – and again, without cheap culturalism – an oriental concept filling poetry, music, films, words and gesture. It is a hopeless, dark situation where *Sıla*, the missed territory, is unreachable. *Gurbet* is being old and looking back while realising that the past has passed.[3] This bitterness is palpable in all interviews but almost never assumed precisely because it's associated in the Turkish culture with an oriental posture and these 'new' intellectuals in 'exile' are everything but 'oriental'. Thus, I understand what Barbaros Şansal means when he states 'No. I have never, at any point in my life, felt like I was in exile'; or Bülent Somay, who says 'I don't consider my own situation exile'; or Can Dündar's caution when he qualifies his situation: 'This is exile; I would have to call it that'; or when Nil Mutluer affirms that she felt herself in exile in Turkey too. I would dare an explanation: these intellectuals do not consider themselves in exile or they nuance their personal situation because being in exile is losing the struggle. Never-theless, many of the interviewees of this book are my friends or at least acquaintances (I will come to my personal situation at the end of this short foreword) and when I talk to them personally – not when I read their scientific papers, their newspaper op-eds or their tweets; no, when I talk to them eye to eye – I hear the discomfort of the exile, the fear of the future, the disenchantment of the struggles. I feel, if I may say so, the bitterness of the *gurbet*.

The last concept that intrigued me while reading these interviews is that of the 'intellectual'. Who is an intellectual in the Turkish context and how does one become an intellectual? And, a naturally subsidiary question, am I one? The path from the classical Ottoman *âlim*, the savant who is a philosopher and theologian (*âlim* is the singular of *ulema*) such as Molla Hüsrev (15th century) or Ebusuud Mehmed

---

[3] Anika Liversage and Gretty Mizrahi Mirdal (2017) captured this double absence of age and exile very well.

(16th century) (Zilfi 1983), to a nineteenth-century *münevver* like Ahmet Cevdet Pacha (1822–95) (Chambers 1973) or an erudite like Osman Hamdi Bey (1842–1910) (Eldem 2012), and from that point to the *aydın* of the twentieth century is tortuous and full of pitfalls. An Ottoman *âlim* is, by definition, religious; a Turkish *aydın* is, by definition, the opposite. An Ottoman *münevver*[4] is a specialist in an art or science, a Turkish *aydın* is a secular intellectual having a comprehensive idea of the world. He/she is necessarily an opponent to the regime and he/she is concerned by all kinds of injustices all over the world.

When I look at these twenty interviews, I can't help but think that in the Turkish context, there is an interdependence between academics and journalists as the main figures of the Turkish oppressed intellectual class. This is, I think, a particularity of the Turkish context because these two professions (should) belong to two different worlds. Academia is specialist and slow, journalism is generalist and fast. Academia is, so to say, somehow private and confidential, journalism is public and open. But in the Turkish case, the means of 'intellectual' oppositions are so limited, and the means of expression are so tightly controlled by the regime, that academics feel the need to act like journalists in order to be heard, and journalists feel the need to teach and research in order to be legitimised. This statement, sad in itself, is unfortunately accurate for me too. Therefore, in a regime hating intellectuals, despising those who think, read, research, write, talk, inform, question, it's regrettably normal to see academics and journalists at the centre of the target. Of course, there are some 'aggravating factors'. If you are a member of a minority such as Hasip Kaplan

---

[4] From the same etymology, by the way, from the Arabic root *n-v-r*, as *munawwar*, 'being illuminated'. This is the exact translation of the French *illuminé* in Ottoman and then in Turkish. But in twenty-first-century French an *illuminé* is a lunatic! Turkish intellectuals don't see themselves as lunatics. On the contrary, they have a very high opinion of themselves.

(Kurdish) or Hayko Bağdat (Armenian) or of an activist movement such as Barbaros Şansal (LGBT) or Jinda Zekioğlu (feminism), you are doubly, triply oppressed! Marx calls this a 'combination of handicaps' (cf. Paugam 1996). These intellectuals in exile cannot be categorised in one single struggle. We are definitely in the area of what French sociology has called, since 1968, *convergence des luttes*, 'convergence among social struggles' (Carrier and Ebermeyer 2014). This is the price to pay to be an opponent and intellectual in the Turkish context: to fight not only for his/her group but also, and maybe more, for other injustices. And this is the most frightening for the regime. An Armenian fighting for the equal rights for Armenians of Turkey is a traditional enemy. But an Armenian fighting for Kurds, for LGBT people, for ecology . . . is an unknown territory. Hrant Dink knew (Simet 2012). A leftist Turk struggling for union rights is usual. But a leftist woman struggling for transvestite prostitutes, for street children, for Kurdish women is more dangerous than anything. Pınar Selek knew (Selek 2010). A prize-winning physicist working for CERN is a cause for national pride, but a writer for *Özgür Gündem* and of social novels is not acceptable. Aslı Erdoğan knew (Erdoğan 2017), like many, many others. I think here we touch on the specificity of this new group on the way to becoming a diaspora of academics and journalists, political activists and intellectuals: unlike the previous exiled people, they fight on several fronts and sometimes not on their own fronts.

These twenty-one wounded but proud intellectual people are interviewed by two scholars, Bahar Başer[5] and Ahmet Erdi Öztürk. Are they themselves exiled academics? Bahar is one of the signatories of the Academics for Peace text, like many others among their peers (and like myself) who suffered from the oppression of the regime (Baser et al. 2017), and Erdi works on very sensitive topics such as the Diyanet or Turkish policy in the Balkans. They are not exiled *per se* but, they are definitely in *gurbet* in York, in this rainy town of Great Britain. I

---

[5] I know Bahar prefers 'Baser' to 'Başer' but I don't.

have been familiar with their works for many years but, I must confess, I was surprised by their capacity as interviewers. It is not an easy task to ask very sensitive and sometimes private questions of these very well-educated scholars and journalists. Obviously, they managed to earn their trust because in these lines, apart from political commitments, I read love, family, children but also fears and angers. This *tour de force* requires not only knowledge and know-how but also a talent, and, let's dare to say, psychological tact. Being able to interview a Kurdish activist such as Faysal Sarıyıldız and a former Gülen Movement sympathiser and scholar (I chose my words very very carefully) such as Gökhan Bacık is not a piece of cake because interviewees are also tempted to return questions! But, fortunately for Bahar and Erdi, they seem hungry to talk, to express their experiences, their anger, and they sound very sincere. I think this book will last.

While reading these interviews and Bahar and Erdi's comprehensive introduction, I couldn't stop myself thinking of . . . myself. Am I an intellectual and am I in exile? Besides the fact that I have lived in France for more than thirty years, I have also found myself in tricky positions vis-à-vis Turkey by, for example, signing the famous 'I apologise' letter from Armenians[6] in 2008. Two of the four initiators of this campaign, Ahmet İnsel and Cengiz Aktar, are also in exile, while Baskın Oran and Ali Bayramoğlu could remain in Turkey despite constant pressures. As I mentioned above, I was also one of the Academics for Peace in January 2016 and I preferred to remain far from Turkey during the two years of the trial. Finally, before the attempted coup d'état in July 2016, I wrote some op-eds for *Today's Zaman* newspaper on minority rights, and I must say, no one intervened in my articles including when I criticised harshly the Gülen Movement. I am not a Gülen sympathiser, but I think that the revenge of the state is beyond acceptable towards Gülen sympathisers or people accused

---

[6] https://web.archive.org/web/20160304054234/http://ozurdiliyoruz.com/, accessed 3 April 2023.

of being such. I am not a Kurd but I think what happened in 2015 in Cizre, Sur or Nusaybin was beyond acceptable towards Kurds. I am not Armenian, but I think recognition of the genocide is a compulsory first step to reconciliation. I am not Greek, Jewish or Syrian, but I think that minorities have been treated unacceptably since the beginning of the republic until today. However, sometimes I find myself a real coward. Did I erase what I started to write on Twitter? Yes. Did I remove my op-eds in *Today's Zaman* from my personal website? Yes. Am I afraid sometimes for my family in Turkey? Yes. Does my heart beat quickly each time I find myself at the passport desk in Turkey? Yes. So, I am in exile. And if reading, writing and teaching is being intellectual, I am certainly one. Contrariwise, I can only imagine what is the insecure and precarious life of a *real* intellectual, really *in exile* like those who are interviewed in this book and so many others all around the world.

Let me finish with a prophecy. I think the intellectuals who have opened their minds and hearts in this book, and those who are not interviewed that I did or did not mention in this foreword, will not form a diaspora. They won't have time. Their eyes, for most of them, are oriented towards Turkey. And I know very soon, the oppressive regime of the country will implode by itself, to leave its place to a democratic regime under the watchful eye of Turkish public opinion who experienced the worst, too experienced to leave the scene to another undemocratic regime. Then, not all maybe, but many of these academics, journalists, political activists, artists, human and minority rights defenders will find the pleasant and unpleasant smells and nice and deafening noises of the streets of Turkey.

INTRODUCTION
DEMOCRATIC BACKSLIDING AND THE NEW WAVES OF MIGRATION FROM TURKEY

The Exodus

There is an exodus from Turkey. Turkish citizens from different ethnic and religious backgrounds and ideological groups and classes do not think that they can continue their lives in Turkey under the current regime and consequently are leaving, either temporarily or permanently. Some media outlets have reported that 'Turks leave in droves' (Gall 2019) or 'Turkey loses its brains' (Weise 2017). Especially since the coup attempt in 2016 which accelerated democratic backsliding in Turkey, the Turkish exodus has featured in newspaper headlines all around the world, highlighting the brain drain and the varied profiles of Turkey's dissidents in exile (*DW* 2016). This is not the first time intellectuals, activists or regime opponents have left Turkey en masse. Each of Turkey's various military coups has triggered a surge of conflict-induced emigration, and the events of 2016 fit that pattern. However, much of this migration was underway before the coup attempt (Baser and Korkmaz 2018). Indeed, we have argued elsewhere that this new wave of migration started with the Gezi protests in 2013 and accelerated after the coup attempt in 2016 (Öztürk & Baser 2021). This time, however, those who are migrating do not constitute a homogeneous group. Their motivations, means of departure and destinations differ drastically depending on their networks, resources and access.

The new wave perfectly mirrors the situation of the groups who are considered as in opposition to the ruling regime: fragmented, disappointed and multilayered. Those groups, which would never come together in Turkey, despite being in opposition, find themselves sharing this new faith which foresees a new life outside the country they were born and raised in. Many white-collar, highly educated, middle-class citizens, students, activists, non-Muslims, seculars, journalists, former politicians, former regime loyalists among others began leaving (or began considering leaving) Turkey to start a life outside Turkish borders both in the Global North and in the Global South, due to their lifestyle choices, future concerns and perceived lack of human security in Turkey. After the coup attempt, however, most of the migration decisions taken by migrants and asylum seekers were involuntary because of their fear of persecution, arrest and torture. The approval rates for asylum applications indicate that the receiving countries also acknowledge the basis of those fears.

What is pushing people away? As Bahar Baser and Emre Eren Korkmaz (2018) explain, 'the government used the coup attempt as a pretext to impose a never-ending state of emergency, whose provisions it has used not only to fight against putschists, but also to suppress the democratic opposition'. The shrinking democratic space to resist and exist became smaller and smaller after the 2016 coup attempt and the crackdown on the opposition. The new wave is perceptible and it is a testimony of the polarised socio-political environment in Turkey. The new political environment is hostile towards dissent within the country's borders as dissidents face human rights violations and the threat of imprisonment and persecution. The new ruling elites have created a dichotomy between desired and undesired citizens. Some of the latter can still find a small space to breathe within the country and survive and resist in Turkey either willingly or unwillingly, but others have been pushed away. The current political, social and economic landscape was suffocating them and they decided they had to leave their homeland behind.

Current statistics show that under this gloomy political atmosphere in Turkey, many Turkish citizens, primarily members of the Gülen Movement (GM) as well as secular Turks, Kurds and Alevis, are fleeing or migrating to Greece – mostly as a transit destination – and to other European countries. Some are applying for asylum while others are buying property to obtain residence permits via the golden visa systems available in Europe. Recent data shows that thousands of Turkish citizens have applied for asylum in Greece, Germany and Sweden. Authorities report that until 2015, applicants were mostly of Kurdish origin, but after 2015, the recent trend shows that the profile of the applicants is usually non-Kurdish (Goßner 2020). The number of Turkish citizens who were granted protection status in European Union member countries rose by 300 per cent between 2016 and 2017 (*Ahval* 2018). About one-third of these applications were successful. According to Lampas (2018: 2), 'recognition rates vary significantly among European countries. Norway holds the highest rate of recognition with 89.7 per cent. By contrast, Poland, Hungary, and Bulgaria have yet to reach a positive decision. Greece has a rate of recognition of 54.5 per cent.' Our extensive research on the new leavers shows that they migrate not only to Europe or North America, but also to visa-free destinations such as North Macedonia, Bosnia, South Africa, Morocco, Tunisia or the Philippines. They use these routes as transit destinations to transfer to other countries with more favourable extradition rights and naturalisation opportunities (Öztürk & Baser 2021). According to the Turkish Statistical Institute, more than 80,000 Turkish citizens emigrated in 2019 (TÜİK 2020). In 2018, the number was 134,740 and in 2017 it was 113,326. In 2016, the year of the coup attempt, it was 69,326.[1] Our field research data indicates that those who have left are only the tip of the iceberg and there are many more people in Turkey who are planning to leave (Öztürk &

---

[1] https://data.tuik.gov.tr/Kategori/GetKategori?p=Nufus-ve-Demografi-109, accessed August 2022.

Baser 2021). Some are staying because they are waiting for the 'right time' to leave or the 'right opportunity' to come, while others are suffering from negative liberty deprivation, meaning the state prevents them from leaving although they have the intention and the means to do so (Haas 2021: 25).

These numbers suggest that the latest flow constitutes a significant wave of migration from Turkey, the largest since the 1990s when displaced and/or politically active Kurds left the country in record numbers due to human rights violations and criminalisation. Turkey's diaspora communities abroad were already heterogeneous along ethnic, religious and ideological lines, consisting of Turks, Kurds, Alevites, leftists and nationalists. This new wave of migration is changing the current profile of Turkey's diaspora in European countries. Recent migrants are not necessarily in solidarity and may have competing interests. These dynamics are carried to the destination countries where the interactions between the newcomers and the older diasporas from Turkey cause new tensions. Moreover, some segments in the diaspora are supportive of the authoritarian measures and there are widening trust issues among diaspora groups from different backgrounds. These new developments have made the diasporic landscape a highly contested space and a playing field for the transnationalisation of Turkey's domestic disputes.

The new wave is different from the previous ones in a number of ways. Migration scholars who study Turkey's migration patterns tend to focus on a few stages such as the 1960s, when the bilateral guest worker agreements were signed between various European states and Turkey, the 1970s and 1980s, when politically motivated migration occurred in response to the military interventions and family reunification, and the 1990s, when mostly Kurds migrated due to the intensification of the low-intensity civil war in Turkey (Aksel 2019). The new wave is more heterogeneous; it includes privileged highly educated middle-class citizens, academics and intellectuals as well as members of the GM who are persecuted in Turkey due to their alleged ties to the coup attempt. A majority of the academics and GM members were dismissed from their positions after the purge starting with the coup attempt in 2016. White-collar migrants, academics and intellectuals might have secular concerns which compelled them to leave the country. Both migrants with cultural capital or wealth and members of the GM from working classes apply for asylum in various countries as a result of pending trials and fear of persecution in Turkey. Therefore, the motivations, fears and disappointments of these new migrants overlap and vary depending on individual circumstances.

Among the groups who are migrating either by choice or by necessity, the intellectuals and public figures constitute the most visible segment of the new wave. They are well-known figures in Turkey for their stance against the current regime and most of them choose to speak up and continue to resist democratic backsliding in Turkey after leaving the country. Some left Turkey exactly for this reason – to be able to raise their voice and not be silenced. They are well networked in the Global North, and they can easily find a readily existing audience outside Turkey's borders. They become *translators* of Turkey's internal dynamics to external audiences and their voice – despite coming from a variety of ideological, religious and ethnic backgrounds – becomes the voice of the dissidents of the current regime abroad.

This book examines the current wave of migration from Turkey with a specific focus on the experiences of Turkey's public figures and intellectuals from varying backgrounds. It scrutinises how the authoritarian turn in Turkey under the reign of the Justice and Development Party (Adalet ve Kalkınma Partisi, AKP) compels intellectuals to go into exile and how they cope with being separated from their homeland in their new host countries. By presenting their stories in their own words, our intention is to demonstrate their return prospects, their interactions with the host society and the conventional and unconventional solidarity networks among different diaspora groups from Turkey.

Democratic Backsliding in Turkey: A Key Driver of Migration

The Republic of Turkey has had a tumultuous political atmosphere since its foundation. This dynamic atmosphere stems from the different institutional structures it inherited from the Byzantine and Ottoman Empires (Heper 2000; Goçek 2011), its young population, the uniquely complex structure of its geography (Larrabee 2010), and the diversity of ideological groups (Çelik et al. 2017). In this context, one can say that Turkey's journey towards democratisation has traversed a bumpy road. The Republic of Turkey, which was founded after the War of Independence with the building of a nation from the top down, was penetrated by the dominant world currents of the second half of the twentieth century, leading the government to attempt to 'Turkify' its society (Aktar 2009) and then to 'make it meekly religious' under its own guidance and control (Öztürk 2016: 621). However, these efforts caused conflict within the state and different reactions in society for the reasons mentioned above. Therefore, while Turkey's politics diversified day by day, they also became more complex. As such, the twentieth century witnessed multiple military interventions, state-sponsored pogroms against different groups, and social divisions. Many political and social ruptures have also caused the state, or the structure controlling the state in Turkey, to constantly create 'others' within the society who are not desired citizens. In each transformation period, Turkey pushed certain segments of its own citizens into exile while the ruling classes defined and redefined the 'ideal citizen' within their own political paradigms. Since its foundation, Turkey has generally excluded Kurds, Alevis, Islamists, non-Muslims, liberals and those that it does not accept as *its own* in a broader framework. This exclusion has been made in the name of protecting the state and the integrity of the nation, and Turkish-style secularism and Turco-Islamic authoritarianism.

This exclusionary power, which some call 'the state' and some call 'Kemalist tutelage', first started to be forced in 2002 (Tuğal 2009).

A group of ex-Islamists, led by Recep Tayyip Erdoğan, who was elected mayor of Istanbul from their party in the mid-1990s, with the AKP, which they founded by assembling a coalition of liberals, pro-European Union supporters and those who wanted to change the tutelage regime, managed to come to power alone in November 2002 with 34.29 per cent of the votes. As Ömer Taşpınar (2012) mentions:

> The victory for the AKP was historic. It was only the second time since the beginning of Turkey's multiparty democracy in 1946 that a political party had won three consecutive elections. And it was the first time that a party actually increased its percentage of the vote at each succeeding election. The AKP received 34.28 percent of the vote in 2002. It won 46.58 percent in 2007. And it scored 49.90 percent in 2011.

This success, which was 'hope' for some (Insel 2003), was 'the beginning of disaster' for others (Haynes 2010). In other words, the AKP's rise to power in a country with traditional patterns like Turkey was accepted by some as a welcome change of politicians, the establishment of large social coalitions, and the ability of Islam and democracy to coexist after the events of 9/11 (Kuru 2017; Yavuz and Öztürk 2019). Others, however, claimed that the AKP government actually instrumentalised many other structures, paticularly the European Union, and that its main aim was to separate Turkey from the Western civilisation it was trying to become a part of (Tepe 2005). When one looks at Turkey during the first half of the 2020s, it is possible to say that the second group was right, and it is easy to argue that the years when Turkey was under AKP rule contributed to the positive change and dynamism mentioned above. It is even possible to take this one step further and claim that Turkey has experienced multiple and different breaking points during the AKP's rule for more than twenty years, and each breaking point has created a different *other* for Turkey. The AKP government, which has become increasingly authoritarian in the process (Baser and Öztürk 2017;

Esen and Gumuscu 2016), has managed to compel these groups to migrate either voluntarily or involuntarily and created a significant new wave of migration out of Turkey. At this point we have to ask two questions: (1) What are the major breaking points? (2) Which breaking points excluded whom, and in what way?

Although the AKP emerged victorious in the elections and placed Erdoğan in the prime minister's seat, it actually tried to govern Turkey after 2002 with a consensus formed from different groups both within the party and within society. The main reason why we say 'it tried' here stems from both the military and the civilian wings of the bureaucracy failing to act in accordance with the AKP government even after it won the election (Özbudun 2006). This forced the AKP, as we mentioned above, to align with the liberals (Onar 2007) and those who stayed away from the Kemalist tutelage, and then to enter into a very important coalition for the history of Turkey: its unoffical and unconventional partnership with the GM (Watmough and Öztürk 2018). The AKP–GM marriage of convenience was doomed to fail, but politics makes strange bedfellows. However, before addressing this partnership, it is necessary to mention the first important breaking point for the AKP government, because this breaking point is considered to be the first time the AKP's collective struggle with certain structures in the state began. It occurred when a lawsuit to close the party was filed in 2008 with the claim that the AKP had become the focus of acts against secularism (Aydın-Düzgit 2008). Although this closure did not take place, the AKP was coerced into saying 'We are in power, but not strong enough to run the state', and after that it began to try to dominate both society and the state. Indeed, this effort was made possible by first getting public support and establishing varying and flexible interest partnerships with different pressure groups. They had all the right to worry. Previous parties with Islamic tendencies had been banned several times in Turkey, starting with the National Order Party, the National Salvation Party, the Welfare Party and the Virtue Party. Similar to the experience of Kurdish political parties, the establishment in Turkey had not allowed these political fronts to flourish and have an equal share of state power since the republic's foundation. However, this time the AKP had a different trajectory. It had the support of Turkey's organic intellectuals and the international community; in other words, it was enjoying a surge in popularity. Especially with regard to the support of liberal intellectuals, Duygu Ersoy and Fahriye Üstüner (2016: 406) remind us that it was 'crucial for the legitimisation of the AKP government [after] it first came to power, as the party lacked its own media and intellectuals'. As the authors splendidly explain:

> Their support was based more on the party's assumed characteristic of being the bearer of change and of democracy which became a prevalent discussion in the media. The focus of the 'liberal intellectuals' was the elimination of military tutelage, the logical consequence of which would be the construction of the 'New Turkey' in which democracy would be established. It was the common belief among this group that the actor that would enable this transformation was the AKP government. (Ersoy and Üstüner 2016: 407)

Besides the support they received from Turkey's liberal intellectuals, the AKP also had a major success in garnering support from external actors. The more the European politicians praised the 'reform' process in Turkey under the AKP and the more academics started publishing articles about how the AKP demonstrated that Islam and democracy are compatible and that we were in the era of 'Muslim democrats', the more the AKP felt confident to play the role of a grassroots resistance movement which would potentially democratise Turkey by erasing the legacy of the military tutelage. It had sufficient *legitimacy* to play politics both at home and abroad.

In 2008, Turkish politics became the scene of a different scandal: the Ergenekon trials. Many military officers, opposition law makers and journalists were tried in court for plotting a coup against the

AKP government. For some authors such as Erdağ Goknar (2020), the judicial process was predicated on a conspiracy theory to supress the opposition to the AKP's rising power and creeping Islamism in Turkey. As he explains:

> The conspiracy trial convictions began to be overturned in 2014 based on procedural irregularities and were fully dismissed in July 2019 when a Turkish court again ruled that there was insufficient evidence to indicate that Ergenekon, a purported ultra-secular, ultra-nationalist clandestine organisation, ever existed. But the arrests and investigations by police, the indictments by prosecutors, and the sentences by judges had long remapped the Turkish political landscape, and the conspiracy theory had served its purpose of censuring the military and political opposition and ensuring the continued rule of the AKP, which had grown increasingly authoritarian in the meantime. Ergenekon, which devolved into a dragnet against all political opposition, ranks as Turkey's second most comprehensive legal case involving coup plans. The first, which is ongoing, is the Gülen mass trials in the wake of the 2016 failed coup attempt (associated with the Mastermind conspiracy). Ironically, the Gülenists were the driving force behind the Ergenekon trials. (Goknar 2020: 2)

However, for others the Ergenekon trials were not a conspiracy, as Turkey has witnessed numerous military interventions and coups in the past. There was also a strong belief that the 'deep state' existed and this increased the possibility of the existence of such an institution. During this time, various liberal intellectuals as well as different opposition groups such as the Kurds supported such trials and asked for further investigations (see for instance Wrigley 2008).

The AKP continued to push back against the military's shadow over Turkish politics. In 2010, it organised a referendum to make various amendments in the constitution, which was the legacy of the 12 September 1980 military coup. As Ersin Kalaycıoğlu (2012) puts it, it was a *Kulturkampf* as it polarised the political environment and even fragmented opposition groups internally. He explains:

> The campaign for the 'yea' and the 'nay' votes focused on the two major issues of the size and composition of the CC [Constitutional Court] and HSYK [High Council of Judges and Prosecutors]. The other amendments got, at best, scant attention, if any. The AKP spokespersons presented the package as a new initiative to democratise Turkey, to empower the nation (instead of the state – i.e. the military, bureaucrats and judges), to undermine the secular elites and their alien ideas, to hold the state elite accountable for the political execution of PM Adnan Menderes in 1961, and to hold the coup-makers of 1980 accountable. The CHP opposition and its new leader, Kemal Kılıçdaroğlu, argued that the AKP's main goal was to stuff the CC and HSYK with its supporters and control the judiciary, ensuring that if in the future the CC works as a Grand Jury and tries the AKP elite the latter will have their cronies as judges.

Although some of the constitutional amendments promised liberalisation, it was obvious that they removed some protection mechanisms against the AKP's rising power. Therefore, as Kalaycioglu (2012: 6) argues, 'the CHP campaign also stressed governmental corruption and the AKP's alleged hidden agenda to create an authoritarian regime in democratic disguise under PM Erdogan'. Although the AKP and the MHP are in close partnership in the contemporary Turkish political arena, during the referendum of 2010, the MHP took a stance against the referendum as it was disturbed by the on-going peace initiatives between the AKP and the PKK (Partiya Karkerên Kurdistanê, Kurdish Workers' Party). The Kurdish movement and the political party aligned with the movement at that time, the BDP (Barış ve Demokrasi Partisi, Peace and Democracy Party), opted for a boycott rather than supporting the AKP's cause in this strategic move (Kalaycioglu 2012:6). While the constitutional referendum resulted in a 58 per cent vote in favour of the suggested amendments, some pro-AKP scholars interpreted the results as saying 'Farewell to the Old Turkey' (Ergil 2010). For Doğu Ergil, for instance, there were two polarised camps in the debates surrounding the referendum: those who were supporting reform and democracy and those who were against it. He argued that the Kemalist/secularist camp did not want to lose their privileges and therefore tried to stop any changes to the old regime. The 'yes' camp, however, represented positive change and further liberties for the people. In his own words:

> After all, the people of the nation had just gone to the ballot boxes and cast their votes, making it clear that their desire was to get rid of a series of laws that had allowed the state to put pressure on society, and instead transform these laws into new ones allowing the people to live in peace and enjoy their rights and freedoms, without fearing a dominant authority. Why is it so difficult to understand this message? (Ergil 2010: 18)

His views clearly explain the package that the AKP managed to wrap the new amendments in. This discourse has been constantly repeated by AKP politicians, Erdoğan himself included, and the party's spin doctors and academics. This is, of course, understandable as it was their job. However, what created a milestone in Turkish political history was the support of Turkey's intellectual circles, mostly liberals but also liberal left-wingers (Tapan 2010), to the 'yes' campaign. A new slogan appeared during the referendum propaganda campaigns, which said 'Not enough, but yes!' The individuals who belonged to this loosely organised initiative supported the suggested amendments but continued to lobby for a new constitution and criticised the AKP government for not lifting a finger on other critical issues that were essential for Turkey's democratisation, such as the election threshold. As time proved their 'good intentions' wrong, many of these individuals were targeted by various opposition groups who made a calling to them to self-criticise their actions. Kemalists, various secular and left-wing groups, as well as other organisations in opposition have not forgiven the 'betrayal of the intellectuals' (Ersoy 2012) to this day. As things have gone south, these intellectuals have been accused more frequently of enabling the AKP and bringing it to its powerful position which resulted in an authoritarian drift and consequently a regime change thanks to the erosion of the barriers ahead of it by changing the constitution.

The AKP was acting pragmatically and strategically. As mentioned above, one of the most important partnerships that the AKP maintained was the interest- and power-oriented one with the Gülen Movement, starting from 2004–5 and lasting presumably until the end of 2013 (Taş 2018). Although the founding cadres and Islamist figures of the AKP and the GM, organised under the leadership of Fethullah Gülen, have historically not had a great partnership, these two parties were able to make room for themselves in the state staff and gradually cooperate to get rid of the Kemalists and opposing structures within the state (Yavuz 2019: 73). This cooperation benefitted both parties. While the AKP used the GM's trained cadres in the state bureaucracy, the GM provided legitimacy to the AKP both internally and externally through the media, civil society and other institutions. Although this partnership marketed itself both in the West and at home as an alliance to get rid of tutelage (for instance with cooperation in the Ergenekon trials), they were somehow secretly staffed within the state and becoming a single body. Although this caused suspicion among the secular and Kemalist-sensitive segments, Turkey was growing relatively quickly in this period under the effect of globalisation and an economy that gave importance to structuring rather than production. Moreover, the AKP, which was victorious in the constitutional amendment referendum in 2010, was further breaking the influence of the Kemalist tutelage (Aydın-Düzgit 2012). However, although these developments were taking place in front of a domestic and international audience as a well-played spectacle, creeping authoritarianism and a conflict of interest between the AKP and the GM were also looming behind the scenes.

Although it is difficult to argue that the AKP became authoritarian directly or suddenly after 2011, we can view this date as the beginning of the AKP's democratic backsliding. This date can also be seen as the beginning of the AKP's getting tough while struggling with the rising economic crisis, its inability to tolerate social diversity, and the beginning of the process of establishing a one-man regime. After this process, the AKP continued on its way not only by conflicting with different segments of society, but also by creating new divisions and polarisations from these conflicts (Kaygusuz 2018). Many segments of society, especially the youth, Islamic structures, Kurds, academics, liberals and leftists, have had their share of this process gradually, sometimes one by one and sometimes collectively. These developments created strong incentives to leave Turkey as a result of lack of human security and basic freedoms. Many people were familiar with creeping authoritarianism from the political atmosphere of the 1980s and 1990s, while others were feeling sentimental about the 'old Turkey' which began to fade away under the new regime.

While we cannot give the date exactly when the AKP started to become authoritarian, we can easily say that the Gezi Park protests that took place in 2013 were a turning point for Turkey. The harsh intervention following Erdoğan's order against those who were protesting against an AKP project to be built in Gezi Park in Taksim, Istanbul, caused further protest actions that would spread to seventy-nine provinces of Turkey and last for more than a month. In the police interventions where loss of life and injuries occurred, Erdoğan used polarising instead of conciliatory language and claimed that the events had occurred as a result of the plans of some Western-supported interest groups (Tuğal 2013). The impact of the Arab uprisings of the early 2010s is important to mention here. The Turkish elite's rhetoric was very similar to the Syrian president Bashar al-Assad's strategic placing of the blame for protests in Syria, putting them in the context of terrorist actions and movements supported by external powers. The AKP's spin doctors managed to create a perception that the Gezi protests were an attempt to remove the AKP govenrment from power. Erdoğan also refused to address the demands for social change and justice and treated the protests as unrest that could potentially cause a political loss for him and his party. Even though it has been almost ten years, the big Gezi case in which intellectuals and artists are being tried continues and people like civil society leader Osman Kavala are kept in prison (Turkut 2020) and artists like Mehmet Ali Alabora are forced to live outside Turkey (Seyben 2019). Moreover, the Gezi events became a breaking point for the younger generations in Turkey. After these, they started to look for a solution other than the AKP's Turkey (Baser 2015; Gümüş 2017). The international community was also astonished by the amount of violence that was used against the protestors and started understanding that the end of the *democratisation façade* in Turkey was near.

It is obvious that the Gezi protests caused a great transformation in the political and social landscapes of Turkey. However, an event that was equally or more instrumental was the transformation of the interest-oriented partnership between the GM and the AKP into an interest-oriented war. Although it seems like an ideological separation on paper, the AKP and the GM, or Erdoğan and Fethullah Gülen, who could not agree on many issues, especially the Kurdish issue, entered into a secret struggle in late 2012 over who would have the upper hand in the state bureaucracy, which became open after 2013 (Yavuz 2018). In this struggle, while Gülen was trying to get the AKP government into trouble with his police and judicial power, Erdoğan was trying to make the movement smaller in Turkey and in the world through public support and political power. In this process, in which both structures were damaged, undoubtedly, it was Turkey which suffered the most. While the AKP criminalised many groups within the scope of this struggle, the securitisation process in the country increased. The rhetoric of the government started to become more religious and nationalistic, and Turkey gradually entered the process of introversion. This undoubtedly affected the already fragile economy even more.

Before looking at the ways in which the struggle between the AKP and the GM remains relevant, we had better mention another issue that runs parallel to the process. This is the story of the broken relations between the Kurds and the AKP government and their reflection on Turkey. In this context, the Kurdish–Turkish peace process and its termination are important. Secret talks, namely the Oslo Talks, started in 2009 between the AKP government and the PKK. In addition to that, the National Unity and Brotherhood Project (Initiative) was put in place by the AKP. As Baser and Özerdem (2021: 1782) write:

> In parallel with the Oslo Talks, in 2009, the AKP government declared the beginning of a process of reforms with the potential to help resolve the conflict. Officially named the 'Democratic Opening: National Unity and Fraternity' in January 2010, this program is now known as the 'Kurdish Opening'. A state TV channel (TRT 6) broadcasting in Kurdish was opened, several departments at universities started teaching in Kurdish, and the existence of a Kurdish Question was openly acknowledged by politicians, including then-Prime Minister Erdoğan himself. The AKP also ended the state of emergency as 'a gesture of goodwill' and prepared an amnesty law for PKK fighters. The government was clearly signaling that it treated these reforms as public diplomacy, but these initiatives were exclusively elite-driven and top-down, and the public remained skeptical about the whole process.

The peace process unfortunately ended in 2015 due to both the intra-state struggle and Erdoğan's embrace of nationalism (Gurses 2020). Some scholars blame the PKK for prioritising its gains in Rojava rather than having a permanent peace deal with the Turkish state, while others put the blame on the Turkish state for not having a genuine intention to end the conflict. Although the process helped to lift the blanket over taboo subjects in Turkey, it still did not create a conflict transformation process that addressed structural inequalities and the societal dimensions of the conflict (Baser and Özerdem 2021). In other words, with the multidimensional negative results, it cannot be said that the process ended due to a single factor. It is possible to talk about factors that triggered and affected each other. However, this ending affected the Kurds and the representatives of the Kurdish political movement the most. The government started a witch hunt and engaged in a massive crackdown on Kurdish political mobilisation in Turkey, which continues today. The arrest of the HDP's co-chairs and leading actors caused some HDP members to flee Turkey. The Kurds, unhappy at home, have sent some of their representatives outside Turkey's borders, although they still hold a key position in Turkish politics. Hasip Kaplan, Faysal Sarıyıldız and many others can be given as examples.

The mid-2010s also revealed that human security in Turkey was not a given due to overt political violence in the forms of urban warfare and terrorist attacks on Turkish soil. For instance, the Suruç bombing of 20 July 2015 was one of the deadliest terrorist attacks in Turkey; 33 people were killed and more than 100 were wounded. The bomb was planted in a cultural centre (Amara), which was hosting young activists preparing to go to Kobane, a Kurdish town resisting ISIS in Syria, to help with humanitarian aid. It made Kurdish citizens feel unsafe in Turkey as many believed that Turkish intelligence services were aware of the attack. Another bomb attack took place at a pro-peace process rally in Ankara on 10 October 2015. Two bombs were detonated, killing over 100 and injuring over 600. The bombings were 'presumably committed by ISIS militants after major intelligence flaws by the Turkish security forces' (Irak 2018: 412). The failure of Turkish intelligence services to stop the attacks had a tremendous impact on how Kurdish activists envisaged the Turkish state's approach towards them.

At this point, it is necessary to address a direct as well as an indirect matter pertaining to the issue, namely Academics for Peace and the government's hostility to intellectuals. After the government became unpermissive on the Kurdish issue, numerous operations were carried out in Turkey's Kurdish provinces. In this context, at the beginning of 2016, under the initiative of Academics for Peace, a declaration titled'We Will Not Be a Party to This Crime', signed by 1,128 academics, against the human rights violations experienced during the curfews and operations in the Southeastern Anatolia region, especially in Sur, Cizre and Silopi, came on the national agenda. Following the declaration, which divided the public in two, Erdoğan called on the 'relevant institutions to do what is necessary' by using expressions such as 'draft', 'dark', 'cruel', 'vile' and 'the fifth column' for the signatory academics. Following Erdoğan's call, some of the signatories across the country were detained for 'propagandizing for a terrorist organization' (Baser et al. 2017; Tekdemir et al. 2018; Biner 2019). Most of the detained academics were released after making their statements. However, the lawsuits lasted for many years, academics were fired from their jobs and the government started to intervene more in the intellectual sphere after this. The purges on academics were accelerated after the coup attempt and many were dismissed from public service with emergency decrees. Many academics began to live in exile in other countries, especially in Germany, and continue their professions there.

In this environment of chaos, perhaps one of the biggest turning points in Turkey's political life took place during the 15 July 2016 coup attempt. This unsuccessful bloody coup attempt, which the ruling party claimed was organised by the GM, but included many other structures within the state, provided Erdoğan with an opportunity to become more authoritarian. First of all, the government, which declared a state of emergency, officially switched to the presidential system in 2017 and started to rule the country with a nationalist wing that wanted to get even more unpermissive within the state (Öztürk and Gözaydın 2017). According to Amnesty International, during this time, more than 10,000 people were detained and around 70,000 were dismissed from their positions in the army, academia, education sector, legal sector and civil service among others. An Amnesty report confirms that 'the Turkish authorities also targeted media outlets and journalists, continuing their crackdown on freedom of expression. More than 20 news websites have been blocked, 42 journalists have arrest warrants out against them, and 25 media outlets have had their licenses revoked' (Amnesty International UK 2020). This caused many people, especially members of the GM, to leave the country in various ways. The post-coup environment caused Turkey to draw further away from the West and to become more isolated. In the meantime, the AKP found new conventional alliances within the Turkish state structure. This time it turned its face towards the ultra-nationalists and the party's rhetoric completely changed; the new strategy was to increase and deepen ethnic and religious cleavages within Turkey in order to legitimise its power and repress the opposition while perpetuating co-optation among its loyal circles. In 2017, the AKP, in coalition with the ultra-nationalist MHP, proposed another constitutional referendum which changed Turkey's regime from a parliamentarian to a presidential system. The referendum was held under a state of emergency, a legacy of the 2016 coup attempt when many civil society organisations were closed and alternative media outlets were silenced. The proposed eighteen amendments decreased the check and balance mechanisms and gave more power to the president by increasing his control over the HSYK, meaning the judiciary among other things. The amendments were accepted with 51 per cent of the votes and Turkey entered a new path from that date onwards.

The shift towards authoritarianism and the unstable political atmosphere deeply affected the economy. The growth rate of the Turkish economy slowed down and inflation rose. This caused economically motivated waves of emigration from the country. Although Erdoğan lost İstanbul and Ankara in the 2019 local elections, Turkey experiences every problem mentioned above differently each day. This causes the departures from Turkey to continue without slowing down as the witch hunt continues, fed on public fears and vindictive investigations.

After the Gezi protests, but increasingly in the aftermath of the collapse of the Turkish–Kurdish peace process, it was evident that international support for the AKP and its leader Erdoğan was diminishing. After the coup attempt, diplomatic relations between several European countries and Turkey became tense as the new migration flow to Europe mostly consisted of dissidents, some of whom were wanted by the authorities in Turkey. European states started questioning Turkey's extradition requests and granting asylum to those who applied for refuge in their countries due to fear of persecution and arrest in Turkey. From signatories of the Academics for Peace petition to members of the GM, Turkish citizens started leaving the country en masse, by either legal or illegal means. The already existing tensions in Turkey's diasporic landscapes (Baser 2015) were transformed with the new wave of Turkish emigrants. As European authorities perceived the spillover of Turkish politics with its conflicts and tensions among different groups across their borders, they started pushing back against Turkey's outreach in the transnational space. Such strategies included banning Turkish election propaganda and closely following Turkish state apparatuses' activities on their soil. Their concerns were validated when Turkey started using tools of transnational oppression, from monitoring and surveillance to threats and proxy punishments. The issue of 'spying imams' in various countries in Europe further securitised the matter in the eyes of the European authorities and Turkey's image has been severely damaged as a result of these developments (Adamson 2020; Baser and Öztürk 2019).

While the ruling elite were securitising their domains at multiple levels by using a counter-terrorism discourse, creating exceptional situations and keeping the state of emergency intact in Turkey, they also slowly Islamised their public discourse. Despite the fact that social religiosity began to decline in Turkey within all this transformation, the state's religiosity nonetheless accelerated and became more discernible. For example, the Presidency of Religious Affairs' budget grew and it seized a growing number of historical non-Muslim structures after 2015. The increase in alcholic beverage prices, and the fact that the representatives of power always brought religion to the fore in many different dimensions, started to cause anxiety in the secular segments of society. Additionally, violations of women's rights and femicides began to increase rapidly after 2015. Studies conducted in this context show that between 2010 and 2020, femicides increased by 25 per cent when every five-year period is compared (Ben-Porat et al. 2021). This has become Turkey's largest threat to security in recent years. In March 2021, Turkey declared its withdrawal from the Istanbul Convention and the Council of Europe's treaty on preventing violence against women and domestic violence. Although women's organisations and collectives criticised this decision and made declarations about its negative consequences on women's lives in Turkey, the government proceeded with the decision.

Various interventions on individuals' lives, as mentioned above, created tensions between the secular and liberal circles and the AKP. Currently, Turkey is categorised as 'Not Free' in the Freedom House Index and the *Democracy Index 2021* explains the situation in Turkey as follows:

> 'Turkey is the only 'hybrid regime' in the region and has recorded a big decline in its total score over the past decade, roughly mirroring the increasingly autocratic rule of it strongman president, Recep Tayyip Erdogan. From a highpoint of 5.76 points in 2012, Turkey's average score has declined by 1.41 points. Its score slipped again in 2021, falling from 4.48 in 2020 to 4.35, owing to weakening public confidence in government. Hard-won improvements in macroeconomic stability (on which the ruling Justice and Development Party had based its previous electoral success) were undermined as a result of rising prices, policy mistakes and a depreciating local currency. Public frustration with widespread corruption has also damaged confidence in the government. (Economist Intelligence Unit 2022: 64)

The lack of human security, the polarised political environment and the return of political violence after the collapse of the Turkish–Kurdish peace process also alerted those who could be less politicised than other groups mentioned above. Many white collar, well-educated middle- and upper-middle-class citizens, groups with secular concerns who were disturbed by the Islamisation of public space, started looking for ways to leave the country by creating opportunities for themselves abroad.

Researching Lived Experiences of Migration and Exile

This book focuses on the experiences of public intellectuals, journalists, academics, former politicians and other public figures. We find their experiences extremely important, not because we think that they are more valuable than those of other migrants, but because we believe that as people who affect public opinion at home and abroad, their experiences are telling with regard to the current situation in Turkey as well as in their host countries, which are stuck between a rock and a hard place when it comes to forming foreign policies towards Turkey, which is on the edge of authoritarianism or electoral sultanism. Intellectuals have an audience at home and abroad. They have certain privileges, such as access to international networks or solidarity mechanisms, that enable them to have a voice when needed. It could be treated as a blessing, but also a curse. They have no chance to hide and act like ordinary people as their faces are known to many. The 'intellectual' or 'public figure' label gives them an obligation in exile too, which can sometimes turn into a heavy burden. In this book, we bring their experiences alive using their own words.

Drawing on over one year of field work and more than twenty in-depth elite interviews this book seeks to illuminate a neglected aspect of Turkey's public intellectuals' experiences in exile. It focuses on the narratives of such individuals who have voluntarily or involuntarily left Turkey since the Gezi protests in 2013. The interviews were conducted in 2021 and the sample consists of politicians, artists, journalists, academics and activists who have migrated to a variety of locations as a result of trials against them and a dehumanisation discourse towards them by pro-regime politicians, as well as no prospects for freedom of speech and assembly in Turkey.

This has not been an easy task. All of the interviewees included in this book are famous in Turkey and thus very busy and most of the time not accessible. We carefully identified potential interviewees and started mobilising our networks to reach out to them. Our intention was to take a snapshot of the current wave and the status of intellectuals in this new diasporic landscape. Therefore, we have included interviewees who come from different religious, ethnic and ideological backgrounds. Most of the interviewees were persecuted in Turkey for their political and social activities, ranging from issues such as the Kurdish–Turkish conflict and the Academics for Peace petition to membership of organisations such as the GM.

As in many qualitative studies which include interviewing subjects on sensitive matters (Brayda and Boyce 2014; Abrahams 2017), we focused on trust-building before the interviews took place. We informed the participants about the goals and objectives of our research and asked them to look at our profiles. The informants were fully aware of our positionality as researchers, and they agreed to proceed with interviews after they fully understood our intentions. As soon as we started the interviewing process, we understood that we were standing in front of a great challenge. Both of us have worked on sensitive issues related to Turkey before. Dr Öztürk has conducted extensive research in the Balkans while investigating Turkey's foreign policy priorities in the region. Dr Baser has extensively researched the experiences of Kurdish exiles in the diaspora. Both research landscapes were politicised and fragmented. Yet, the qualitative research endeavour for this specific project turned out to be harder than we envisaged. We immediately understood that the polarised political atmosphere that exists in Turkey among several dissident groups was reflected in how some interviewees approached our project. For instance, before the interviews, some people asked for a list of participants who had agreed to take part in this book. If there was a member of the GM in the list, they withdrew from the interview. For others, the participation of former Kurdish politicians was an issue. They did not want to be associated with such names who belonged to pro-Kurdish circles. As our intention was scholarly rather than political, as political scientists we wanted to present a true portrayal of Turkey's transnational landscapes in the light of the debates surrounding the new wave. The migration of GM members is a reality. Even if we do not agree with their ideological stance or methods, we still perceive them as part of the picture. Their experiences are also important for us to have a comprehensive picture of the current migration flows and what we make of them. Leaving their narrative outside the book would not be ethical and would not be justifiable to the scientific community.

In the same manner, we were burdened by the responsibility of knowledge production on a sensitive topic. As academics, we have assessed the situation and included all colours that are represented in the current statistics describing Turkish migration trends. Therefore, we need to underline that we were not guided by our own political stances but by our scholarly curiosity. We therefore included public intellectuals from different backgrounds such as Turkish, Kurdish and Armenian, and we included the voices of journalists and academics who are considered as secular and liberal, or leftist and Gülenist. Another important issue to mention is the rapidly changing political atmosphere in Turkey. Some participants decided to withdraw their interviews for fear of persecution or undesired visibility. Some of them decided to return to Turkey or had to do so (due to the end of fixed-term appointments) and therefore reconsidered their participation. Others have learned that they have pending trials after they were interviewed by us. This also showed us that their precarious situation remained constant throughout the year. During field work, we followed the ethical procedures approved by Coventry University and we allowed participants to withdraw if they so wished any time before publication. The interviews were firstly transcribed in Turkish and then translated into English. Both versions were sent back to the interviewees for confirmation.

The questions revolved around issues such as motivations to leave, how they define and experience exile, and how they mobilise in their respective localities. We asked them what kind of Turkey they left behind. We had interesting discussions about the meaning of exile and the psychological burden of the label 'asylum seeker'. Furthermore, we delved into debates about their prospects for returning to Turkey, interactions with their host society and conventional or unconventional solidarity networks among different diaspora groups from Turkey. The main aim of these interviews is to show how exile takes shapes and forms in contemporary political space where communication technologies are advanced and how globalisation makes it easier to stay connected to the homeland compared to previous decades. Each interview touches on aspects related to political realities on the ground in Turkey, the political, social and economic impacts of authoritarianism, the multiple meanings of exile, transnational repression mechanisms put in play by Turkey and potential scenarios for reconciliation and normalisation in Turkey. The book, therefore, provides a snapshot of a new layer of intellectual diaspora in the making.

This process, meaning how the new wave is slowly but surely transitioning into a new diasporic condition, was remarkable to witness for us as researchers who focus on diasporas and transnationalism. We could see how suffering surrounding the departure from the homeland is human and even those we perceive as privileged can mourn for their loss in different ways. During the interviews, there were times when our interviewees became emotional, had teary eyes or needed a break. There were also times when we found ourselves tearful listening to their individual stories. We are extremely grateful for their trust and for their sharing of lived experiences with us. We hope that the book makes a mark on the research on democratic decline in Turkey and its consequences as well as the transnational politics of Turkey in diasporic landscapes.

Feelings of Hope and Despair: What Do these Personal Tales Tell Us?

In this book, our aim is to bring the participants' own voices to the fore. We believe that understanding and representing migration and exile can be more meaningful if we go back to people's own story-telling practices. Each interview provides a different narrative about motivations to leave but they have many aspects in common including leaving a beloved country behind without knowing when and how they can return. We posit that a combination of these individual accounts reveals larger political, social and cultural realities, not only about the participants' country of origin but also about their country of residence.

The interviews revealed that the concept of *exile* does not have the same meaning for all. It is a loaded word; for some it means libera-tion and for others it is a ball and chain that represents vulnerability and victimhood. Mario Sznajder and Luis Roniger (2009: 11) define political exile as

> a mechanism of institutional exclusion – not the only one – by which a person involved in politics and public life, or perceived by power holders as such, is forced or pressed to leave his or her home coun-try or place of residence, unable to return until a change in political circumstances takes place. This definition covers both those directly persecuted by the authorities or by other violent political actors, such as paramilitary groups and guerrilla organisations, as well as those who choose displacement and expatriation as they sense an existential threat or problem originating in political quarters; and those who, once abroad as voluntary sojourners, discover that the changed politi-cal circumstances prevent their return. Ostracism, forced displace-ment, and exile are, in our view, the result of political settings prone to exclude a myriad of actors, whose political voice the power-holders

cannot digest and contain within the polity. We thus consider exile to be a major form of institutional exclusion, a tool profusely used by states to ban political dissidents.

Although most, if not all, of our participants fitted in this definition, their self-perception and identification varied. Some produced concepts such as *voluntary exile* or *semi-exile* to define the situation that they found themselves in. We found that the concept of exile was usually associated with non-belonging and loneliness in their new countries of residence.

Interviewee accounts also showed us that each depicted a different Turkey when we asked them about the homeland that they had left behind. Each narrative pointed to a different breaking point which had an impact on their decision to leave and this showed us that the dissident community abroad is so diverse and multilayered that their reading of Turkish political history varies immensely, reflecting their view of their current situation through the lens of their ethnic, religious and ideological backgrounds.

What is the obligation of intellectuals in exile? Do they have to turn into permanent activisits to justify why they left the homeland behind? Do they have to keep their ties to Turkey? Are they allowed to focus on their lives only? During the interviews, we observed that most of our participants were dealing with such questions in their minds. For some, exile meant an opportunity to speak up and be the voice of the silenced masses in Turkey who are 'trapped' in a country that wants to repress them. For others, the struggle became impossible and they turned inwards and focused on their families. One way or another, however, they formed new relationships with their host societies and its authorities. In some cases, this brought more visibility and responsibility, leaving them with a burden of obligation in exile and for others the attention they received made them resist not only Turkey's democratic decline but also their host country's labelling and victimising discourses at the same time. Being away from Turkey did not mean being away from its polarising atmosphere but it gave them space to 'breathe a little'. New tensions and struggles occurred as they got embedded into their new homes, either within Turkish diaspora communities or with the wider society. Sometimes they found that common interests and sufferings brought people from different walks of life together and in other cases they were betrayed by those who they thought were 'in the same camp'. The attention they received in the host society, either from the authorities or civil society or from their peers, made them feel trapped in a cage that they could not break out of: an exile from Turkey whose only job is to explain how bad the situation in Turkey is to wider Western audiences. The interviewee accounts reflect these dilemmas – new battlefronts against social injustices and new interactions such as unconventional solidarities and adversaries.

Although the individuals we interviewed could be considered as privileged, partly because of their material assets but mostly because of their intellectual capital and networks, we have observed that their experiences varied according to different factors including the motivations to leave, what they left behind (a family, a job, a set of pending trials . . .) and the opportunities in the host country as well as their return prospects. Our impression from these interviews is that many migrants of the new wave are now here to stay as *the right time to return* might never come in the short run or their children are now adapted to their new environments.

Just like the exiles of the 1970s, 1980s and 1990s, they will be creating another layer of transnational community, a periphery of Turkey's diaspora(s) which will slowly but surely be amalgamated into the core. While this is happening, we will observe how new waves are absorbed by already existing diasporic structures and how the already existing diasporic structures are transformed by the newcomers. In this book, we take a snapshot of the current moment, the present-day realities of Turkey's intelligentsia in exile, and shed light on the transformation of Turkey's diasporic landscapes in the years to come.

1

BARBAROS ŞANSAL

When I look back on my performances, I performed a miracle in the desert in Turkey, but that flower can't survive in the desert; I realised that as I matured. You leave a cactus in the desert and walk away.

Barbaros Şansal was born in 1957 in Ankara. He studied business management at Marmara University and gained a master's in design and chromatics at the Royal Academy of Arts in London before becoming an apprentice to prominent fashion designer Yıldırım Mayruk. Besides being a fashion designer, Şansal is also a famous LGBT rights advocate and an anti-war activist.

Barbaros Şansal took part in the Gezi Park protests in 2013. On 1 January 2017, while at his residence in North Cyprus, Şansal shared a video on social media in which he criticised Turkish society, stating: 'While scores of journalists are in prison, while children are sexually harassed and raped, while corruption and bribes are everywhere, while extremists are distributing shit to you in the streets, are you still celebrating the New Year? I am not ... Carry on your celebration in disgrace, misery and dirt. Drown in your shit, Turkey.'

Because of these words, the Turkish Republic of North Cyprus Interior Ministry detained Şansal and deported him. On landing at Atatürk Airport, Şansal was physically and verbally attacked by people on the tarmac. He was taken to court and charged with 'inciting the public to hatred or hostility' under Article 216 of the Turkish Penal Code.

Şansal was released from prison on 2 March 2017, and he wrote a book about his arrest, his attempted lynching and his treatment in prison. Şansal closed his business in Turkey and moved to Cyprus.

Could you tell us when and why you left Turkey?

I actually first left Turkey in 1980. I was accused of being a communist and arrested because of my red Converse shoes during the military coup era. The first time I emigrated was 7 October 1980. I wasn't able to return for nine years. Later, with the arrival of the Özal era and the alleged return of democracy to Turkey, I returned in 1989 and continued my fight where I had left off. But ten to fifteen years after the AKP regime came to power in 2002, the system in Turkey had changed completely. I was subjected to attacks, kidnapped and targeted dozens of times. An organised network of the state at the international airport finally frogmarched me from another country to lynch me, and I was thrown in a cell. I had actually decided to leave Turkey before that, after that 15 July nonsense.

While watching television one night, I saw a neo-Islamist, Ottoman man shout 'Their property is lawfully yours, their properties are your spoils, take these and use them' in front of a Turkish flag unfurled on a stage set up for the media. I decided to leave when I realised that the culture of pillaging, plundering and occupation that had always existed – the ill fortune of that geography in 1915, the 1920 Izmir auctions, the 1919–20 Pontus issue, the 1934–35 Thrace incidents like the Jewish incident, the 6–7 September 1955 Istanbul incidents in which part of my family were victims, the 1974 incident, the 1980 insurrection, the 24 April decisions – and that radical, political Islam – they express it as such, so I use it like that as well – that sleeping serpent was always waiting, coiled up.

Changing my investments, property, occupation, career and international connections all in one night was incredibly difficult. I wasn't eighteen or twenty anymore, like in 1980 when I just grabbed a bag and left. I needed at least two lorries to move my things, and I was forced to move to a new location. I won't go back to Turkey again. I won't go back regardless of the circumstances. In fact, the leader of the main opposition party, Mr Kılıçdaroğlu, Mayor İmamoğlu of the municipality of Istanbul and my dear friend Canan Kaftancıoğlu invited us to a goodbye dinner two days before leaving Turkey. That night, as Yıldırım Mayruk and I expressed our sorrows about leaving Turkey, they said, 'You'll return when things improve.' But we don't have that much time anymore. I had to dedicate myself to other targets and ideals, because bringing peace to Turkey requires facilitating peace in the eastern Mediterranean. That's why I produce projects to work towards a unified Cyprus with the governments of both North and South Cyprus, with prominent figures in culture and the arts, and with journalists. This is my story in brief. I mean, my reason for leaving Turkey was the words of a man on state television sanctifying pillaging, plundering and occupation in front of the flag. After that, there was nothing left to do.

You've chosen one of the most interesting places among those who left Turkey. Why Cyprus?

Because I have fought for years as a defender of rights and within civil society organisations and because I am known globally after the incident at the airport for those hideous images, many countries have tried to grant me the right to asylum and residence. Sevim Dağdeviren or Cem Özdemir, who are MPs in the German Bundestag, Kati Piri from the Netherlands, Theo Francken from Belgium and many individuals from the UK and Washington have offered this to me. I have one passport, from the Republic of Turkey, and I reside here with my Turkish passport. That is my hunchback. But our hunchbacks must be our gear in life. If we dismantle and try to dispose of those hunchbacks, it would be like severing the hump of a camel. And you then wouldn't be able to pass through the desert. Geography is not destiny. You change that with your own behaviours, positions and actions. I am a citizen of the Republic of Turkey. That's how I was born, and that's probably how I will die. That's why there were two reasons why I chose Cyprus. First, I have visited the island since 1965. Because I have been the tailor for prominent political figures like Özal, Çiller and Erbakan, I have had to experience intimately all the processes including the 1974 Cyprus operation with the public figures of the political, commercial and artistic worlds by the nature of my profession.

The problem in Cyprus is that Niyazi Kızılyürek from the south is now in the European Parliament and the constitution of the Republic of Cyprus is in Turkish and Greek. But what facilitated the Republic of Cyprus's entrance into the European Union was that its constitution was previously translated because of Greece and the Turkish constitution of the Republic of Cyprus was ignored. If we are to view Cyprus within the European Union federally or as any other form of collective whole, we must insert the native language of the Cypriot Turks and the Turkish citizens of the Republic of Turkey among the languages of Europe. Language is important. You must make love in the language in which you think and battle in the language of your enemy. I believe that the greatest obstacle preventing the citizens of the Republic of Turkey from becoming European citizens can disappear the moment that Turkish enters the European constitution. And I have seen numerous injustices, pillage and similar things on this island. Because of my sensitivity, I want to compensate and treat those. That's why I chose Cyprus. Whether it's Finance Minister Petrides, Foreign Minister Christodoulides, or the chancellors of any number of universities, my acceptance and dialogue is better than in the north, unfortunately. Because there are pressures such as Islamisation, advanced fascism and almost a vassal system – like Turkey's back garden – in Northern Cyprus. I chose the right place to oppose this. I withdrew my investments there. I'm building a gallery now. I built my home, and I got a residence permit. Despite everything, Cyprus is probably fifty years ahead of Turkey in terms of human rights despite its colonial laws. Because rights such as the safeguarding of bodily integrity and sexual orientation are under considerable protection in the Turkish Republic of Northern Cyprus, and the law is not significantly impacted by capital and politics.

Cyprus is an island for women, and as a women's tailor who has worked with ten thousand women, I believe that I know women. The ombudsman is a woman, the general director of security is a woman, there has been a female prime minister here, there are female ministers. So a Turkish land where there is male–female equality is different from all Turkish geography in the world. Maybe that's also a reason why I chose Cyprus. It's a place I love and know. The Cypriot Turks here need more people like us. I mean, rights and liberties are guaranteed in advanced democracies like Germany, Belgium, France and the UK, but this is a place where more nonconformist lives can emerge. The conditions here are more challenging, but I think I like the challenge.

Especially after 2017, Turkish academia was introduced to a new concept known as transnational repression. This concept expresses certain instances of repression that some Turkish

institutions and fanatics of the current regime have imposed on people outside Turkey who are described within Turkey as dissidents and traitors. Have you been subjected to these sorts of practices, directly or indirectly, by the state or its supporters in Cyprus?

On 2 January 2017, even though I have residence in this country, I was deported unlawfully and subjected to that heinous incident at Atatürk Airport. I filed a lawsuit against unlawful deportation, and I won. Turkey had me deported after so much injustice, and it tossed the entire crime into the back garden. Now the chief public prosecutor has accepted and opened an action for compensation for up to 2 million Turkish lira as a dissuasive punishment against the interior minister, the general director of the police and security forces commander at the time and two under-secretaries. I mean, yes, but I was still a victim in a way. Once while drinking coffee at a café, a few Idealists [ultra-nationalists] verbally assaulted me. A case was opened against them, and they were banned from leaving the country. The law functions in Cyprus. Although Turkey attempts to intervene, it can't because the rule of law functions. By contrast, interestingly enough, there are incredibly positive approaches from Cypriot Turks, Maronites, Armenians and Greeks. Not more than fifteen minutes ago, as I was coming home, I opened my window at the police checkpoint but was waved on as they said, 'The king has arrived. You are a god for us. You fight for this island's freedom. You fight for the Cypriot Turk. I won't look at your licence.' It's a very small community here. There are 60,000–70,000 Cypriot Turks. And there have been systemic efforts to assimilate them both culturally and economically since 1974. So the motherland perspective of the Cypriot Turk for Turkey is a bit different. There's not such a reaction here; to the contrary, I see more tolerance, acceptance and assistance than what the Cypriot Turk shows for another Cypriot Turk. Because this isn't something I'm particularly accustomed to, it really makes me happy. So, I'm thankful for the Cypriot Turkish people.

Didn't you go to London from Cyprus after a short while?
I went to Westminster as a speaker for CEFTUS.[1]

So, you didn't plan to reside in London for a longer period?
No, I didn't come to stay. I had previously participated in CEFTUS events, in İbrahim Doğuş's ballroom events. The British Kebab Awards are one of the most pleasant events I attend in the world. I'm going again this year. I sat with Jeremy Corbyn once. I'll probably sit with Boris Johnson this year. Yes, I have frequently gone to London, Berlin, Zurich and capitals around the world because of my commercial, political and cultural connections. I lived in London between 1980 and 1984, and I received an education as an exile.

Have you encountered any reaction while travelling the world, especially after the coup?
One time in Berlin a Turk pulled out a knife. Şafak Salda was at my side. It was something polemical between him and Şafak. Once while my dear friends were seeing me off at Berlin Tegel Airport, a man came up and taunted me. I spoke with him, and we flew together all the way to Brussels. When we landed in Brussels, he said, 'I should drop you off at home.'

There's something where Turkish citizens learn about what happens in the world to the extent that it's translated for them because, unfortunately, of their foreign language deficiencies. Miracles in the Republic of Turkey aren't things that transcend the arrangement. I see the cultural structure in the country a bit like Fecri Ebcioğlu's writing lyrics over stolen music. It's always established over a theft, over a shakedown. The most recent example of this is the project of Gülben Ergen's husband and Yılmaz Erdoğan's brother, who emerged under the name 'The Sultans of Dance' and was actually obliged to change

---

[1] CEFTUS is an independent and non-partisan organisation based in London. Its mission is to build bridges between the UK and Turkey and the region.

it to the Anadolu Ateşi folk dance troupe. The names already tell the whole story in this sentence. So I don't blame those people because Turkey has citizens who are not cosmopolitan and because they view the world through a lens they create with biased, one-sided and fake news which is broadcast on news channels on which they watch scandals such as Müge Anlı and Esra Erol or which is seen on *A Haber* or in *Yeni Şafak*. They're people who are made to believe. I see the AKP somewhat like the Crusaders, something like missionaries, like colonisers, because they're writing a non-existent history and trying to erase the local history. Of course, society is affected by this and is filled with hatred because of their prejudices. There is no sexual satisfaction, no cultural satisfaction, no sport or art, no economic might; life continues merely in front of a monitor and television screen, and so these reactions form quite naturally.

I met with Can Dündar at an event in Berlin. The police were there, of course, because of Can. But I joked around a bit with the German police. I know German because I studied at a German high school. A fan came up and wanted to hug me, but the police pushed them away. I explained the situation, hugged them and took a picture. We went out to eat after the event. The police told me, 'The Turkish organisations here described you so differently that I understood when I recognised you what kind of lies they told, I was embarrassed. You are a completely different person. That's why we won't come with you to the restaurant. You're safer than us.' Everything is resolved through dialogue. This too will pass. And our nation, the Turkish nation, has a certain characteristic; they applaud – they applaud their own – make them heroes, lift them up but grab their ass while they hold them up. When they get shit on their fingers, they throw them off and rise up to grab at someone else. This is our story of creating heroes.

Do you feel like you're in exile? What does exile mean to you?
No. I have never, at any point in my life, felt like I was in exile. Perhaps this was because I always went on my own accord. I have a

sexual orientation and lifestyle preferences. I mean, they can't pressure me. I stayed fighting in Turkey for years. I was one of the first figures of Gezi Park, I was one of the first people to start the LGBTI parades, I was on the streets, like a guard activist every day with a lollipop in my hand protesting the 5199 animal rights issues, and human rights issues. I'll tell you an ironic story about my reason for leaving. I left Turkey because of violent intra-family discord. I couldn't bear the violence any longer, and Turkey is a place that supports violence, not dialogue. It's always about taking a hostage, blackmail, threats, slander, neglecting to listen to who's in front of you. I couldn't tolerate this anymore. I made this decision and left on my own, even though I have lower standards of living and economic conditions than before. And I won't pay alimony.

You said you left in 1980 and couldn't return for nine years. What is the difference between your departure then and your departure now?

If I would make a comparison, my sexual performance, economic status, educational situation, and life experience at the age of twenty in the 1980s are incomparable. It's very different. But there was hope for that day in Turkey. Everyone who left – Melika Demirağ, Şanar Yurdatapan, and I can list more names – when our friends left, they existed as people fighting for their country in different lands. I'm that way as well. I was attending university while residing in London and also working on women's clothes on Monday nights at the Hippodrome. I would go shopping in the streets of London, get cotton, sew shirts, press them with scouring pads and sell them. The conditions were challenging. There were no mobile phones or credit cards at the time, but there was hope. I achieved considerable professional success nationally and internationally after I returned. I dressed the Congolese president, Denis Sassou Nguesso, and his family. I held grand weddings for the family of OPEC founder Zeki Ahmed Yamani. I reached the peak of my career, but during my career in

Turkey, I saw that the Republic of Turkey was no longer being worn. It was being covered or taken off. They didn't need me anymore in a professional sense. Politically, unfortunately, the regime and opposition transformed into a bloc mass at any criticism about the alleged opposition because they had donned names and titles like patriotism, nationalism, sensibilities and values. It was a befuddled land that had lost control. It was now a dangerous land. The conditions are the same today. That's why I gave up the fight. I gave it up for Turkey, but I haven't given it up for the rights of Turkish citizens in the international public and legal system of the future. But as a citizen of the Republic of Turkey, I become upset during international trips when I see the struggles of my friends who are living in exile – by necessity or voluntarily – and who have set up new lives for themselves, when I realise the country's considerable losses. So perhaps those who want to return one day will do so.

There is no right to cremation in Turkey. I don't want to be buried in a casket in a mosque with the *selâs*. I don't want my ass to be grabbed. This is my body. I want to be cremated. And the Republic of Turkey says, 'No, you cannot be cremated. We'll absolutely cram you into a mosque.' We're almost at the point where blasphemy laws will be issued in this country. You have seen what has happened recently. I'm in the eastern Mediterranean because of the nonsense about sensibilities and values. I'm twenty minutes away from seven countries by plane. The heart of Israel is twenty-eight minutes. Tel Aviv's beaches are wonderful. Cairo is there, Jordan, Lebanon are there, Syria is there, Greece is there and Turkey is there. I can go wherever I want in the world. So the homeland is not where a person's stomach is full but where their hopes flourish.

Every different group in Turkey has its own distinct perception of Turkey. And there is one reason everyone points to as the reason for their being where they are, but they also have different critical junctions. Some say 15 July, others say

17–25 December and others say the Kobane protests. Which incident drove you there?

First, your conclusion is quite pointed, everyone has a Turkey they dream about belonging to, because Turkey is actually a country with an invisible caste system, like India. You belong to a religious organisation, or an athletic club, or a neighbourhood . . . there's a question in Turkey where people in Istanbul ask you, 'Where are you from, neighbour?' I mean, you're in Istanbul, and they're asking you where you're from. Turkish citizens feel the need to cling to a place to complete their own lack of belonging, because all the ideals prioritised in the efforts to create a nation-state ignored the others. Kurds, Zazas, Armenians, Jews, the Orthodox community, Protestants, homosexuals, Jehovah's Witnesses, they have all been turned into infidels and demonised . . . The upper class has always been constructed beneath the maximum interests. But it needs to be the lowest common denominator. Turkish citizens are not people who consider the lowest common denominator. It's a society that considers the maximum interests, those of itself, the family, the lover . . . I mean, they park their car in another's parking spot in an apartment car park. 'Theirs is more in the shade,' they say. 'Why is mine more in the sun?' they say. They're always in a state of interrogation. The capacity of Turkish citizens for acceptance and producing a result is low.

Why is it like that?

Because from the moment of birth [Turkish children hear]: 'Show your uncle your penis, son', 'Get up, young lady, do ballet', 'Come on, young lady, belly dance', and later on, 'Don't sit with your legs open' and 'Get your hand off your penis, son'. You can't raise a healthy individual in this society. It's very easy to analyse Turkey when you view it from the streets with the basic public. Look, I've worked with ten thousand women. These are the wealthiest, most famous and most powerful women in Turkey and the world. There are names from Victoria Beckham to Maria Schneider who are known around the world. I have worked with the best models in the world. I have contact with the best companies in the world. I have contact with all the largest media organisations in the world. I have done television programmes. I have written books. And when I look back on my performances, I performed a miracle in the desert in Turkey, but that flower can't survive in the desert; I realised that as I matured. You leave a cactus in the desert and walk away. Orchids bloom in humid, tropical climates. Chasing your dreams is beautiful, but when you return to reality, those dreams can come true when you are able to build them. The dreams that others present to you and shoot down pick you up and carry you away from life. Our friends living abroad right now don't care much for the struggle in Turkey, perhaps because they don't realise this. When you look at the flow of daily news in Turkey, an academic, an activist, a prominent figure in society whom you recognise, know and trust . . . you look and, in the morning, say 'Good morning, have a blessed Friday'. Towards midday we say 'Boy, did we beat Fenerbahçe!' And after midday, 'No to child abuse', and after lunch, 'No to animal cruelty', and towards evening, 'Look, I ate lunch here; look, this is my new ring', and towards the evening a bit more erotic, a little longer until night . . . When you look at that parabolic graph, it becomes a place in which the lives of imbalanced people are granulated. It's a place that grinds up people's lives. And the primary, underlying reasons for this are that great economic powers of the world like the United Kingdom, United States and European Union overlooked some things and transformed Turkey into a temporary refugee depot and gave this as ammunition to the hands of the government. It also touches on cultural hegemony and on economic capitulation. This world order – I'm not saying this in a critical sense. It's valid for every country. But the Republic of Turkey has transformed into a hungry chicken which thinks it's a grain storehouse. There aren't many things left that I could do. I will continue my life in Cyprus, which I have made my own, where I live and where I believe I can exist and produce, and where I should be able to do something for the people. Turkey has reduced my capacity to such a great extent.

Perhaps if Turkey was a secular, democratic, social law state, perhaps if it was a modern state, I could have made my fight there more internationally forceful, but Turkey didn't permit this. The newspapers made me into a Gülenist terrorist because I went to their event at the European Union Press Club in Brussels. I mean, it's impossible for me to be a member of the Fethullah Gülen Movement; I'm an atheist. I haven't ever believed in religion. More ironically, I was declared transphobic, as a gay man in Turkey, because I fought with Bülent Ersoy because she didn't pay me. Bülent Ersoy has been my friend for forty years. We always fight. They interfered with her. And I've grown weary of this.

I'm continuing from where I'm at now, but this time for the bodily integrity, belief, conscience, and the freedom of thought and expression, not just in the Republic of Turkey but around the world. And I'm not saying this in a heteronormative sense. The environment, of course, is my first target right now, because you see what the situation is in Canada. The earth is warming; the freshwater reserves that are being depleted are critical for our vital assets. Natural fibres are incredibly important. There are a lot of people for whom I will fight. I won't do this for a single society anymore. I am weary of that society.

The reason you won't return is because of this weariness and intimidation, as far as I understand.
No, it's not just because of the intimidation. I won't return. I mean this isn't intimidation. I won't return to that cesspool. That place is a cesspool in every regard. That place, for me, is a characterless geographic space with its politics, opposition, bureaucracy, security, military, police, mafia and art. Why should I go? It has no qualities. The pharaoh projects don't interest me. They made the canal, the bridge, the mosque, the cultural centre. The buildings don't interest me. The people don't interest me. My childhood was very cosmopolitan

together with Jews and Armenians. I mean, could you consider living in a city where 30 per cent of the population in the 1930s was Orthodox but is now just 1,200 in a city of 18 million? What is there for me in that space? I won't spend my money there. Hakan Uzan had a lovely quote, he said, 'Look, Barbaros, you attempt to do the impossible and earn money, work under difficult conditions. When you spend your money, don't do it in countries where the average annual income is less than $20,000; it's not worth it.' This angered me. One day at a bazaar where I was going to drink coffee in Cameroon, they wanted $5 for a cup of wretched coffee in a cracked cup; that disgusting coffee explains something about Cameroon, the homeland of coffee. If I can drink the same coffee on beautiful boulevards in Paris for only $2, why should I go to Cameroon?

A new layer of Turkish diaspora has formed recently in Europe. It would probably be the most diverse migration wave compared to diasporas in the past. Have there been groups from the new or old Turkish diaspora that have supported you significantly, offered to cooperate or invited you somewhere else – to Germany or the UK, for example?

They have all invited me, but I don't believe verbal declarations or promises. I look at life very professionally. I carry as much as I can. I can't always satisfy the requests of others. Many have invited me, but those invitations are not actually for my struggle. Those invitations are because I'm Barbaros Şansal, because I'm famous, because I'm accepted despite being a member of the LGBTI community and I could be a key for them. In other words, I see it as the reflection of genetic nepotism in Turkey.

I don't trust anyone who sends me an invitation. Nobody does in their home country what an expat does abroad. Citizens of the Republic of Turkey have immediately begun living in a more communal state. Where are the Turkish neighbourhoods in Brussels or Munich, for example? They're right behind the train stations, because those who arrive get settled in the first place they find immediately after stepping off the train, and they try to create their own communities. We can't break ourselves off as a nation. We are incapable of acclimatising to the idea of living independently, as an individual, and of advancing by adapting to new cultures. I'm a little different. If you notice my speeches and terminology, I don't use words like 'but', 'contrarily', 'however'. I'm a man of yes and no. I never get hung up on 'I wonder'. While eating at the Bundestag, an MP said, 'Live in Berlin for two months, your citizenship is ready.' I said, 'No thank you.' The MP was shocked. Those things aren't important to me. I learned to stay far away from societies that try to copulate in the dark and in silence but dream of others, turning their partners into masturbatory implements.

Do you think that the Turkish diaspora can change the world's – North America and Europe's especially – degraded perception of Turkey? Or are we going to experience the projection of a vertically and horizontally polarised Turkey?

The latter is more probable, but I'll offer an example: regardless of how successful it is in Britain, the owner of Alligator beers is an Indian lord, and the locals say 'Deal'. After all, that racism, belittlement, self-righteousness is in every nation. The families leaving Turkey as the first-generation worker migrants were never integrated. They worked, saved up money, made homes in their villages and tried to return. But they had children in the meantime. Their children became relatively integrated. They became teachers and government officials. But the third generation – their children – have broken off entirely from this integration in the past twenty years. Because the ministry formed something called the YTB (Presidency for Turks Abroad and Related Communities). These religious organisations, *cemaat*, foundations and so forth. So Turkey began to implement the strategies that the colonialist order had implemented 150 to 200 years earlier. The strategies of nationalisation, Ottomanisation, Islamisation and amassing voters living abroad poisoned Turkey's international image. We were travelling visa-free to Britain before 1980 with a Turkish passport. My first trip to London was without a visa. The visa requirements began in 1984 and in 1994. They are quite new for Turkish citizens. Moreover, without reaching an agreement. So they don't have to get a visa to come to you, but you have to get one to go to them. This is a violation of international law.

Although Turkey's diaspora – whether Gülenist or PKK member or LGBTI individual – may appear to be unified in the fight due to the common denominators brought about by living in exile or far away from the country, they are not. Because the maximum interests are to the fore and they are unable to meet at the lowest common denominator. It's impossible to enter a collective battle without determining the lowest common denominator.

So this sort of division will make post-Erdoğan restoration impossible, don't you think?
It's already like that. What will you restore now? There must be work on hand for us to be able to restore. But there is nothing on hand to restore. Are you going to restore the TOKI buildings? What's available? There is nothing left of value. What would happen if you restored a precast concrete tower? What if you didn't? There's that, and a whole new regime has been created by abolishing the principles, the values of the Republic of Turkey, though they've been debated for the past twenty years, and there's this regime's fanatical electorate of 30–40 million people. Removing Erdoğan from this system won't change anything. The underlying hierarchical structure will continue to nourish this system. Özal had said, 'My official knows how to do his job.' That's where everything started. You look now, and men, businessmen say at their meetings, 'I was stealing the remaining *döner* while working as a *döner* salesman, I was putting it in sandwiches and selling it to my customers. I was caught.' This is applauded in Turkey. There aren't any left like Suna Kan, İdil Biret, Ferit Edgü, İbrahim

Çallı, journalist Ümit Deniz. But in Turkey there are Demet Akalın, Bülent Ersoy and Safiye Soyman.

You said you'll continue working for everyone living in Cyprus and for Turkish citizens. You're not hopeful, but you're also working for these places. Do you have no hope left for Turkey? At the current conjuncture, feeding my own hope for Turkey is a bit of a visionary mindset. I can't know what time will tell. Of course, my dream is that people coexist healthily in togetherness, tranquillity and peace in a secular, democratic, social law state and a powerful Republic of Turkey. This is also true for Uganda, and for the UK, and for Singapore and for Saudi Arabia. This is true for everyone in the world. We are in the twenty-first century now, and we are preparing to pass into a brand-new world order after this pandemic. And this is irrefutable. But for this, you must determine whether returning is worth the cost. You must determine the price you'll pay. When others begin to estimate the price for you, you fall into the proletariat, the oppressed class. That's why I will continue my fight internationally in line with the ideals and truths I believe in, and it is impossible for me to do this in the Republic of Turkey. Because there is no longer any freedom of expression, life or property in the Republic of Turkey. A polar bear can't live in the desert for the same reason a frog can't. You choose your geography, you know your capacity, you measure your opportunities and you fight based on that. Revolution does not occur simply by shouting that the only path is revolution.

2

BÜLENT SOMAY

**If I don't trust my students, this relationship has been
broken for me. The moment I began to see my students as
potential informants, potential rogues, that meant that
I would no longer be able to teach classes well.
I decided there and then.**

*Born in Istanbul and with BA and MA degrees in English language
and literature, Bülent Somay was a lecturer in comparative literature and cultural studies at Istanbul Bilgi University between 2000
and 2017 and was the director of the Cultural Studies Graduate
Programme between 2006 and 2017. His main interests are Marxist
theory, psychoanalysis, psycho-cultural analytic theory, postcolonial
theory, and utopian literature and science fiction. He earned a PhD
in psychosocial studies from Birkbeck College, University of London,*

in 2013. He has published seven books in Turkish (Geriye Kalan Devrimdir *('What Remains Is the Revolution'), 1997;* Şarkı Okuma Kitabı *('Song Reader'), 2000;* Tarihin Bilinçdışı *('The Unconscious of History'), 2004;* Bir Şeyler Eksik *('Something Is Missing'), 2007;* Çokbilmiş Özne *('The Subject Who Knows Too Much'), 2008;* Tarih, Otobiyografi ve Hakikat *('History, Autobiography and Truth', ed.), 2015;* Cinsellik Hakkında Vazgeçmemiz Gereken Yüz Efsane *('A Hundred Myths We'd Better Give Up about Sexuality'), 2016), four books in English* (The View from the Masthead: Journey through Dystopia towards an Open-Ended Utopia, *2010;* The Psychopolitics of the Oriental Father: Between Omnipotence and Emasculation, *2014;* Something Is Missing, *2021;* The End of Truth: Five Essays on the Demise of Neoliberalism), *and one book forthcoming* (Beyond Family: A Case for Another Regime of Reproduction, Sexuality and Kinship). *He was a research fellow at Université Libre de Bruxelles (2017–18) and the University of Oslo (2018–19), an Academy in Exile fellow at Freie Universität Berlin (2019–21), and is currently working at Off-University, Berlin.*

Can you tell us when and why you left Turkey?

I left Turkey in September 2017. Right before this, I resigned from my various positions at Bilgi University. Coming to the question of why I left, there are a few reasons. First, I was actually one of the lucky few who left during that time in Turkey. I mean, I wasn't the worst victim. Why? Because they didn't fire me.

I was on the Academics for Peace team. I was among those against whom a case was filed and who were acquitted in late 2019. I think they couldn't file all the lawsuits yet; there were 600 people in the case I was in. The figures may not be accurate; I'm not entirely sure. But they were able to open a case against 600 people whom I remember, because they were filing them piecemeal, and they didn't file a single, massive lawsuit. I was acquitted in October or November 2019. Another lawsuit had been filed in 2017. I first went and gave my statement to the police. I gave my statement to the prosecution remotely because I was abroad. Bilgi University, unlike a number of other private universities, didn't immediately fire us. I think they implemented a tactic where they first got the views of the Faculty of Law. Because the Faculty of Law provided a report, saying there was no justification for opening an investigation, no justification for firing the signatories, Bilgi used this in later months and years against the Council of Higher Education (*Yüksek Öğretim Kurumu* – YÖK). It said, 'While our own Faculty of Law gave such a report, if we do what you want and open an investigation, we won't have taken our own Faculty of Law seriously.' I remember that the Council of Higher Education accepted this justification grudgingly. One of the two chancellors was called, and I remember him/her saying, 'Come on, open an investigation into them.' I don't know the details. So Bilgi didn't fire us. But on the other hand, they didn't approach us with much empathy either.

I received a post-doc position from Université Libre de Bruxelles in mid-2017. At that time, I had requested unpaid time off for a year, because I had already taken a sabbatical in 2012. The dean's office accepted it, the chancellor's office accepted it, the university senate accepted it, but it got stuck in the board of trustees. The board of trustees – what I'm saying is gossip, of course, since I wasn't at the meeting and didn't see the meeting minutes – said 'This person was a peace signatory and didn't accept our request, don't give him this position.' So I said I'd resign and I submitted my resignation. What I was doing for the next year was already clear – I was going to Brussels. I left and went to Brussels in September 2017.

There weren't any notices or limitations placed on your passport as far as I understand.

No, there weren't. My passport expired sometime last year (2020). I applied to the Berlin consulate. They renewed my passport. So there weren't any problems.

There's no special reason why you went to Brussels probably. You went to Brussels on the fellowship you received, correct? What happened then?

A year had passed in Brussels. It was guaranteed that I would be unemployed if I was to return to Turkey. Returning to Turkey wasn't going to be a smart decision. I submitted a couple of applications. This time, Scholars at Risk found a position for me at the University of Oslo. I spent a year there. My postdoc could have been extended in Oslo. It couldn't have been extended in Brussels because it was a limited one-year fellowship the university itself provided. Oslo was providing it through Scholars at Risk, so I requested an extension. The department didn't want to extend it.

What was the reasoning?

The reasoning was that I was not a good fit for the department, which was true, because unfortunately – not to belittle the department – I really wasn't a good fit. I was in the Media and Communications Department there, while my subject was first in English language and literature and then in psychosocial studies. So however I looked at it, it wasn't a good fit. They weren't wrong, but Scholars at Risk insisted, and they extended it for another year. But at the same time, Academy in Exile offered me a year-long fellowship in Berlin. I opted to go to Berlin rather than staying in Oslo, thinking it would be more colourful, more social, a life where I would meet more people. We couldn't have predicted the pandemic at the time.

Did you say you were a signatory of peace and that you didn't have opportunities to work in Turkey while applying for these funds?

It was exactly like that. I mean, I didn't invent stories as if my life was in danger. Because then it would have been much exaggerated. I said that I was a signatory of peace, that I was pushed to resign – I didn't even say I was *forced*, because I could have stayed at Bilgi. The reason

I didn't want to stay at Bilgi was because during my last year there, they suddenly decided to fire Zeynep Sayın, whom they had hired part-time.[1]

Wasn't that after students recorded what she said in class and leaked it to the press?

Definitely. It leaked to the press, I think the news was in *Yeni Şafak* or *Yeni Akit*. YÖK probably sent a signal when that happened, saying, 'What's going on?' She was fired immediately. It wasn't very easy for us to fight this decision because they made a new agreement for each course, since she was on a per-course contract. So, there was no terminated contract. The department was told she would not teach another class; it ended, and she left. I think it was the Faculty of Architecture. They had no chance to resist because the board of trustees approves part-time courses. It won't happen if it's not approved. It wasn't a decision that the department could make on its own. So that happened and we talked among ourselves and wrote something of a protest together to the chancellor. I caught myself the very next day wondering whether I should gather the students' phones as they entered class, and I decided at that moment to leave. Because I'm not a very assertive person on issues of academia; I do not exactly consider myself as an academic. Although I taught for seventeen years at Bilgi, I describe myself rather as a writer than an academic. So I wouldn't call it 'academic etiquette', but rather an ethical stand: if I don't trust my students, our relationship is broken. The moment I began to see my students as potential informants, potential rogues, was the moment that I would no longer be able to teach classes well. I decided there and then. We live in an incredibly divided society. There were a few incidents like when a group of students attacked female students who set

---

[1] For more information on Zeynep Sayin's case, see BIA, 'Bilgi University lays off academic over "insulting president"', Bianet, 16 June 2016, https://bianet.org/english/freedom-of-expression/175905-bilgi-university-lays-off-academic-over-insulting-president, accessed 27 February 2023.

up a booth on 8 March – Women's Day. I say this symbolically. Ultimately, the students have been divided. I must teach divided classes because I can't pick and choose the students in my classes. With this sharp division, I thought that the university would not be able to be managed reasonably and because I don't see myself very much as an academic. I mean, I love to teach, but I have never been a professional researcher. My subjects weren't generally research topics. So, when I wrote, I usually published outside academic venues. If there was research to be done, I did that outside of the university. Coming to teaching, I thought that I would find a way to teach freelance classes as much as possible, and I decided to resign.

You left Turkey couple of times for your studies in the past. But this departure is different from the others, no? Leaving Turkey, being dismissed, feeling unwanted, choosing to go . . . How is the psychology for this? I'm asking this of someone who didn't leave in their twenties for their PhD.

You're correct. I have left Turkey three times to live outside the country. I was twenty-six the first time when I left to do my PhD. Of course, I left immediately after the 12 September coup, and it was a similar departure, because it was the end of 1981, and we didn't know what would happen in Turkey. We didn't know how things would develop. I didn't know if I could even do a PhD at a university in Turkey. I didn't know which of my friends who had been detained, arrested or imprisoned were tortured and forced to speak and gave my name, because nobody has to be silent when being tortured. Such heroism wasn't a given for me. I would appreciate it, but I wouldn't be angry with those who did [speak]. So there was always a risk in that way, and I left to escape from the 12 September regime, because I didn't see an opportunity to stay in Turkey and do my PhD. I didn't know for how long I would be abroad. On the other hand, I had some financial problems, and on top of these, my mother was very ill. I returned to Turkey in 1983, and I think we lost her four months later in December 1983.

I have always been a little bit of a mummy's boy. I was an only child, and the money we were earning in Montreal was really not enough. We went as husband and wife. That's why I returned.

I broke off my relationship with academia after returning. I said I wouldn't continue at the university. I worked at thousands of different jobs. These included as a musician, a journalist, a columnist, as a copywriter at advertising agencies, as an editor at publishing houses, whatever you could think of. Then, in 2000, I thought I could teach at Bilgi University. I spoke with Murat Belge, then the comparative literature chairperson, and said, 'I could teach such-and-such a class for you.' Murat said, 'Come, teach.' I began teaching in 2000. I started with one course per semester, which became two per semester in 2001, and four in 2003. Dean Alan Duben called me and joked, 'You're swindling us, because you are making more money than you would have if we had hired you as a faculty member.' I said, 'Okay, then hire me as a faculty member.' Alan opened a spot for me on the faculty, and I began to teach as a faculty member starting in 2003. I taught about three or four classes per semester from 2003 until 2017. It was a long time, and it could be said that I accepted academia in a sense. But after 2016, when cases were opened against us after the statements of the chap intending to 'shower in our blood'[2] and the president declaring that we were traitors, and when we were tried for aiding and abetting a terrorist organisation, it didn't have much meaning left. But as I said, teaching has always been important to me. I saw teaching not just as professorship but as a sort of performance art. And this wasn't something to give up on. I love teaching, although I write as well. My books were published during this period. I'm still writing.

[2] 'Notorious criminal threatens academics calling for peace in Turkey's southeast', *Hürriyet Daily News*, 13 January 2016, https://www.hurriyetdailynews.com/notorious-criminal-threatens-academics-calling-for-peace-in-turkeys-southeast-93834, accessed 27 February 2023.

I went to London in 2011 for my PhD and spent a year there before returning. I finished my PhD in two years and three months. And that was because Bilgi University was sold to an American conglomerate called Laureate Education. They tried to set up a more official, more hierarchical structure. I didn't have the opportunity to continue my job as a faculty member without a PhD then. Being a faculty member without a PhD would have been difficult financially, and I wouldn't have been able to perform any administrative duties. But at the time, I was the director of the Cultural Studies Department. Various friends urged me to go and get my PhD. The former administration that sold Bilgi said, 'We'll give you a fellowship, go and get your PhD.' I left, went to London and did my PhD at Birkbeck. This is a new doctorate. My old, unfinished doctorate was in English literature. This one was in psychosocial studies. I had left Bilgi on sabbatical for a year, and that was the agreement I made with Birkbeck. I was going to spend a year there and a year at my own university, and they were going to monitor whether I was at a university. They wouldn't accept it any other way. But I was already going to be out there, because I would be teaching there. I wrote my dissertation in a hurry. I completed my dissertation and went back to London for the PhD viva in November 2013. So, I finished my thesis in about two years and three months. Thanks to the British system! They didn't tell me to do my PhD and take a bunch of (mostly unnecessary) courses like in the American system. This last one was my third departure.

What are the psychological differences between these?
It wasn't much different from my first departure.

In terms of uncertainty and so forth?
Of course, because the second time I had simply gone to do a PhD. The first time I had gone to Canada, where PhDs last approximately five years. I took on a loan to fund my PhD. There wasn't any possibility of paying it back if I returned to Turkey. So after I finished the PhD,

there were options like staying in Canada or the US, paying that debt off and maybe finding a good job opportunity and staying long term. That's why that departure was uncertain. But it was a very open-ended departure. I mean, if it hadn't been for my mother, I could have continued my PhD, continued going into debt. It wasn't that much debt. I was an assistant, a teacher's assistant, and I earned a wage, but it wasn't enough. That's why I went into debt each year, little by little. This last time is a different departure from that because it wasn't open-ended. I went through a review every year. Let's see, are you under threat? We go through reviews each year about whether this is working out for us, and of course, I came across another problem that wasn't an issue during my first departure, that popped up as a raised eyebrow when I left for my second PhD and that hit me like a cannonball this time. And that was ageism – in other words, 'You're too old for this shit. Many young people in your position will be the future of academia. Why should we give this money to you?'

How do you defend yourself?
Well, no one has ever said this to my face explicitly.

If someone were to?
I would say this is ageism.

You said it hit you like a cannonball. If no one said it explicitly, how did you understand? Are you going off a hunch?
I understood from the nature of the rejections. I submitted forty-four applications between 2016 and 2017. One was accepted. Human resources responded to about thirty-five of the forty-four applications. Although I'm not much of a quantitative social scientist, I know a little about analysing data. If, out of forty-four applications, thirty-five come back from human resources, it means you're not being evaluated academically. So, what are they evaluating? I have the experience. I have the references. Where could I be losing out? With my age, of

course. So that was the basic challenge here. I fell into the position of an elderly man dashed from here to there. Is this fair? Partly, and I consider my age when I look for places to apply. There are already distinctions like junior scholars. I have an advantage there, because only a short period of time has passed since I got my PhD. But I don't use this as much as I could. Rather, I apply to positions that look for senior scholars or at least that don't make such a distinction. I gave up on quite a few places for this reason.

Fourteen years between 2003 and 2017 is a serious length of time – fourteen years in an area like academia where stability is very limited. It almost became something like a permanent job. After that – I'm saying this because you did – did falling into precarity with fellowships at this age, being sent away from the country evoke any sort of fury, anger or resentment?
Because I struggle to consider the situation with an academic perspective, it evokes not a resentment – we don't hold grudges – for the country, but anger. Ultimately, I had written seven books in Turkish by the time I left. I taught for years. I did everything I could to be active, respected, productive. The word 'useful' is always suspect for me, but I tried to be useful in the cultural world in Turkey. 'Useful' is a dangerous word. Useful to whom? One of the topics I'm studying right now is the distinction between useful and useless information. There's a great book on this topic by Nuccio Ordine, they also published it in Turkish, under the title *The Usefulness of the Useless*. Today, if you provide a use, an input to the neoliberal capitalist order, you are useful. And this isn't a principle that has become valid just for Turkey but for the whole world. That's why I didn't really want to be someone useful in this sense; in fact, I thought it would be better if I wasn't. But in the sense that Ordine uses the word, if use is to benefit all human culture and, gradually, the survival of the planet, I think I have one or two uses on this issue. That's why there's a regime in Turkey completely ignoring this 'use'.

Am I furious with Turkey? Yes, I am. There's a political adminis-tration that has entirely neglected how I, like thousands of academ-ics and intellectuals in my position, have contributed to the cultural world in Turkey so far without considering what I have done, what I have taught, and says, 'This person signed this. He's already a leftist, we've known this forever. Let's throw him aboard.' But this isn't just happening in Turkey. I'm about to have spent four years here, and one thing that being abroad for four years and being swept around like a broom has taught me is that the situation in Turkey is not much different from the trajectory around the world, although I'm not say-ing that we're exaggerating it, because the situation in Turkey is truly terrible. Moreover, what I mean when I say the trajectory around the world, I'm not talking only about the world of right-populist totalitar-ians and, in fact, autocratic regimes in the countries in the 'moderni-sation process' – I'm definitely saying this in quotation marks – like India, Brazil and us. To the contrary, I lived in Germany, Belgium and Norway. You should spend some time in Norway, for example, to see very clearly how Nazism was able to emerge in northern Europe.

Do you feel like you're in exile?

I don't consider my own situation exile. Why? Because when I say 'Let's go', I am able to return to Turkey. At least since the end of 2019 – for a year and a half – since the acquittal and because they didn't rise up to launch another case, if I return to Turkey today, nobody will stand at the gate and say 'Why are you coming?' or stop me and not let me in. I'll go and be unemployed. I have a small pen-sion coming from Social Security. I wouldn't be able to get by just on that, but I could do this and that, some freelance work, and I'd find a way to get by. I'm not someone who prefers to live luxuriously or extremely comfortably anyway. I can live under any circumstances. That's why I could return. So if I'm saying that I can return, I think this means I shouldn't call this exile. I should call it semi-exile. Why? I could return, but if I return, my life will be poor in two ways: in terms of money, because I don't have any savings – I survive as long as I am able to work; and in terms of politics, because nobody knows what will happen politically in Turkey tomorrow. I'm not sure that they won't break down my door with a battering ram at 5.30 in the morning because of a tweet I shared. In Germany, at least, I'm sure this won't happen for another three or four years. Based on the rise of the AfD, however, we can't even be sure that this will not happen in three or four years.

You're witnessing the process of Turkey's most diverse diasporas emerging, and maybe you're progressing towards being one of those. There are intellectuals, leftists, Kurds, Alevis and Islamist movements. There are youth movements and the elderly. There are former AKP members and a lot of people who have recently left the AKP. There are members of the CHP. You're a part of a circle that stands a little more to the left in Turkey. But you're encountering many different structures now. How have your relationships with different groups in the diaspora been in this process?
I had been in contact with hardly any Turkish people in Belgium. Other than friends coming to visit from Turkey, I didn't have any connection with the Turkish nationals in the diaspora living there. It happened once; I went to vote in the Turkish presidential election and waited for hours in a marvellous queue. I had the chance to see Alevis, Kurds, Turks and Muslims living in Molenbeek all together. I saw the discussions and near-fights among them. The division there is frightening. But there isn't much of an academic diaspora there. I mean, there are very few people.

Oslo is the same. It's not really possible to talk about the academic Turkish diaspora there. There are some people who found an academic fellowship – in fact, I know a few people who found work directly at a university. But I've come across maybe two or three people. That's why I wanted to leave Oslo. Berlin is almost like the centre of the world for the Turkish diaspora, but Covid-19 didn't permit socialising there either. I was shut up inside for a while after coming to Berlin. The Turkish diaspora lives mostly in Neukölln and Kreuzberg. I opted for Steglitz, because I wanted to live in a calmer, cheaper area. It's in the south-west, very middle class. There are Turks here of course, there are all types of people, but it is essentially a middle-class, white German neighbourhood. It was an old Jewish neighbourhood, by the way. I chose to live there, but at the time, I didn't know that Covid-19 would come, of course.

The groups in the Turkish diaspora became more active on social media when Covid-19 came. Have any of these different groups approached you?
Yes. There are groups of friends from the old diaspora here – not the diaspora of the AK Party era – but the older diaspora. They're leftists. 'Come, let's meet up,' they said. 'Okay,' I said. Because they're my age or older and struggle with adapting to social media and the digital environment. But after the pandemic started, those invitations stopped. I joined the BAK (Academics for Peace) Germany email list as soon as I arrived. But I don't interact with them much. I usually follow what happens, but that's probably because I don't have much to say . . .

Everybody has a different Turkey, so the incident that they view as the breaking point that led to their being in Germany or France right now is different, and they generally connect this breaking point to a specific reason. For you, what is the breaking point that caused you to be in Germany today? Was it only the signature?
It wasn't only the signature. To be honest, even if I hadn't been a signatory, I would have eventually left the university after 15 July. But there weren't the living conditions available for me to leave the university, and I hadn't saved up any money in the various jobs I did after

returning to Turkey in 1983. Sometimes I earned a little and spent it. Sometimes I earned better money, and I spent that too. I didn't save up money, nor did I buy a home. I see from this that I'm not a good investor. I didn't establish any networks. That's one of the things I haven't been able to succeed at in life. I lived like this for seventeen years, between 1983 and 2000. After that, I worked for close to the minimum wage but with a commission as a faculty member without a PhD at a university, and I had just enough money to get by: 'Take that extra fee from this administrative task, take a bit more there.' So the only thing I could do from the moment the idea not to remain at this university occurred to me was to get some teamwork under my belt and find an academic job outside the country. This didn't have to be a 'job' as such, because I had already turned sixty when I began to think about this. Who would give me a permanent job after I turned sixty? And would I want it? I'll work, I'll live, I'll watch what happens in Turkey from abroad. I'll try and do whatever I can for what happens there. And I'll return to Turkey when the situation becomes a bit more breathable there. This was always my plan. As of 15 July 2016, I saw that they wouldn't let us breathe any longer. And yes, that's why, like most of the people you spoke with, I can tie this to a person, but it is not only because of just that person. As I said, when I came here, I saw that I was out of the frying pan [and] into the fire – a proverb the English really love. I got caught in the sleet as I ran from the rain. Why? Because here it is almost impossible to exist outside academia. Because I had no intentions of applying for political asylum, it's also impossible to stay here outside of academia. The situation for academics here – and when I say 'here', I mean Belgium, Norway and Germany – is terrible. I think there's a serious threat. I prefer to call this 'neoliberalism goes to college'. Of course, although they may not appear to be as dangerous as the threats to liberties or the freedom to live as there are in Turkey. But look at the UK universities, where redundancy debates push people out of work and force them to reapply to their old positions for less pay and on more precarious contracts . . .

Goldsmiths?

It was Goldsmiths, but there were others too. In Hungary, Orbán shut down a large department (Gender Studies I think). That's why the entire university is literally fleeing to Austria, because he's sacking the staff. It's clear this reaction will come. In the US right now, based on my calculations, adjunct professors are teaching more than 60 per cent of classes, people who can't get a contract longer than a year, whose fates are uncertain and who are working for truly low wages. Students in the US, on the other hand, are $1.8 trillion in debt. So there's a system that is taking astounding amounts of money from students and failing to give one-tenth of that to the academics. The American educational system has collapsed in this respect. It is a bit more humane in the UK. Germany is another story. There's a neoliberal attack in Germany, but the country has a more established university structure, which is a sort of a guild structure and is very closed off. So a number of people do their PhDs there and say, 'This professor came in the 1980s, do you know if they've died?' expecting a place for themselves. Positions don't open up. Faculties don't open up. And there's a certain story in Germany: six years after you get your PhD, if you haven't been able to draw up a long-term contract for yourself, the validity of your PhD disappears. It's a very old story. So every country has its own unique differences but, ultimately, has problems that are the product of the neoliberal attack on higher education over the past thirty years. We are experiencing the worst of it in Brazil, India and Turkey, of course, because they are coming along with a political attack. But it's not wonderful in other places either. Yes, there is a series of solidarity networks (I'm saying this for everywhere I've lived) but these solidarity networks quickly turn into charity rather than solidarity, out of necessity.

Would you return to Turkey?

My prediction is that If I return to Turkey, I will retire on my pension, as I said, which is very little. I may be teaching classes freelance here or there – the possibilities have increased a little in Turkey right now – I would teach classes at independent academies or non-university institutions, earn a little money. I could also do pro-bono work. There's almost no possibility of earning money through publications. Not in Turkey, nor elsewhere in the world. Still, I think I'll find a way to get by. I mean, we'll find a way to get by, husband and wife. Ezgi Keskinsoy (my wife) is working right now. I could return; it's not that I don't want to return. I've moved house five times in three countries in three and a half years. This isn't practical at my age. It really wears a person down. It wears you down psychologically. So I want to return, but I can't predict what will happen in the period between June 2021 and June 2022 very well. I mean, I don't view the period until autumn 2022 in a hopeful way. So I'm not very enthusiastic about the prospect of returning Turkey after September 2021 and spending that year in Turkey. That's why I'm waiting for the result of a few applications. The regime won't go away without a struggle; we all know this. It's very clear that Erdoğan won't go quietly, but everyone's view of going away with a struggle, setting boats alight or leaving wreckage behind is different. I didn't expect that they were going to leave behind wreckage this terrible, but they did. This latest pressures on the HDP indicate that. They won't leave without using at least a bit of that paramilitary strength they have amassed so far. I see that they will use this in some way. And this isn't a good thing for the country, of course.

So, the possibility that you would return is somewhat based on Turkey's future?
Yes. I'll probably return by the end of 2022. There's no point in resisting here any longer. All the fellowships I've applied for are two-year fellowships, from September 2021 until September 2023. But I'm considering returning provided that they don't truly strangle Turkey into a civil war, even if I get a two-year fellowship, and say I'll use this year and let someone else use the second. I'm very serious about that.

I could be forced to return this September. All my applications could be pointless, and I could be forced to return. But I don't think I'd have a very good year in Turkey. The crisis of academia in Turkey and the crisis here are two sides of the same coin, and so you aren't saved from the crisis when you flee. We could have talked about saving time, but that's not the topic here. We are only barely surviving here.

3

CAN DÜNDAR

When you are exiled, they define you through your identity
as a Turkish dissident and there you go to another prison, at
least ideologically. This is a little disturbing. After a while,
you only get asked about Erdoğan and Turkey, and this puts
you into a tailspin eventually. It's coming to such a point
that it's as if without Erdoğan you would disappear as well –
as if you exist through your opposition or are
allowed to play on a playground.

Can Dündar has been working as a journalist for the last thirty-seven years for several newspapers and magazines. He is one of the best-known figures in Turkish media and is described as possessing impeccable republican credentials. He has produced many TV documentaries focusing particularly on modern Turkish history and cultural anthropology. He has worked as an anchorman for several news chan-nels. He stepped down from his post as the editor in chief of the daily Cumhuriyet *in August 2016, after he was sentenced to five years ten months of imprisonment due to his story on the Turkish Intelligence Service's involvement in the Syrian war. He is a columnist for the German daily* Die Zeit *and commentator for the German radio organ-isation WDR's Cosmo channel. He founded the news website called #Özgürüz in exile. Dündar was nominated as a candidate for the Nobel Peace Prize in 2017. He has written more than forty books, one of which,* We Are Arrested, *was published in the UK in 2016.*

Mr Dündar, the whole world has heard about your story but could you kindly briefly tell us the reasons why you left Turkey?
I left in the summer of 2016. It was early July. I had just got out of prison in February. I had been working again at the newspaper for four or five months. It was a very busy period with hosting visitors and the ongoing trial process. It was incredibly chaotic at the newspaper. After a period of about four or five months, I asked for time off from the newspaper to go on holiday for a bit to write my book. I went on holiday to Barcelona for a month in early July. The coup happened fifteen days later. I saw the events of 15 July on the television and spoke with my lawyers the next day. They advised me against return-ing because there were signs that the entire regime would change in the country. Indeed, we saw once we waited a couple days that Turkey entered a state of emergency on 20 July. One of the first actions to be carried out was to arrest the members of the Constitutional Court who had issued the ruling for my release. Two members were arrested immediately. All the signs indicated that, if I was to return, I would not be able to leave again for a very long time. There were also violent attacks, and as such there would be issues in terms of personal safety. My family didn't want me to return. I decided to stay for a while and monitor the situation, and this 'for a while' will turn into five years this summer.

Your passport wasn't revoked after staying at home due to the National Intelligence Organisation (Milli İstihbarat Örgütü, MİT) lawsuit, was it? You left with a regular visa.

No, it was not. The Constitutional Court issued a very historic ruling and said that the work that had been done was related to press freedom. As a result, there were no limitations implemented regarding our travelling abroad.

How did your passage from Barcelona to Germany take place? Why did you choose Germany?

I observed the situation for some time in Barcelona. My son was in London. My first goal was to go to London. Indeed, I did go to London and stayed for a while and looked at the situation. England, for a long time, had not talked about anything apart from Brexit. It had almost severed its relations with the world. At the time, I considered this more intensely. They considered Turkey as almost another continent and as completely irrelevant. Later, I received an invitation from Paris. Reporters without Borders proposed a scholarship in Paris. But Turkey was not on the agenda in Paris either. Nevertheless, while I was still in Barcelona, the famous German newspaper *Die Zeit* suggested that I write for them. I immediately accepted. Meanwhile, a film crew came from ARTE to shoot a documentary and made a joint proposal for a documentary. As you know, I am known in Turkey mostly for my documentaries. For us, ARTE is something like the highest attainable standard. I was overjoyed when this proposal came. Later, I realised that German politicians were showing keen interest, frequently calling and trying to get information about what was going on. I understood then that there was an unbelievable degree of interest in Turkey in both the media and in politics. In Germany, I realised that I would be able to exert my authority on behalf of those imprisoned or living in Turkey and that I would at least be able to provide some kind of information. I also saw that I would be able to work in my profession better there. I realised that I could be of service explaining to Germany what was going on in Turkey and explaining to Turkey what was going on in Germany. For those reasons, I decided to move to Berlin.

How are you able to sustain yourself in Berlin? Were your possessions in Turkey seized? Were you able to retrieve your possessions? What is your legal status here?

The decision to seize [my] possessions is more recent. It was made three years after I arrived. Previously, this was an action that predominantly targeted members of the Gülen Movement. I would guess that it was applied to very few people in our position, and one of those was me. I already had no income coming from Turkey. We had a home that they seized. We were still paying off the mortgage. For the first year, I received a stipend from PEN and I later received a stipend from [Reporters without Borders]. But, to be honest, this was only paying my mortgage. I worked a lot outside of that. I probably worked harder than I ever did in Turkey, and I continue to do so. I got two books published here. Later, they were published in various languages: Italian, English and even Chinese. There were royalties for those. I began writing regularly for the website of the Gorki Theatre. I was already writing for *Die Zeit*. And then the documentaries started. We later formed #Özgürüz ['We Are Free']. I had a regular income through #Özgürüz. As a result, I was in a position where I had to do six or seven different jobs. I truly worked a lot, but I am not really complaining.

Right now – as far as I know – there are two actions being taken for those in a situation similar to yours. The first is the application of pressure coming from Turkish legal institutions, what we call transnational repression. The second is the pressure that members of the AKP in the diaspora or the organised group of those who favour the current regime apply to people like yourself. Currently, what is your legal status in Turkey, and are you feeling acts of transnational repression in any way?

I'll first say generally that, more than those two categorical groups you mentioned, I think that the first determines the second. By this I mean that if the official approach of the government demands that you be threatened or attacked, you will be attacked. I don't think that there's much outside the government's control. I can say this not only for myself but on behalf of all journalists who have been attacked in Turkey. From Uğur Mumcu to Ahmet Taner Kışlalı, all the way up to Hrant Dink, I don't think there is a single attack that the government was not involved with. As such, these are things that take place entirely at the discretion of the state, under its observation, with its contribution or acquiescence. The attack perpetrated against me was one of these. So as a result, if the state takes a step back – I mean, there is certainly going to be harassment at work and such – but if this provocation disappears, I don't think that I would experience any serious issue of security. Coming to my personal situation, the threats skyrocketed after Erdoğan came and, during a press conference with Merkel, he said, 'He's an agent.' It was clear that there was a mechanism that was mobilised after that, and both the threats and the harassment became more intense. I think that it later diminished over time. I am, of course, more careful. I have had the opportunity to become more familiar with Berlin. But [the threat] remains.

The polarisation in Turkey is reflected in Germany. There is no escape from this. This is an exported product of Erdoğan's. I see that campaign of polarisation and hatred as it is and, in fact, more profoundly here. This is because Erdoğan's supporters living in the diaspora know very little about Turkey. They know the country as well as A Haber tells it. As such, whoever is shown as an enemy on A Haber, they view as an enemy. That's why it's a bit more difficult to tell the facts here compared to Turkey.

As for my legal status, I was sentenced to five years ten months in prison. The Court of Cassation struck down this decision to my detriment, saying, 'This punishment is not enough. He must be tried for espionage.' After that, I received an even longer sentence. It was twenty years seven months, I think, but I don't remember all the details anymore. It hasn't yet been finalised at the Court of Cassation. That's my biggest case. But apart from that, I have three or four other ongoing lawsuits, as far as I know. One is the Gezi Park case. I was a defendant in the Gezi Park case, where I was tried together with Osman Kavala. I am a defendant in the Özgür Gündem case. I think there's a *Cumhuriyet* case. And then there's a couple of cases about insulting the president.

As far as I know, you don't have a relationship with any Turkish institution, correct?

No, I have no official relationship. It's not recommended. Ultimately, the moment you enter, you're setting foot on Turkish soil. And there is a warrant. The Turkish government has applied serious pressure to Interpol. Thankfully, regarding the issuance of red notices, Interpol understands what the Turkish government is trying to do and doesn't take these sorts of applications seriously.

The German government is aware of all these pressures. You are a well-known individual. Has the German state taken any precautions against all these state-based pressures?

The fact of the matter is that they get word of all this before we do. Sometimes, they end up learning things that I don't know about, because there is a flow of intelligence to them from various channels. Sometimes they alert me: 'We've become aware of a threat against you.' Because it's like this: someone they apprehend confesses or they obtain something in development. Sometimes they end up knowing things we don't know, and they take their own precautions. Sometimes we are aware of this, sometimes we aren't. But for a time – I can say this comfortably since it was reported in the press – there was a warning disclosed by Garo Paylan that a serious assassination team had been dispatched to Germany. They took that one seriously and, for a while, took serious precautions. This happens every so often.

Have you applied for asylum in Germany?

No, I've never applied for asylum. Right now, I'm working as a freelance journalist. I have a work permit, and I'm not thinking about applying for asylum.

There's a perception of hate towards you among A Haber viewers. And then there are some Turks who admire you. What are you doing in terms of solidarity? How do you receive support and from which groups?

Actually, there have been many who have done something, who have offered support, who have rung the door[bell] and asked what they can do, seen me on the street and hugged me. Like you said, we experience these sorts of things a lot. And also like you said, at least, there are dissident circles. A new diaspora is forming. There are people coming from Turkey amid the 'brain drain'. There are Kurds and Alevis who have lived here for years, for generations. There are dissident figures in exile. All of these individuals are aware of the situation; they know what has happened, and they are mobilising to do something. As such, this boosts their morale and it balances out the campaign of hatred on the other side. Sometimes it can turn into something exaggerated. Certainly, there is a need for something. People are trying to do what they can because they have ended up here. Sometimes, a taxi driver won't want to pick you up. Sometimes, you fight to be able to pay for another taxi. Truly, you can experience these two or three situations in taxis all in the same city. But I must say, these are all wonderful relationships that form on a more disorganised, cluttered and personal basis. There's an opposition, a diaspora – or whatever you call it – that is not institutionalised, operates more through personal relationships and frets about what to do. I'll say that there are quite a few humanitarian efforts that are political and, in reality, unable to evolve into solidarity.

There is currently a group of individuals, such as yourself, who have been forced to flee Turkey. There are Kurds, Alevis, leftists,

a segment we can call new middle-class youth and members of the Gülen Movement. How are your relations with these groups? And second, have you contributed to this solidarity network?

First, this is something very new for all of us. Everyone got by with the residence permit for a few years, completing the documents here and [making] efforts to create a new life in a new country. As such, we haven't been able to do this by gaining strength from one another. For a long time I have been saying to those who have been here for a while, 'If only there had been a setup that welcomed new arrivals with open arms, showed them around, helped them and thought about where they could find housing, daycare for their children, where and how they could show solidarity and what kind of organisations could be established.' I don't know if there was an organisation that would do these things, or at least I never encountered it. But to a serious degree, I felt the lack of such an organisation. When academics arrived, they tried to establish connections with universities. There was a solidarity initiative for them at first, but it didn't continue as far as I could see. These all became disconnected. Suddenly, there was a decaying landscape, like each of the prayer beads on a chain were scattered outside of the country, unfortunately. And I still don't see any serious sort of recovery. We held a couple of meetings, as the Turkish nationals in the diaspora. A few of them were successful. It was a search for something we could do together that never played out. There are a few reasons for this. First, people are truly struggling for their lives under grave circumstances and are occupied with their own problems. Second, everyone has reservations. They have serious reservations with the Gülen Movement and members of the HDP and CHP, and academics sometimes have reservations with one another. That's why uniting here is a bit like uniting in Turkey. However, we must be able to do here what we couldn't do in Turkey – that is, unite, come together, take account of the past and look to the future. We must be able to have hope for Turkey's future. But, unfortunately, it didn't happen. There were efforts by the Gülen Movement to grow closer, but I must confess,

I didn't feel much like partaking. Without criticising the Gülen Movement, I don't find their approach of saying 'Oh! Are you here too?' to be very sincere or believable, as if nothing had happened. I also don't find it to be politically correct. But after a bit of self-reflection, we can sit down and talk about where they went wrong, why they did what they did and what they can do so it doesn't happen again. I would respect a community and people who are able to confront the past. I can do this for that cause. But, to be frank, I am a bit distant because I have not yet seen any efforts in this regard.

What is the situation for your family? As far as I know, your wife's passport was confiscated. You mentioned that your son is in London. Are they with you at the moment? What is their legal status?

This has been a very difficult process for my wife in particular because in effect they took her hostage in a way that isn't seen too often. That lasted for three and a half years. After I decided to relocate to Berlin, she came to Barcelona, we spoke and made a certain plan for the future. She later returned to Turkey. She was going to come to Berlin. We were going to keep an eye out like that for a while. Either I would return, or she would move to Berlin. But as she was leaving the airport, they stopped her, saying it looked like her passport was lost. We haven't been able to get any response to the legal steps we've taken since then. We tried other ways, pressuring political channels, but nothing came of it. It's clear that she has been taken hostage to target me because there was no legal accusation directed at her. In the end, it became clear that we would not be able to produce any results and that they wouldn't let her go. By then, we had lived apart for three and a half years. Our son was in school in London. She was unable to see our son's graduation ceremony, his most valuable years. It's almost as if I left prison and was released but we're still in a situation where that never happened. Ultimately, she was forced to leave illegally, and we brought her to Berlin without a passport, and now our son has joined us. He left London and moved to Berlin. Finally, the family was united in Berlin after being apart for so long.

You were able to attend your son's graduation, correct?
I was able to go. I was in Berlin and went to London. I live-streamed it for my wife from there.

How were you able to go? You need a valid passport.
The Germans gave me a travel document for the week that I went. I can travel with that. I was able to go anywhere in the world except Turkey.

Do you consider yourself in exile?
This is exile; I would have to call it that. This is the situation of humanity that everyone who knows the history of Turkey recognises. Or not so much a situation of humanity but a situation of dissidence. If you're a journalist in Turkey, your career path follows these steps: you enter [the sector], work somewhere for a while and get exploited as an intern. Later, you slowly climb upwards. If you're courageous, you write something that will tread on the government's toes. When you write, you become an issue for the courts. Then you go to prison, and later you go into exile. If you go a little further ahead, you get killed. I mean, this is our career plan. So there are no surprises in this. When I entered Silivri prison, the truth is that I was psychologically ready. As I was coming here, I was ready for whatever surprises there may have been. I'm not complaining much. And I won't complain now. Because, for one, it's of course better than prison. Ultimately, Silivri is the bearing point I use for comparison. If you ask 'Berlin or Silivri?' I will certainly say Berlin. Besides – and I'll admit this – Berlin was a career boost for me. For the first time, my book was published in other languages here. Plays were staged for the first time from books I wrote. I made documentaries with Germans. In a sense, I tested myself in the international arena. Maybe I tested my standard. I don't

know if the documentary I made meant anything in Turkey, but it had meaning here. I saw here that I'm able to make documentaries in a foreign language. And whether I could sell a book I wrote in German, whether an article I wrote could be read. For me, the truth is that this disadvantage has, in a way, become an advantage. I mean, there is danger, of course, when you are exiled; they define you through your identity as a Turkish dissident and there you go to another prison, at least ideologically. This is a little disturbing. After a while, you only get asked about Erdoğan and Turkey, and this puts you into a tailspin eventually. It's coming to such a point that it's as if without Erdoğan you would disappear as well – as if you exist through your opposition or are allowed to play on a playground. However, I feel that I am about to overcome this, because we're preparing new documentaries and books about issues that are unrelated to Turkey. As such, I think that I've found the opportunity to produce works on issues such as Europe, the future of the world, the future of the opposition and the status of those in exile and, accordingly, the opportunity to step out into the international arena. This, for me, has become a process that has transformed into an advantage. That's why I'm not complaining.

You work a lot, and there are security-related issues. How is your social life? I remember you saying in an interview on You-Tube that you don't know Berlin very well. How do you spend your days?
I spend them here, in this room. I don't go out much. The corona-virus has already prevented this for two years, but even before that I was mostly either at the office or at home. This doesn't bother me much. Ultimately, being in exile or being from Turkey under these circumstances evokes a strange feeling of responsibility and guilt. If you drink a beer at a bar in Berlin or have fun somewhere, you feel as if you'll spend two or three hours away from the issues of your home and this causes feelings of guilt, in a way. It's very troublesome. You can't do much – I mean, your mind goes right back home. Especially

if you spent time in prison, however briefly, or if your friends are there . . . I was able to have fun like crazy at the Silivri prison, for example. I danced by myself – I felt I had the right to do so. But now I don't do that here. It's an interesting psychology. If I spend an hour doing nothing, I begin criticising myself and thinking, 'What am I doing? Why aren't I producing or working on anything? Why am I not serving some use?' But this has made me more productive, and I have felt myself to be a more prolific worker here than have been recently.

You have been in the news in Turkey ever since your article about the MİT trucks. How did your friends and social circle react?

This process became a litmus test. This happened in prison, but the solidarity at the time was much higher. I felt that it diminished after arriving here. There are people who are wary of being listened to on the phone, who avoid meeting, who meet me and say 'Let's take a picture, but you won't use it, right?' We are seeing all of these. It's an interesting experience. People know their friends or their future friends. I acknowledge a portion of these are justified. I mean, there's certainly a fear that after taking a picture with you something will happen to you. A portion of these are things I expect, some are a surprise. And things have happened that have caused me to say 'Come on, that too?' Despite this, there are things that cause me to say, 'Come on, did they do that?' and with which I saw an abnormal level of support from people I didn't expect. A few surprises, it's part of the experience. Truly, at a time like this, people know, differentiate their friends a lot better. And in the end, we feel that there aren't many but that those who are left have really fitted that sort of character. I'll mention something that just happened on Sunday, for example, a documentary aired on Halk TV. It was a documentary we made with some friends. I looked, and a ten-minute segment had been cut, the person who was asking questions wasn't there, only the answers. That's because the person asking questions was me. Some people find it difficult.

Did you react to this?

Generally I do something like this: I sleep on it for a night. My first reaction is a lot of disappointment and to say 'What a shame'. But I trained myself for a while, I don't respond without sleeping on it. After I sleep on it, it becomes less important. You start to say 'If it's like that, then that's the way it is, it's not important', and you learn to appreciate what you really value. When you reach this point, you say 'It's not important' and move on. I didn't react to that, but these things happen. My arm is visible in some group pictures, but my body isn't, for example. Or my documentaries are broadcast, but my name isn't published. My writing is circulated under others' names, and so on. I see things like this. But it's not very important. I consider myself luckier than others living in exile throughout Turkish history, because technology has brought a lot of opportunities. I can meet, talk and debate with my readers. And I can closely watch their reactions. I can watch Turkey much more closely. Actually, I've been watching Turkey closer than I ever have since I arrived. I go around with an antenna in my head.

You said that most of the reactions to you coming from the diaspora relate to colluding with the state or the state's sending signals. You also mentioned that your friends are wary of the current political atmosphere. In your view, would everything resolve itself if the state backed off this policy? Is there a lynching culture or is it easy to demonise someone in the nature of Turkish society, like Tanıl Bora said? When you lived abroad, did you start to view Turkey in a different light?

Let's not confuse this, but the threats I mentioned were attacks. If the state wasn't engaging in provocation, I think that threats, attacks like this largely wouldn't be as prevalent. Let's look at Maraş, it really shows that there is serious provocation – provocation perpetrated by the state. These are unbelievable state organisations. I don't want to say that there isn't a lynching culture in Turkey, but if the state wants something, it can prevent it, and if it wasn't engaging in provocation, something like this wouldn't happen to this extent. I believe this seriously. Also, this tells us that if there was a different state that opened up doors of mediation and dialogue rather than hatred, this society might not develop such a culture. I mean, lynching culture almost turns into a genetic thing that is in our DNA when we talk about it, it makes me uncomfortable. I think that it's passed down through generations in this way. It is something that is cultivated. If the state works towards this with all its ideological apparatuses, media, family, mosques and military facilities, society certainly will be poisoned, and such a reaction will develop. But if we can change, transform all these outputs, I think that society can rapidly transform and conform to this.

This, if I'm not mistaken, is the longest experience living abroad in your life.
Yes, it is.

Do you view Turkey differently when living abroad?
I think I do. I can't really measure it. Because I work with documentaries, I have always tried to view events through a historical lens and with historical depth. This has expanded to a more international dimension. I mean, it's helped me see things in terms of world history, the world's trajectory. After all, you have greater access to foreign publications, and you have a greater chance to see things happen. Accordingly, it positions Turkey not within itself but within a certain context, maybe a certain geography or historical period, and a reflex of interpretation is developing. I think this is very beneficial. Although the thing we actually experience is what is experienced by a certain period in time or a certain geographic territory. I think that if we read this correctly, we can better see how this will be created in the future. In that regard, I'm doing something I can say is not seeing Turkey better but seeing better what kind of juncture Turkey is at, what kind of

geography, what kind of historical period and in what direction it is going. A situation like this is brought about by living abroad or, especially, living in Europe. And this also offers an opportunity to better study Europe. It is truly different to see Europe from Turkey than to see it from within.

Everyone has certain breaking points regarding the recent period in Turkish history. What is the breaking point for you?
The breaking point for me was 2013. A lot of data shows that 2013 was an important turning point in Erdoğan's personal life story, not only politically but also economically and in the sense of international relations. It was the Gezi protests and the subsequent developments. I think it was like this in my own personal life as well, because in my opinion, the Gezi protests had a greater impact than would have been guessed that transformed my life and the life and history of Turkey in a way that we still can't see today. It created a few things. For example, it was an incredibly hopeful thing for me in terms of revealing a potential I wasn't aware of in Turkey. For Erdoğan, it was probably an incredibly frightening thing in terms of revealing a potential he also wasn't aware of. And we all experienced and are still experiencing in waves the repercussions of the fear that appeared that day. It was actually that day that Turkey began to be ruled with a militaristic mindset. Gül's removal, Erdoğan's assumption of all positions, martial law in Turkey, the beginning of preparations for a police state, surging oppression and more began to appear in waves. That's why I think that the change over the past eight years began with the Gezi protests, especially in 2013.

Do you think you'll return to Turkey? Do you think that there may be a Turkey where people like you will at least be able to live freely?
I think it could happen tomorrow morning. Turkey is a country of great surprises. It can change that quickly! The Gezi protests were

features of the type of Turkey I wanted to live in. But two weeks later, that heaven transformed into hell. Similarly, it could be the exact opposite. I saw that one morning, I was in Taksim, walking, news broke that Turgut Özal had died, and a completely new Turkey was born that day. 1993 was a year that altered the history of Turkey. That was the year Turkish history changed, as if a button had been pressed in Turkish history, though I don't like this phrase. Turkey changed very quickly as a result. I'm not a pessimist. A one-man state was constructed. Imagine that this one man went away tonight, but something else would begin tomorrow. I don't believe that Erdoğan was able to establish an institutionalised regime. He created a personal network of power, linking everything to himself. As he revived himself, he was simultaneously destroyed. Because I don't think that he can be replaced when he's no longer there. That's why Turkey can be quickly rehabilitated if the opposition acts a bit more wisely. There will certainly be a long process of rehabilitation, I can see that. But I think a lot of people in exile today are keeping their eyes peeled, and many are ready and willing to return. Maybe I should add that I think those in exile here are prepared to return the day after he falls. And I don't mean to sit and wait for that but to weave and back and prepare and, in fact, make plans to return and create a roadmap afterwards. This is what's missing in Turkey. These days, I've been reading the memoirs of academics who left Germany in the 1930s for Turkey, and I'm seeing that they offered an unbelievable contribution to the formation of Turkey's new republic and made preparations for Germany after the war. If you were to ask German academics in 1936 or 1937 'Are you considering returning to Germany?' they might have said 'No, I will probably spend my life in Turkey'. If you were to ask this question in 1944, Germany would have been finished. The Germany of 1945 is incomparable to Turkey, no? We're talking about a country that was in a shambles. That country recovered. Those people returned. As a result, whenever I become overcome with hopelessness, I turn to history books and find hope for myself in history. What's important is preparing for the day after.

Maybe there is a network of academics who have come here with the brain drain in a way that was never destined with earlier generations of migrants. There are economists, cultured individuals and sociologists who might be able to do this. The Kurdish movement is here, the Alevi movement is here. What are Turkey's bleeding wounds? The issues of religion, secularism, the Kurdish question, the Armenian question, and all the components of these are actually here. Right now we need to rack our brains and do what we can't do in Turkey. We need to think about answers to the question 'So what will these problems become after Erdoğan?' How will we confront this police state afterwards? The police in this country need to be completely disbanded. And what will replace them? All the judges have been politicised. And what kind of justice mechanism will be established? The media has been nullified. How will a new media be constructed? We need to be talking about and preparing for these issues. I personally am prepared on the topic about how the media will be and what we can do. I see what the Germans did in 1945. A propaganda mechanism collapsed, and you need to create a new media to replace it. The German media today was actually created on that day. The principle of public broadcasting was implemented step by step. We will do this. We must. We need to lay the foundations for this. Accordingly, I think we need to consider how we can use this process more productively for Turkey.

The people we have interviewed so far have generally been more pessimistic. You are really the most hopeful of all of them.
Their reaction is justified. The fact that the country is still in this state so long after the coup is disappointing people. I'm not saying that just for the sake of conversation. There is a rationale for this. Moreover I'll say that we've started to work on this issue. We're setting up an organisation like a think tank right now in Berlin. We've submitted our application. There are figures settled here active in German politics for this, newly arrived academics, and some individuals with ideas about Turkey's future. We've come together with them, and my

hope is that in the near future – I mean a future that could be measured in months – they will work on topics like the environment or women's issues in which it's easier to reconcile with the media. But over time, we'll reach a point where we produce papers, put our heads together and invite individuals from Turkey and think about what we can do on more chronic issues like judicial independence, a constitutional state and the Kurdish question. I mean, we're preparing the ground for talking about what we will replace the regime with when it changes tomorrow. Our goal is not just to stand around but to do something, because some people think that we are living under very miserable circumstances. Some think that we're living lavishly. The essence of the matter is to think about a life you're starting from nothing. Everything you have, your career, has disappeared. Your belongings have vanished, the climate you live in has changed. The ground has changed, and you're trying to prove yourself in a whole new climate. Starting from scratch at this age is a very serious challenge. But can we turn this into an advantage? Yes. I feel rejuvenated. I'm not going to cry about this. You start to think 'We worked for forty years and bought a home – that went away too. This means that we will start something new here. A home isn't that important.' These are the psychological aspects of all this. But we continue to work here – yes, under difficult circumstances – but with the belief that we absolutely have to do something. But my ultimate goal really is to return home and to write my book somewhere in peace.

For the first time, you're closely encountering the diaspora, and for all of our conversation, you've differentiated between those in exile and the diaspora. When you return to Turkey, how will your relationship with the diaspora be in Turkey during the revision and restoration period?
Here, a binary project is possible for the diaspora. The issue of explaining this place to Turkey is important, because there is a serious misperception here regarding Turkey. It is important to fix this.

In this sense, I don't see a very strong diaspora in Germany. I don't see anything that will explain to this country what has happened in Turkey. It's imperative that this be constructed. Partisan members of parliament are coming, and we're meeting with them. And although the photographs we take aren't shared on social media, you're still meeting with people. On the other hand, another missing aspect is explaining the real Turkey to the people here. There is an urgent need for a diaspora that can pursue these two missions. This is a sort of lobby, actually, not just a diaspora. We need to construct this kind of lobby. There's no need to wait to return to Turkey for this. If we can institutionalise this now, this would benefit both Europe and Turkey. This feat is possible. All of the data for this is clear, but for some reason, it hasn't been assembled. I hope that we can create a new core. And those who will stay here will serve from here in the process of constructing the new Turkey.

4

DENIZ (PSEUDONYM)

I left Turkey in 2017 after the 'We Will Not Be a Party to This Crime' petition. Every cell in my body, in my brain wants to forget that process.

Thank you so much for agreeing to give an interview. We appreciate your insights. Can you tell us when and why you left Turkey?

I left Turkey in 2017 after the 'We Will Not Be a Party to This Crime' petition. Every cell in my body, in my brain wants to forget that process. When Tayyip Erdoğan targeted us after the first wave of signatures, I was suddenly forced to leave. I was working for the National Education Ministry, as a teacher, in a small village in a small city at the time. Everyone was looking for me there. They found a 'marginal' picture of me from university and targeted me in the local newspaper. I was the only signatory at the time in that small city. There were 10–15 signatories in another city nearby, and they would get together every week and talk. That was some support, at least, but I felt very alone during that period. I joined them once or twice. But you could imagine the fear and anxiety we had been facing. An inspector was sent to the institution where I worked. You could guess the reaction of the school staff, always a sort of 'Oh look, there's a terrorist in our midst'. I was already marginal compared to them, and this further consolidated that. The inspector came to the school later. They reprimanded me, but the demeanour of the inspectors was a separate kind of aggression. Then a case was opened in another city in the context of the fight against terror. I was forced to go there. I gave my statement. I felt very alone there, because one of the signatories directed me to a pro-bono lawyer to look at the case for this group – that is, Academics for Peace. Because I had never gone to a police station in my life. I was going to go with that individual to the lawyer's office and go with them to give my statement. They asked standard questions: 'Why did you sign it? What was your objective?' and so forth. The lawyer asked me if I thought the PKK was a terrorist organisation. I didn't want to answer this question or, even if I were to answer it, I just wanted to say yes. Ultimately, when I said I have a different view and I could explain it, the lawyer said to me, 'If you consider the PKK a terrorist organisation, I'm not coming with you.' I was left alone crying. I was already traumatised. It was already challenging for me, and I was left there alone. I went alone, crying. I gave my statement and left.

Did you leave the country after being fired or did you quit?
I was reprimanded. I took unpaid leave and left the country. I stayed for a year in a European country.

What was the reasoning behind choosing a city in Europe?
An academic friend who was a signatory received a fellowship from that country. That friend said to me, 'This is the situation here, try your chances if you want to.' They helped me in the application

processes. I didn't have much of a Scholars at Risk network, and my English was awful. I had never had a plan like this in my life.

But you did your PhD in Turkey?
When I signed the petition, I was in the final stages of my dissertation. I experienced extreme mobbing there, because my advisor was apolitical and was probably pressured after the signature and then pressured me. Our relationship changed completely. In the last three or four months, I was forced to bear everything just to finish. After I finished my PhD, I received a fellowship from a European city. It was quite a coincidence, because I was working for the National Education at the time, and Scholars at Risk fellowships were given to people working at the university. I think a wealthy businessman had volunteered and said 'Let's give one to this person'. I received the fellowship at the last minute. That's why I chose the city. I didn't have any other options.

You went to the country where you stayed, opting to go legally without having your passport revoked, didn't you? Did you feel like you were in exile when you went to that country?
Yes, of course. I left feeling so traumatised . . . I mean, I see what I experienced, and someone else could say 'What did you experience? We all experienced that.' My family isn't political. Some people's families support them, but because I knew that I would struggle there, I hid it from my family. My father, for example, was in a car accident, and I feared that there would be a problem. I would have some difficulty at the airport if I went despite being so scared. There were already three or four peace signatories in this European city. We were together. We experienced that psychology. We tried to be as active as possible there. Turkey was always on our minds; we were always talking about Turkey. What would happen? What would we do? What is the situation right now? We were there, but our conversations, our discussions were always about Turkey.

You said that you were together with other peace signatories for a year when you stayed in the first country you went to. Did you ever get together with other groups from the diaspora which had just arrived or that had been there for a while? Or were there groups you didn't want to meet at all?

We were generally together with peace signatories while there. Because I'm gay, the only groups where I felt like I belonged in the country where I went were NGOs. It was a safe space for me. But I created a space, engaged in activism not with the white queer community in the group, but with queer minorities from different ethnic backgrounds. I met with other Turks, a few political groups, but it wasn't a very safe space for me. So I can't say I'm in contact with other people who have come from Turkey. I found that safe space more within the queer community.

During this period and especially after 2016, we know that certain practices we call extra-territorial authoritarianism in the literature were imposed on Academics for Peace, supporters of the Kurdish movement and supporters of the Gülen Movement. We hear and read about practices such as harassment by AKP supporters on the street, profiling and harassment by certain institutions such as the Diyanet and the Yunus Emre Institutes, the revocation of passports and consulates refusing service. Have similar things happened to you? Or if they haven't, you must have at the very least some sort of relationship with the consulate, as you've been abroad for years. How have these transpired?

We were scared to go out alone in the city where we lived. We felt that threat.

Was there something specific you know about or is it because of what you've read or heard in the news?

Probably because of what we read and heard about in the news. We internalised that fear. Even if there wasn't a real threat – and I didn't experience any problems myself when I went – I knew things had happened. So even when there's normally no threat for you, you can internalise this. Going there can take time. And you think to yourself, 'What if something happens?' Think about if something were to happen, I notified Scholars at Risk when going to the consulate. I was forced to return to Turkey after the country where I'm living, because I was unable to find another fellowship.

So you went to Turkey and came back?

I initially received a one-year fellowship from a European city. I went on unpaid leave from National Education. I wanted to stay in the city where I first lived, and I applied for a number of fellowships. But I didn't receive any of them. So I was forced to return. I started again at National Education, because I had taken unpaid leave. I worked for 4–5 months, but an inquiry was launched against me because I was researching sexual identity and orientation discrimination. Then an inquiry was launched at National Education. I wrote again. 'Look,' I said, 'I already tried to stay, but I couldn't find a fellowship. I returned. You see that there is no space. I'm an Academic for Peace, but I'm also a gay academic. I have no freedom of expression. I can't do my job, and I've been targeted.' It was terrifying. After a national paper published an article, the comments in that paper were awful: 'Ah, she looks more like a man than me', 'She should go to [. . .] and do I don't know what' and so forth. I received a one-year fellowship after that for a different country. While in that new country, National Education reprimanded me again.

Did you take unpaid leave again?

Yes, and when I went to the new country, they called me from the consulate. They said, 'You have a letter. You need to come.' I wrote to Scholars at Risk. I didn't know anyone in the country. I notified them. I didn't have any friends, so I contacted them to let them know if something happened to me. But nothing happened. They gave me a room there. I wrote my defence. They acted politely. Nothing insulting happened. But what I'm trying to describe is that you can't help but internalise that fear. You experience that anxiety. Even if it's not true, it feels like it is.

What has been the difference for you between the two countries where you've stayed?
There was solidarity in the first country I went to, but at one point, constantly getting together was disheartening because everyone was depressed. Everyone was forced to leave the country. I mean, what seemed like solidarity began to drag me down after a certain point. Beautiful things were happening in my life there, for example, but you can't experience that, because even if you forget, the person next to you reminds you through their depression. What are we going to do? What's going to happen now? You constantly feel this uncertainty. In the second country I went to, I distanced myself from this a little bit. I was still following Turkey, but not that closely. I began to get used to where I was at, to adapt, to engage with the queer community there and work in activism – similarly, not the white queer community but within the ethnic minority queer community.

Every different group interprets Turkey differently. Our interviews revealed that the big split for the Gülenists occurred around 17–25 December [2013]. For more liberal or left-leaning individuals, this break occurred maybe near 2011 or even 2009. But if there's a shared breaking point, it's the Gezi movement. For some groups, it's the coup attempt. What are the processes that brought Turkey to this point for you?
Right now, I'm in a third country. I received a two-year fellowship. It's a fellowship from Scholars at Risk. It ends in January. I'm sending out job applications, because I'm planning on staying. I could say that something happened with Gezi for me, but I'll add that I haven't been very active or political in those leftist organisations in my family

history or in my personal history. I'm a standard, ordinary and, perhaps, apolitical type of person. With Gezi, I said 'Oh, look what's happening in the country!' When there's no such awareness in your circle, it can be late for you to recognise this. If you're gay, you can internalise this heterosexism. Even though I'm gay, I have normalised what I would call violence, what I would call homophobia today. So Gezi invoked a sort of awareness in me. After that, when I lived it up close and personal myself . . . The 'We Will not Be a Party to This Crime' petition was something that I signed with all my human emotions, saying 'Yes, that's exactly right' after reading it. Otherwise, it's not this date or that act of state oppression, because I don't know the history very well. I mean, yes, I knew it, but I hadn't read much about it before. I began to read more about what forms of violence the state inflicted on different groups throughout Turkish history. I wasn't really aware. But after leaving the country, I began to read more and talk with people. I became more political. So I'm a bit of a pessimist when looking from the outside. Okay, we have hope in some places, we're already fighting for that. I still have an organic relationship with the queer community in Turkey. I write articles, and we hold workshops. But most of the time, my pessimism dominates.

You were saying that you felt like you were in exile in the first country you lived in. Has anything changed over the years? Do you still feel like you're in exile?
No, I've begun to think that this is my home, because I've been abroad now for 3½–4 years. When you taste this freedom . . . I don't want to say that these countries are wonderful, I have problems here too. I write about racism here. I still write about heteronormativity. But there is a certain space for freedom up to a point. When you taste this, wherever you are begins to become your home. So I'm not in that psychological exile any longer. A country isn't missed, but the relationships are; of course I miss my relationships, but I have slowly begun to feel like this is my home.

Where has Turkey come for you during this period? Why are you fighting for a place that is no longer your home?
It depends on what you consider to be a home. I don't consider home as a singular thing. This could be my home, but Turkey could still be my home too. I mean, perceiving this place as my home doesn't mean that I've given up on perceiving Turkey as my home as well. So my sense of belonging to Turkey won't ever end. Regardless of the privileged conditions we live in here, at least for me, I have friends there, old lovers and a family. So my solidarity with the fight there won't ever end. It's still my home.

Would you return to Turkey?
Not from a nationalist position, but ultimately, if people leave where they were born and raised, the place they are accustomed to, it doesn't mean that they left voluntarily. Of course I would choose to live in Turkey. It's a place you know, whose native language you speak, where you have your own network, which you feel and think provides you with a safe space because you know it and are familiar with it. But we are going through a terrible period right now politically. We're going through a harsher and more fragile period. There is no space for me there. They tell me 'Don't come here, we don't have any space for you'. I mean, I want to go, but they won't accept me. So I came here because I have to create a space for myself.

Are you considering returning?
If I feel like there's a space for me, then of course. Why shouldn't I return? Because my reason for leaving was that they said 'We don't want you here'. But if they say 'There's a space for you here', if Turkey's socio-political conditions grow more mature, then I would want to return. Why shouldn't I want to return?

5

ENGİN SUSTAM

**When I listened to the experiences of the generation that came
here after the 1980 coup, I didn't want to apply for political
asylum because I didn't want to fall into that
trap of victimisation as an intellectual.**

*Engin Sustam completed his undergraduate studies in sociology at
Mimar Sinan Fine Arts University (2000) and completed a master's
degree in the same faculty (2002). He then completed another master's degree (2005), and a PhD (2012) in the Department of Sociology at EHESS (École des hautes études en sciences sociales). Next, he
worked as a full-time philosophy and sociology lecturer in Turkey.
From 2013 he was an assistant professor in sociology at Istanbul Arel
University until he was dismissed in summer 2015 because of his work
on the Kurds and his political approaches. He then taught part-time
at İstanbul 29 Mayıs University but this time his contract was not*

renewed following his signature with Academics for Peace in January 2016. He is an associate researcher at IFEA (French Institute of Anatolian Studies) in Istanbul, was invited by Queen Mary University of London as a guest lecturer, and has worked as a visiting scholar at the University of Geneva, EHESS, the École normale supérieure and Paris 8 University. His main works include 'Kurdish Art and Cultural Production: Rhetoric of the New Kurdish Subject', in The Cambridge History of the Kurds *(Cambridge University Press);* 'Ecological Self-Governmentality in Kurdish Space at a Time of Neoliberal Authoritarianism', in Ecological Solidarity and the Kurdish Freedom Movement *(Lexington);* 'The Kurdish Political and Artistic Making by the Transborder Perception in the Interstitial Spaces'; 'Decolonising Exile with a Photographic Image in Times of Insecurity'; and 'Criticism of "Colonial Modernity" by the Kurdish Decolonial Approaches', in Global Modernity from Coloniality to Pandemic *(Amsterdam University Press). He participated in the monthly collective seminars of 'Critical Epistemologies and New Thoughts of Politics and Conflict' at Paris 8 University and 'Thinking on the Society: Identity and Citizenship' at the University of Geneva (lecturer). He is the author of the book* Art et subalternité kurde: l'émergence d'un espace de production subjective et créative entre violence et résistance en Turquie *('Kurdish Art and Subalternity: The Emergence of a Subjective and Creative Production Space between Violence and Resistance in Turkey'), published by Harmattan in 2016. He published his new book,* Kırılgan sapmalar: sokak mukavemetleri ve yeni başkaldırılar *('Fragile Deviation: New Insurgency Spaces'), with Kalkedon Edition, Istanbul, in April 2020. He will soon publish two other forthcoming books: 'The Unexpected Uprisings' in French and 'Decolonial Aesthetics and Kurdish Contemporary Art' in French and Turkish. He is an independent curator and an art critic for contemporary art exhibitions on micro-politics, counter-culture, gender and memory. He is currently managing, with his collective team, a Kurdish contemporary art project at nGbK (Neue Gesellschaft für bildende Kunst) Berlin, 'Bê Welat – The Unexpected Storytellers'.*

What made you decide to leave?

I actually have a little bit of an ironic story, being an academic who was fired twice during his academic career. In June 2015, I was fired a week after the HDP's electoral victory from Arel University where I taught classes. The peace process was still ongoing. But I was an active scholar, especially on the Kurdish question and other political issues. I was also on the Peace Commission, which was an academic commission pushing to organise discussions between the Kurdish political movement and the state. The reason I was fired from Arel was because I spoke at a conference about the history of modern Kurdish literature and had given another presentation on Rojava together with the human rights associations the students had formed. These two conferences were fairly dangerous for a private university, especially a university with extreme Kemalist tendencies. A nationalistic reaction stirred up. I wasn't aware of this. It reached the office of the chancellor of the school, which ended my contract in June when it was due to be renewed. I told them that their rationale was political and that I didn't acknowledge the decision. We got tangled up in a lawsuit that I won. But I didn't return to my job. I later started teaching at 29 Mayıs University.

At the same time, I was preparing my assistant professor dossier at Mimar Sinan Fine Arts University. A whole staff was going to be set up for me at Mimar Sinan. I sent my dossier to Ankara, and the ministry approved it. I was also teaching in the Philosophy Department at 29 Mayıs University. That was a period when political battles in Kurdish geographical spaces were surging. I was constantly coming and going to Kurdish regions, especially Diyarbakır. The day Tahir Elçi was killed, I was presenting at a conference at Dicle University – the Radical Democracy and Autonomy in the Middle East Conference. I was sentenced to between seven and fifteen years in prison about nine months ago because of that conference. I already couldn't return to Turkey because of this actually, not because I signed the Academics for Peace petition. There were three cases against me. The first was this one. The second was based on my speech at an HDP rally. Because of the Academics for Peace petition, a rally called Everyone for Peace was held in Şişli. My speeches there were noted, and a lawsuit was filed against me. That one was dropped. The third lawsuit was the Afrin petition. A group of 101 intellectuals, including me, sent an email to AKP MPs, and we said that the occupation of Afrin was not a just occupation and that this was something that would poison not only the peace process but also the friendship between the two nations and that it was unacceptable. That lawsuit was dropped too.

I want to discuss the 2016 process. We were in a period when the war in Kurdistan had intensified, when on the one hand there were rebellions for autonomy, and on the other hand the state had amassed the army with all its strength. We had begun to debate what we should do as Academics for Peace. I was one of the activists in Academics for Peace, which was established in 2012. There was the peace process at the time, and Academics for Peace was first founded to defend the right of native-language education for those serving prison time. This was an important pledge for the peace process, and we appeared with a declaration, asking for native-language education for Kurds and that the requests of prisoners be met. As one of the actors in that process, we started a debate about how the war in Kurdish territory was unacceptable, how violence is unacceptable, and how we needed to return to an exceptionless and undisputed peace process. I was teaching at 29 Mayıs. In the meantime, I was offered a two-month scholarship and invited to the School for Advanced Studies in the Social Sciences (École des hautes études en sciences sociales, EHESS). I arrived at EHESS in December.

Was your passport revoked or did you travel normally?
No, I travelled normally. The Academics for Peace declaration hadn't been announced yet. While I was at EHESS, the debates about the Academics for Peace petition began, and we published the petition

on 11 January 2016. I was fired from 29 Mayıs University as Recep Tayyip Erdoğan launched a serious attack and a process began that branded us. I returned from Paris around that time and held my final exam at 29 Mayıs. I think there were thirty-five of us who were fired at first. But we were still in Turkey. A serious witch hunt began. The Diyarbakır lawsuit was launched. A lawyer from Diyarbakır and a student from the School of Law called me and said, 'Professor, I think you should leave the country, because serious lawsuits are coming. You're getting sentenced to between seven and fifteen years by the Diyarbakır public prosecutor because of the Radical Democracy and Autonomy Conference at Dicle University.' I was shocked, of course. Later, my friend Çağla Aykaç from Fatih University, which was shut down, set up a fellowship for me through Geneva University, and I quickly left. I had a Greek visa in its last month. I left quickly.

What was the legal process like afterwards?

Geneva University was aware of the risk. As soon as I arrived, I applied for Scholars at Risk and was immediately accepted. But the Geneva canton – the federal structure – told me, 'You can't accept a fellowship at a university with this visa. You have to return to Turkey. We'll give you a visa from Switzerland; this will become both a worker's visa and a residence permit.' I said, 'I can't go. This is impossible for me. Here you go, this is the letter that arrived at my house from the Diyarbakır Public Prosecutor's Office.' Because the police had come to my parents' home two or three times and said, 'We're looking for Engin Sustam. He has to come and give a statement.' We know what it means to call someone in for a statement. Later in April, there was a meeting at EHESS about helping Academics for Peace. For these academics, a scholarship was set up at that meeting called PAUSE – like Scholars at Risk. They called Çağla and me to that meeting from Geneva. At the time, my visa had ended in France, and I was stuck in France undocumented. I had neither a French visa nor a Swiss visa. Then Geneva University went to work and got me a one-month worker's visa from the Swiss consulate in Paris. You apply for residence with that as soon as you enter Switzerland. I got my visa and returned to Switzerland. I applied for a residence permit, and they gave me one that would last for one year. I was able to work with that, and I could travel in Europe with a Turkish passport. The Geneva canton government asked if I was going to apply for political asylum. I said, 'I want to think about it. I'm not entirely sure about it. Give me a little time.' I wanted to wait a little bit, because applying for political asylum entails a completely different psychology.

Have you ever interacted with the Turkish state while abroad or did you try to go to the consulate?

Because of the Diyarbakır lawsuit, the police – a special team, at that – came to my house twice. 'He has a lawsuit in Diyarbakır and he has to go and give a statement to the Eyüp Public Prosecutor's Office and, if necessary, go to Diyarbakır,' they said. My family said that I had left the country, that I wouldn't be able to come. On hearing that, the police chief said, 'We know he's in Geneva, but tell him not to talk too much.' That's because I was still giving speeches here. I was invited as a speaker three times to the United Nations. There, I explained that Turkey had been drifting towards totalitarianism, a *drift totalitaire*, as we say in French, that this war system was producing a regime of violence in the biopolitical and necropolitical sense exactly as Foucault and Achille Mbembe described and that this regime of violence was actually settling scores with intellectuals. I later started teaching at the University of Geneva. But the harassment continued through my family and through some of these types of interactions in Geneva.

You're saying that you encountered different transnational arms of the state, not only on one occasion at that conference but a couple of times?

Of course we encountered it. We were threatened, in fact. The Breton Association of Kurdish Friendship (Amitiés kurdes de Bretagne) organised a conference in Rennes. There were ten CRS – special intelligence and gendarme – vehicles in front of the municipal building where the conference was held. Because the conference organisers had made posters that read, 'When will dictator Erdoğan stop talking?' and placed his face on Hitler's head. Beneath that, they put photographs of me and Çağla. Those men officially branded us, making us targets of the government and their institutions. We were already furious that they would make a poster like that. 'You can use our names, but we don't want to use this title,' we said. I still don't think that Turkey has a dictatorship. It's a totalitarian regime, but a totalitarian regime doesn't have to be a dictatorship. It could be liberal, there is a clientelistic and liberal totalitarianism in Turkey. We normally would have stayed in a hotel there, but after this incident we stayed at the home of a Kurdish friend who was an HDP member. There were five HDP bodyguards at that home besides us, they were friends. They stayed to protect us in case there was an attack. It was an odd situation like that.

I want to ask two things. First, what happened to your legal status? And second, something has emerged from the interviews we have conducted so far, which is that Kurds and Alevis are in a certain state of solidarity together. The Gülenists, on the other hand, have been ostracised. We have data that older arrivals are not pleased with the new arrivals, the intellectuals and more visible types, and that there is somewhat of a clash between the new and older arrivals. What do you think about this?
I did not apply for political asylum despite the lawsuits against me because my wife is French. We decided to get married, so I got a normal residence permit through marriage in France. Right now, I have a ten-year residence card. I'm still not a citizen, because it takes time. But I have a ten-year residence permit, and I can comfortably move around. I only have one problem, which is that my Turkish passport is expiring this summer. I haven't gone to the Turkish consulate in five years because my lawyer said that there may be restrictions on my

passport because I'm active abroad and that I may not get my passport back if I go to the consulate. Right now, I can travel with my Turkish passport in Europe, but even if there is a restriction, it won't appear internationally. So this is addressed as a domestic issue, a domestic security issue. So I handled my residence permit without applying for political asylum, because I didn't want to fall into the psychological trap that political asylum creates.

What do you mean by the psychological trap?
I mean applying for political asylum here creates a regime of victimhood and, as a political identity and intellectual, I did not apply for political asylum because it would limit my mobility and would force me into certain processes of victimhood. I am still not considering applying because applying for political asylum means getting stamped by the actors and apparatuses of this system – the system in Europe. This bothers people. When I listened to the experiences of the generation that came here after the 1980 coup, I didn't want to apply for political asylum because I didn't want to fall into that trap of victimisation as an intellectual. Perhaps if I had been a militant or activist it would have been possible, but I won't apply for political asylum because I wouldn't have another chance. Coming to your other question, there wasn't any direct clash with the old generation. To the contrary, I have had a very close dialogue with them, but there is a tendency to experience conflict with, for example, intellectuals from the militant generation coming after 1980. I guess this is the experience of the Kurds and the Turkish left (and also the Palestinian, Berber and Kabyle anti-colonial movement). Intellectualism has been branded as a cursed identity. In any case, you are stigmatised by certain ideological identities as an egoist, a pedant, a know-all. This is an unavoidable process.

So, you're experiencing conflict not only with the older generation but also with the current one?

Of course, I'm fighting with the current generation. I've been in a state of conflict even with all the actors within BAK (Academics for Peace). I believe that beautiful things can emerge from harsh debates. But of course, we went through a difficult period, and a number of people lost their jobs. I have been fairly active in Europe, especially after the coup in 2016. I participated in close to eighty-four conferences – local and public gatherings – in 2016, 2017 and 2018. I calculated this and was shocked. In fact, we organised a conference after the coup with Ahmet İnsel in Geneva called 'Where Is Turkey Going?' The entire generation that had come to Sweden in the 1980s was there. The event space was packed, maybe 700 to 800 people. That conference was interesting, because it brought two or three diasporas together. The first was from the 1980 coup, the second was from the 1990 war in Kurdistan and the third is the generation of exiles we are a part of. As these debates continue in some way in Germany, France, Switzerland and Britain, you join a dialogue with the older generation, but there is a current departing from the older generation. The intelligentsia coming from the 1980 coup is a more militant generation. And this generation of course has ideological troubles. On the one hand there's the presence of Kurds, Alevis, the LGBT community, but this generation also engages in intellectual activities. They can be both activists and intellectuals. This generation works with art and, like you, studies Islam.

More intellectual, you mean?

Yes, it's true that they experienced certain intellectual conflicts through episteme. But honestly, I am more in a state of dialogue with the older generation rather than distance. The experience in Germany may be different. While there's more of a worker-, a villager-based, diaspora in Germany, there's a more political diaspora in France. That's also the case in Switzerland; all the applicants to Switzerland are predominantly university-based militants. They left – or completed – university during the 1980 coup and left in some way. As such, the dimension of the disagreement, in my opinion, changes based on the dimensions of the understanding. For example, those in Switzerland have helped me immensely. All the Alevis in Switzerland know me. All the Kurds know me. There was a conference the HDP organised in Austria during the 'No' campaign [in the constitutional referendum]. While speaking there, one would say, 'as a Kurdish intellectual' and another would say 'as an Alevi intellectual'. I said, 'I'm sorry, but I am an intellectual above all else; don't be angry. Kurdishness and Aleviness are identities I've been burdened with. I could have been born French, but unfortunately, I was born with these identities. I'm participating in this fight over identities, as I have to since it's imperative to reconcile with these identities. Otherwise, I have never produced policies from these identities – I want you to know this.' But it's necessary to talk without forgetting about the issue of exile. I mean, because I'm someone who speaks without forgetting about the Turkishness, Sunniness and masculinity issues in the 'Turkishness Contract', I unfortunately carry these two identities.

Do you have a relationship with the other groups who are leaving Turkey en masse? There's always this sort of impression in the media: the signatories, Kurds and Alevis, are leaving Turkey. There's an unbelievable escape by Sunnis. There's an unbelievable number of MHP members fleeing as well. There are also others who are not involved in politics as much as you are but there's a segment not from our world who sold their Volvo and went to study at university for a second time. How are your relationships with these groups?
For example, I came across the Gülenists. I don't think about the Gülen Movement in the same way that other chronic leftists do. But I know that in the war against the Kurds in 2015, there were also their soldiers or lieutenants. Ultimately, I'm aware that they were decimated by the government after the coup. I'll note that Amnesty International had a meeting in Brussels after the 2016 coup, and they

called me on behalf of Academics for Peace. At the meeting, I met five senior officers – NATO officers – who were political asylum seekers. It was comical to me, that encounter. Remarks about Kurdistan were flying about in that meeting. The five people were listening to me, taking notes intently. I think they were definitely from an intelligence agency. One spoke later, he had an accent but spoke French well. 'Mr Engin, what do you think about the coup?' he asked (and I really had no idea on this coup d'état). I spoke about the coup, saying that it was a process to consolidate the hegemony in the governance system's own internal battles, that the Gülen Movement may have been behind the coup and that the government was definitely aware of it but that we won't be able to know anything with certainty. We don't know, we truly don't know anything. That's the problem. I said that it was only important not to fall into the trap of conspiracies. Afterwards, they invited me out for coffee at the end. 'Who are you?' I asked. 'We're NATO officers,' they said. 'Uh-oh,' I said. 'I did my short-term military service. I don't like you. And let me say, I'm an anti-militarist Kurd.' They laughed. 'How did you do it?' they asked. 'Your law says that you have to finish your military service to work in academia in Turkey,' I said. So I did it out of necessity. In fact, I was threatened while in the military.' I was doing my short-term military service when Hrant was assassinated. I had an Armenian friend at the time, Sarkis. We made a big effort to protect him, because he was attacked a lot in the military. They also targeted me. They later learned that I'm an Alevi-Kurd. When they learned that I'm a dissident ... they asked, 'What do you think about us?' I responded, 'Look, I understand this process you're going through, I understand your thinking right now, but I don't find it very sincere. I'll be honest, you have been one of the actors in this system since the 1960s. You experienced a hegemonic conflict in the process, yes. But during and after the 1980 coup, you didn't want to take very serious steps for the Kurdish question, the Alevi question or any of the other issues as one of the state's actors in a series of processes. In fact, even while reading a brochure from a Kurdish individual, you acted in a pan-Turkist manner without acknowledging that they're a Kurd.' I said, 'I'm standing in a different position than you are as an actor, I am with you here in this exile process (this is a bizarre tragedy for me, a Kafkaesque story). I'm not against this. But your soldiers and officers were at the forefront of the war in Kurdistan. So what do you say about this?' One of the officers said, 'Yes, you're right. We want to talk with you about how this process will be in other ways, Professor. We are very curious about what you think about the future of Turkey.' I went on to say, 'I'll tell you that the future of Turkey is not very good.' In fact, I joked with these officers, 'There will be someone who will see me with you and take pictures. You're soldiers. It's interesting that I'm even here as an anti-militarist, and you are with a Kurdish intellectual and opponent.'

What is your daily life like in France?
I meet a lot of French academic or artistic people in daily life at the university or in the field of art. My relationship with the Kurds is limited in exile. I come across political events like Newroz of course (or during cultural events), but apart from that, I'm someone who prefers not to come together too often with the Kurdish (of Turkey, Iraq and Syria) and Turkish diaspora. I am currently in contact with the University of Rojava for university and artistic events (or for film festivals like Duhok in Iraqi Kurdistan, which I went to twice).

Why is this the case?
The first reason is because I do not want to limit my own intellectual activities and because I want to study more. Second, I was threatened in 2016 and 2018, and this worried me a bit after having a child. Especially when my child was born in 2017, I told myself, 'I think the time has come to distance myself from dark avenues and only walk along lit streets. Engin Sustam, you should be more careful.' My wife was saying that I've become more visible, and that my visibility could be dangerous. She wanted me to withdraw a little. And of

course, I didn't want to appear more militant. I wanted to appear as an academic and an intellectual. I didn't want to be someone talking about everything. It was like this for a while; I was being called everywhere. Also, you can establish better relations with people when you put a little bit of distance in between. The dissident left wings of the Turkish diaspora and the Kurdish diaspora are active and political. The Kurdish diaspora in particular is radically more active and political. As such, I believe it's necessary to establish relationships a little more carefully. If you establish distance as an intellectual, you don't fall into a certain trap of ideological belligerence. I really minded my distance with political organisations. I say this in particular: 'Look, I can talk about certain issues.' I am certainly a dissident intellectual and academic, but I don't like having the privilege of speaking everywhere and on every issue, and I don't want to do this. 'To be amid political activism (which I am not against), this limits certain intellectual activities for me, limits my studies, and inhibits my standing.' I am a social scientist, curator and academic. Although I am politically involved in the Kurdish question, as a scientist, I must place myself in another space of interstice. I am an intellectual activist, but not engaged like Sartre or others in the history of the left. I am preferably a 'singular, Kurdish intellectual' who defends the rights of emancipation of his oppressed people.

I knowingly created this kind of distance, because being in exile comes with the trap of working to rescue the country from abroad. I don't want to do this. If we could have rescued the country from abroad, those arriving from the 1980 coup would have done so, and I don't think we would have experienced all this. Because anyway I'm French and a foreigner – not a foreigner, I mean – I'm one of them, I see myself like that. I see myself as a specific intellectual, not as an organic intellectual – a 'global' one. I'm ultimately a 'singular' Kurdish intellectual ('singular' is a term used by Deleuze and Guattari), but I'm in a dialogue with global French, English, German, Italian intellectuals (like Antonio Negri, Eric Fassin, Marie-Claire Caloz-Tschopp, Slavoj

Žižek, David Graeber etc.), and I want it to stay like this. I don't want to be someone stuck with the Kurds, with the Turks.

We want to understand how your exile situation affects your perception of Turkey. You completed your PhD abroad and have always had connections abroad, but that process is different from your current predicament. After doing your PhD with Nilüfer Göle in Paris, you came to work at Arel University. There are sayings such as 'You get a better perspective when you take a step back'. Do you think you interpret Turkey differently now that you are abroad?

That process was different for me. Actually, I went to Mardin Artuklu University after finishing my thesis as a guest lecturer to set up the Department of Political Sciences. I stayed in Mardin for four months, set up the department and invited all the professors. The establishment in Ankara didn't come for me. My process began like this: I was going to return to Paris in 2013, when Arel University set up the Sociology Department with a team of Mimar Sinan graduates, and they invited me to join. I was unemployed, so I was a little bit forced to go. I was shocked at why the establishment didn't come for me from Ankara. I later learned from Kadri Yıldırım, the deputy rector for a period at Mardin Artuklu but later an MP for the HDP, who told me, 'Engin, we couldn't figure out what had happened, but they said you were attacking the AKP.' 'I don't understand,' I said. Attacking the system is one thing, but I never directly targeted the AKP in my writing. I only had one piece of writing in which I mentioned that a new biopolitical Islam had emerged from the AKP's clientelism. As such, I fell into the trash bin at Arel University. If I add here, for me, this university is a toxic place that is completely nationalist and racist. But Arel was temporary for me, since a faculty was already going to be set up for me at Mimar Sinan University.

Of course, the situation is a bit different now. We're only reading what's in the newspapers after five years. For example, I was asked a question at a sociology conference. We'd been away for one-and-a-half years. A methodological question was asked about how I create dialogue from afar in my own field. I said, 'You're right in asking this question, this is a methodological issue.' Without walking in the streets, as you said, without breathing the air there are some things you can't understand. But on the other hand, of course, there is a theoretical background that helps us study Turkey externally. You, as a person who has come from Turkey, talk about a country you are familiar with from its capillaries to its politics, economy and social structure. When you leave, something happens where you burden yourself with the mission of being a saviour. A conference was held in Berlin after the coup in which academics, intellectuals, MPs, journalists, film directors and people from diverse backgrounds came together. There were about seventy-seven people, I think. It was the first time such a big meeting had been held, I think; the old generation, new generation and different dynamics all came together. Only the Gülenists were absent, of course. We set out with a maxim to save Turkey, a democratic Turkey. Erdoğan will fall tomorrow, we will all return to our work and a democratic Turkey will appear. 'We're flying high like this, and it's beautiful. If only there was a rebellion and we could return to Turkey, but what if we listen to those who arrived after the 1980 coup?' I said. 'Because in my view, Turkey is heading for a very different place right now. Because no one intervened in the system while its foundations were being consolidated in 1980. They only tried to get the system to settle. The system is changing right now, and we aren't aware of it,' I said. 'A new Turkey is emerging from the clash between internal dynamics and hegemonies, and I don't know what it is, but it will be a despotic system. So I'll say here how I interpret Turkey externally. It's very clear that we are heading for a more neoliberal and despotic Turkey, I don't acknowledge the concept of dictatorship. The concept of dictatorship is a very shut-off concept. But right now, Turkey is not a dictatorship, the HDP is still fighting,' I said. It's still like this today – imagine the struggle Gergerlioğlu is pushing in the parliament. Turkey is a regime of violence – this is very clear. I don't think this process is new. The system of today can be consolidated in a way by accumulating a system that has neglected to confront the 1915 Armenian genocide, the Kurdish political uprisings or revolts, identity, the Alevi identity, the 1955 pogrom or Gazi or Sivas. That is to say this has a history, a memory, a collective total of values. This didn't appear spontaneously. This system is actually the renewed state of a previous Turkey that arose as a result of accumulations. This is not a new Turkey. This Turkey already existed, but it consolidated itself with the neoliberal system in the twenty-first century; a new clientelist system was born, and this clientelist system has certain various foundations. It significantly pertains to a spirit into which the world has fallen, because on the one hand, a fascist individual rises to power in America while Bolsonaro comes to power in Brazil. The Macron government, despite being liberal, attacks demonstrators, and a police state emerges. Turkey is heading towards a regime of violence and is trying to attack in every space, to start wars everywhere and to open new fronts. Russia is already like this. The Middle East is heading towards another place where a new type of regime is born, and an unbelievable weariness of violence has settled in. The world is actually heading towards an ideological polarisation in which regimes of violence and global authoritarian regimes appear, as was the case during World Wars I and II. There's an economic, political and social crisis. Turkey is being impacted by this. Under such conditions, the migrant crisis with the EU doesn't originate only from the political battle between Europe and Turkey. I think it also originates from calculations between authoritarian regimes. This is how I interpret Turkey externally. Right now, I don't think Turkey is moving in the right direction. To be honest, it could reach a more frightening point, but we could be wrong, of course. We have to wait a bit and see, but I think that the system is consolidating the foundations of the newly created regime. I mean, it's not like the AKP will collapse here or there. In my view, one of the points many dissident friends ignore is that

I think the opposition that has been trying to overthrow Erdoğan is unable to understand Turkey. Okay, yes. Erdoğan is a symbol, but this system has unbelievably dynamic actors. It has wartime branches, economic branches, political branches, a social media branch called its army of trolls. This government is pan-Turkist and Turanist and rises up to defend the Muslim community, and I think it is trying to organise itself within a new imagined state. Didn't Erdoğan say it himself, '2023, 2054, 2071' – meaning 1923, 1454, 1071; reading these dates in reverse chronological order is quite interesting.

He is reincarnating constantly.
Exactly right. It's not very accurate to only call them idiots. These people are developing a range of policies, I believe, in a very systematic manner and by truly playing off this idiocy and, in fact, by playing off this regime of stupidity. There are two things these policies are coming to terms with right now. The first is perhaps the Kurdish question. In my view, the AKP government – thankfully – made the Kurdish question international, the issue has emerged from Turkey. When we mention the Kurdish question, we can't talk about it without mentioning its international character. If there is a peace process again one day, this problem will no longer be solved only by Turkey. Turkey is no longer the sole actor. The AKP enabled this, because the Kurdish question had evolved into a global issue. There is a significant diaspora with serious diplomatic support. I'm studying Turkey a bit from here. As for the second point, I don't think that Turkey's dynamics of violence are very heartwarming. You said that people from many different segments of society are looking on the one hand for a homeland, for a nation, and, when you mention Sakarya, on the other hand (the motto of Turkish nationalism is 'Homeland, nation, Sakarya', as you know), they are looking for ways to flee the country. Everyone knows that the Turkish bourgeoisie – especially the upper-class bourgeoisie – took their assets out of the country. We are seeing that the middle class has completely melted away and vanished, that a great impoverish-

ment has appeared along with communities that are unable to define or express themselves or live outside the system's actors. We are facing this system, which is attacking everything everywhere, including the 'White Turks'. We are facing one bloc – I mean a Kafkaesque, post-Kafkaesque bloc – and it is wearing us down, because it can extend its hands into the diaspora and blacklist everybody.

In what ways?

Men are being kidnapped. You write something on Facebook, go to Turkey, and they seize your passport. Because you're also a Turkish citizen, they can take you and send you to prison. I, of course, think that this regime is unlike any that have appeared before. In fact, I didn't believe in the AKP's peace process, and I said this at the commission. One of the AKP's actors was there, one of the recognised journalists, Abdülkadir Selvi. He was there at our peace commission, and we fought with him. I said, 'As a Kurd and an Alevi, I don't find you sincere at all, because my body is in this territory, and it was subjected to violence in the Ottoman Empire and all the practices of the republic. How can you get up and say "Come on, try to understand me too", when my body has rights that have been situated within a regime of victimisation? Why should I understand you? You are competent. You're a Turk, you're Sunni,' I said. 'I am a Kurd,' he said. 'Okay,' I said. 'You are a Kurd and Sunni and an AKP supporter. But you are competent in a way, and I do not want to understand you. You need to understand me. Why should women understand men?' I said. Men must understand women – it's that simple. If you want to understand this violence, you must first understand women, you must act in solidarity with them. 'You don't act in solidarity with Kurds, Alevis, Armenians, Jews. You constantly impose yourself in some way over the religious community through Sunnism. This is an authoritarian regime, as you know; it will not create a democratic Turkey,' I said. A meeting was held in Berlin after the victory in Istanbul. I was the moderator. The AKP press targeted us after that meeting. Yes, and because we were targeted there, we couldn't enter Turkey – I forgot to say that. My friend from the lawyers for Academics for Peace said to me, 'Don't come anymore. In fact, don't come for a while.' They allegedly wrote something along the lines of 'PKK supporters, Gülenists and members of the Good Party and CHP came together to make a plan to divide up the region under the moderation of Engin Sustam, one of the Academics for Peace'. Wow, I had said, what kind of plans are in motion. Turkey actually has this kind of paranoia, a regime of paranoia.

Final question. Would you return one day?
Right now, I'm not considering going back because of my child. I think I'll settle here. I miss Turkey. I have never seen exile as a space of refuge. For me, exile is a place of rebellion. This is a space of re-establishment, in my view. I'm not someone who fell victim to the traps of that victimisation, and I already don't like that. Because of that, another life happened here for me. This is how I think about it: in 1978, my family migrated from Erzincan to the Istanbul diaspora. Istanbul is a diaspora for the Kurds. Similarly, I left there and migrated to the European diaspora, and my child was born here. Would I return to Turkey after this hour? Maybe one day if things improve, become more democratic. Maybe one day I can return to visit, because I miss my home, my grandfather and my village. I haven't seen my father or sibling in five and a half years. We only brought my mother here when my child was born. I haven't seen anyone in three and a half years due to the coronavirus, and I miss them, I miss my friends. My hair has truly grown white, my beard has grown unbelievably white. I'm definitely under a lot of stress. I miss Istanbul a lot, I miss the times I spent there. They were very beautiful times. The process between 2012 and 2015 in particular was unbelievable. There was an unbelievable political synergy originating from the peace process in Turkey. We attended some unbelievable meetings. We encountered a lot of terrible things with people from

the younger generation. You know, I lost my own student in Suruç. Murat Yurtgül was my student. He wanted to go to Kobane, and he was in Suruç with all those students who were killed for peace in 2015. My process of trauma actually began there when he was killed by that bomb. That kid with big glasses in my Facebook photo is Murat Yurtgül. I posted that photograph the day he was killed, and I decided not to change that photograph until the day that the people who committed this crime are brought to justice, so it's still there. Everyone thinks it's a picture from my youth, but it's not, it's Murat Yurtgül's photograph. I'm not partial to returning without a reckoning for Turkey's regime. And when I say regime, I'm not just talking about the AKP. I'm talking about a regime that we have truly grown sick of. I'm talking about a regime that must face the 1915 Armenian genocide. I'm talking about a regime that must confront the Kurdish question. I'm talking about a regime that must confront violence against women, femicide, violence against and killings of LGBTI+ people. I'm talking about a regime that must face the Alevis. And I want a democratic Turkey. In the end, I'm not a Kemalist, I'm not secular in that sense. Of course, I'm a laicist, and I defend secularism in the sense of *laïcité*, but I am not in favour of that chronic secularism in the sense the Kemalists have created or the Islamophobic secularism in the sense the French have created. I'm against political Islam, and I say this very clearly and explicitly. I'm against all interpretations of political Islam. I am someone who will fight it and who views it as fascism, but I'm not saying that I am against the interpretation of Islam that is for believers and Muslims. I'm just saying that this powerful Islam must accept my body, please. I am an atheist, but my family considers themselves Alevis and constructs it in different ways. The Yazidis construct themselves in different ways. The others construct themselves in different ways, and please let it become more democratic. Let this Islam become more democratic, let this country become more democratic and let us please not talk about these things anymore. Let's tend to our own business. Let our business be something else. I would certainly want to return if I saw a Turkey where I believed that our business could be something else. But I know that this would be difficult because my child and spouse were born and raised here. They won't return. I just think that when a Turkey like that appears, I'll have a Turkey I can come and go to.

So, you're saying we'll live a two-legged life?
We'll live a two-legged life. I hope that Turkey will one day appear. I'm not very hopeful at the moment, truthfully. So, I'm politically pessimistic even though I'm a positive person. But it really worries me.

You're not alone in your pessimism.
Yes, that really worries me. That's it.

6

ESER KARAKAŞ

**A considerable proportion of my assistants didn't call me.
I helped them earn their doctorates and served as their
lecturer. They cut off our relationship as if it had never
happened. I have close friends in Turkey who didn't call me
even once after I became unable to return to Turkey. I don't
make this into a problem, but it makes me sad for them.**

*Dr Eser Karakaş is an adjunct professor at the University of Stras-
bourg, where he teaches law, economics, and economics of public issues
at the Institut d'études politiques. He was a professor of economics at the
University of Istanbul between 2014 and 2016 and head of the Department of the European Union at the College of Business Administration
at Bahçeşehir University between 2010 and 2014. He worked as the
dean of the College of Business Administration at Bahçeşehir University between 2000 and 2006 before becoming the vice president-provost
there between 2006 and 2010. Dr Karakaş was a professor of public*

economics at the University of Istanbul between 1986 and 1996. He
received his PhD in public finance from the Faculty of Economics of the
University of Istanbul in 1986. He earned a master of economics from
the same university in 1981. Dr Karakaş's main research interests are
public economics, public choice, public finance, European finances, pub-
lic policy, law and economics, and good governance. His work has been
published in journals such as Public Economics, Public Choice *and*
European Union Budget.

**Professor Karakaş, thank you for your time. We want to start
with asking why and how you left Turkey.**
I didn't flee Turkey. I was a faculty member at the university. I was
supposed to have a green passport. But on 15 July 2016, they banned
anyone with a green passport from leaving the country. At the time,
my ex-wife was the Turkey magistrate at the European Court of
Human Rights (ECHR). As a result, I received a diplomatic passport
through my wife. After 15 July, I left and entered Turkey several times
with that diplomatic passport. There were never any problems at the
border. We have a daughter, a faculty member in America who lives
in Washington, DC. I went to see my daughter. I was going to return
to Istanbul again; I had classes. But in the morning, as I was sitting
with my wife, daughter and son-in-law at a cafe in Georgetown, I got a
message on my phone saying I had been dismissed from the university
through a statutory decree. My daughter immediately found the issue
of the Official Gazette, opened it, and I saw it there. I read the statutory decree. It said that the passport would automatically be revoked.
The revocation of a passport means a ban on leaving the country. I got
a French passport not long after that day and became a French citizen.

**Had you applied for French citizenship as a precaution or were
you already considering applying?**
No, I was already considering it since I had been living in France
since 2008, which meant that I had the right to apply for French

citizenship. But if this 15 July catastrophe hadn't happened, applying for French citizenship wouldn't have been on my mind because I already had a green passport. I had a long-term American visa. I was comfortably able to go anywhere in the European Union. I had a diplomatic passport at the time, too, but when my Turkish passport was revoked, I was left all of a sudden without a passport in America. I returned the very next day. Our tickets were through Frankfurt. There weren't any problems upon entry, but I was thinking if I enter Turkey, I won't be able to leave again. That much was certain. But what would they do to me in Turkey? I wasn't sure. My wife at the time was a magistrate at the ECHR, and they probably wouldn't have touched her, but I wouldn't have been able to leave Turkey again. My daughter was in America, my wife was living in France. Returning to Turkey became pointless, so I became a French citizen and got a French passport. I still have friends in Turkey, family in Turkey asking why I didn't go to Turkey with my French passport.

In a country of which you're a citizen, your French citizenship is invalid. They could arrest you if they wanted to.
Suppose I wasn't arrested. I look at the e-state online portal occasionally, and no lawsuit has been launched against me. But if I came [to Turkey] with a French passport, I wouldn't be able to leave. I could enter with no problem, But because my Turkish passport was revoked and I'm still a citizen of the Republic of Turkey, they wouldn't let me leave the country. Every morning at six o'clock, I sit and wonder who's going to come to my door, and this isn't pleasant at my age. Ultimately, I decided not to go to Turkey.

Have there been any lawsuits filed against you apart from the statutory decree?
No, but you can't know of course, since it emerges when you go there. Something like that happened to a friend of mine. You're entering at the border, and they say 'Go ahead', and they bring you to Vatan

Emniyet[1] for a tweet you sent or an article you wrote. What would happen there? Perhaps the prosecutor would take my statement and let me go – that's another matter – but I definitely wouldn't be able to leave Turkey. As a result, I don't want to take any risks. I have a daughter and a granddaughter, and they live in America. Why shouldn't I go and see them and come back when I want to? This is of course a bit of a paradoxical issue. I can go anywhere in the world with a French passport. I was saved from visa processes like this. It's almost like there aren't any countries that require a visa for a French passport. But I can't go to my own country – to the place I was born. I didn't flee the country. I left normally from Yeşilköy with my diplomatic passport, and I still could have returned, but I didn't because of the statutory decree issue.

I normally would have to ask you why France, but as far as I understand, you didn't have any alternatives, and there wasn't a situation where you could have made a choice.
I live in France. I have been teaching classes at Strasbourg University since 2008. I was also employed as a professor at Istanbul University. I was coming and going to Istanbul every week.

When you were dismissed with the statutory decree, you weren't given your pension or other personal rights as an employee, were you? Were you able to retire?
This is why I wasn't able to retire: I had taught at the university for thirty-five years. There was an article in the social security law – at the time there was the State Pension Fund and the Social Security Institution – that stipulated that you could retire from wherever you taught if you had worked half of the past seven years plus one day. When I moved to Istanbul University, I hadn't worked there for three-and-a-half years yet. I worked as a professor at Bahçeşehir

---

[1] The police headquarters in Istanbul.

University. I moved to Istanbul University so I could get a pension from the state, I had that right. If I had been able to work there for three and a half years, I would have got a pension from the state. The statutory decree went into effect with one year left. As a result, I received my pension from the Social Security Institution. But I want to receive a state pension. If I can go to Turkey after all this is over, I'll file a lawsuit.

You are famous in Turkey because you are a well-known professor with a significant media presence. Strasbourg is a region with a significant and diverse Turkish diaspora. After you began living there permanently, did you have any positive or negative public encounters? It could be with a supporter of the current regime or someone else who knew you. Was there ever an incident in which you encountered some kind of reaction or reactions?

Nothing too troublesome happened. Every once in a while there are people who come up to me and want to talk; there still are. I don't really like to leave home, but sometimes when I do, people come up to me. But I haven't encountered anything too troublesome or threatening.

Was there ever anyone who supported you? With which groups and which structures in Turkey do you have more relationships?

Yes, that happened more often. There are some who look for me and ask me to appear on programmes, mainly from the 'liberal segment' like us. I don't like that expression actually because I don't identify as a liberal. I have a more heterodox understanding. I believe in market economics and of course I believe in freedom of thought, but I also believe in a social state. There isn't much of an organised liberal circle like this, but my relationship with Turks living here is good. There are some from the Gülen Movement who seek me out.

Only the ones in France or Strasbourg, or do members from elsewhere in the world seek you out?

From all over the world. I have been invited a few times on programmes that Turkish Kurds in Brussels have organised. These sorts of offers come from Gülenists across the world. Apart from that, there are people who don't have much of a sense of belonging. People with no sense of belonging to any group but who are aware that this treatment that we have faced is inhumane.

So you've encountered more solidarity?

I won't say solidarity, but I haven't had any troublesome encounters. I have more cordial relationships. Of course, the position of the state is more unlikable here. Because I was impacted by the statutory decree, no one from the consulate or embassy is looking for me anymore. But worse is that they cause problems when trying to give someone power of attorney. There was an application needing to be filed with the governorate regarding the statutory decree. I needed to give someone power of attorney to be able to do this. They even caused problems there.

Could you describe this a little bit?

There's nothing to describe here. It's illegal. Giving power of attorney to someone is the most natural right of a citizen. I lost my father four years ago. A document must be produced to be able to receive my father's inheritance. They caused problems even with that.

Like what? Like not being allowed in a building, not completing your request?

I can't get a certificate of inheritance. As a citizen of the Republic of Turkey living here, I am entitled to get that from the consulate. There were problems, but they were resolved later. There were people at the consulate who helped. I have to hand it to them. But, for example, the young people working at the consulate would have known, they would have heard that I was going there. They never said, 'Professor, come, let's have a cup of coffee.' I never committed any shameful crimes. I don't know why I was dismissed with the statutory decree. I don't know what crime I committed. It was probably because of the programme I hosted. We organised a really successful programme – Mehmet Altan, Şahin Alpay and I. We did it for ten years. It started in 2006 and continued until 2015. We organised 600 episodes without disruption. When the programme started, the AKP and the Gülen Movement were incredibly close. Their relationship later deteriorated. We spoke among ourselves; the fight between the AKP and the Gülen Movement wasn't a matter that was relevant to us. We were calling out to citizens from here. And I had one or two interests. One was the Court of Accounts, and the other was the procurement law. One was the fact that the Court of Accounts no longer functioned in Turkey. And the other was this terrifying situation that the procurement law found itself in. I think that these were Turkey's most important problems. The AKP changed Article 160 in the constitution regarding the Court of Accounts, but it didn't pass a law. I am a professor of public economics, of property. I saw this as a mission for myself, and I absolutely connected every issue to the Court of Accounts and the procurement law. But we didn't have any bad relations with the channel.

It was Samanyolu TV, right?
No, it was Mehtap, not Samanyolu. Mehtap is Samanyolu's sister institution, but it is separate from Samanyolu. They didn't distinguish the three of us from the Gülenists. They would have known that we weren't part of them. Just once, they asked us not to ridicule Aliyev so much because they had schools in Azerbaijan. We never encountered anything apart from that.

Four years have passed since you started living there. The staff at the consulate changed during this period. I know that the consulate changed in 2018. Although the consulate and its

staff may change, the state's approach to you remains the same, correct?

I wasn't harmed. I no longer have any relationship with the consulate. I don't have a Turkish passport. I have a French passport. I only went to the building once to declare my French citizenship to the Interior Ministry. They were helpful with that and didn't cause any problems.

European media constantly report that Turkey's transnational state apparatuses such as MİT and the Diyanet implement certain repressive policies such as monitoring and surveillance. Have you ever experienced anything like this during this process? Have there ever been any times when you've been threatened or have felt unsafe?

I'm not terribly familiar with the issues of religion and the Diyanet. There is a very powerful Diyanet here, a Diyanet neighbourhood. It's an amazing thing. There are Diyanet hotels, schools, mosques. I don't go to the mosque, so I haven't had a problem with the Diyanet. Thank God I haven't had any problems with the National Intelligence Organisation. But I know that they are very powerful in Strasbourg. In fact, I think Turkey's intelligence centre in Europe is here. The reason the newly built consulate building is so big is probably because of that. The state is like a stomach, Mehmet would say. If your stomach is strong and tough enough to dissolve a stone, you won't even know where in your body it is. Because your stomach never hurts or burns. A well-functioning state is like this. It functions very well but doesn't show itself. Poorly functioning states are like a diseased stomach. It makes its presence known every minute. It burns, it hurts, you take medication. You can't digest food, you grow uncomfortable. You'll get sick. Our state is like a stomach with an ulcer.

Do you still have relationships with other intellectuals who left Turkey like yourself? Yavuz Baydar lives in France as far as I know.

I do, of course. I speak with Yavuz Baydar almost every day. Some live in Canada – Ergun Babahan, for example. Celal Başlangıç is in Germany with his wife Ayşe Başlangıç. Both are very old friends of mine and we still talk.

After being dismissed by the statutory decree and being forced to leave Turkey, did anybody turn their back on you or put a distance between you and themselves because of your political views or the position the state put you in?
It hasn't happened here, but it did happen in Turkey unfortunately. A considerable proportion of my assistants didn't call me. I helped them earn their doctorates and served as their lecturer. They cut off our relationship as if it had never happened. I have close friends in Turkey who didn't call me even once after I became unable to return to Turkey. I don't make this into a problem, but it makes me sad for them, because this is a very unpleasant view of people. I wouldn't have wanted to be in their place. I'm happy with where I am. Their situation is very perilous, they showed an immense weakness in terms of humanity.

You've lived continuously in France for a while after spending a great deal of your life travelling between Strasbourg and Istanbul, and you're observing Turkey from afar. How do you see it? What differences are there between Eser Karakaş's understanding of Turkey in 2015 and his understanding of Turkey today?
There aren't many differences. There may be a quantitative difference in the gravity of the problems. The degree of severity may have changed. The problems have become more dangerous, but I'm not saying this only for the AKP era in Turkey. I think that past continuity, between the sixteenth and seventeenth centuries, for example, was even more important and treacherous than change. The problems are always there; the essence doesn't really change, and especially throughout the history of the republic nothing has changed. If you asked a scholar what the two most important problems facing

Turkey in 2021 are, they would respond with the Kurdish question and *laïcité*. When the Law on the Maintenance of Order (*Takrir-i Sükûn*) went into effect in 1925 it was due to the Kurdish question and *laïcité*. A hundred years – a whole century – has passed and we are still debating these two problems. I go on Artı TV nowadays on Friday evenings, Artı Gerçek's TV channel. Celal Başlangıç is also on the programme. Celal says, 'I'm preparing a two- or three-page weekly agenda. Nothing like this happens anywhere in the world.' Mehmet, Şahin and I did 600 programmes. Şahin would prepare the programme agenda and I would present it. Mehmet would bring the issues and Şahin would prepare the agenda, each week he would bring a three- or four-page list of topics. We never were able to get to even the second page. The programme lasted for an hour and a half. Şahin lived for ten years in Sweden. Şahin would say the same thing: 'This agenda I've brought is a yearly agenda for Sweden.' It seems like there's a certain dynamism in Turkey, though the country appears to be rolling idly. There's a completely unproductive dynamism. I mean, a country which is this dynamic could go places. It seems like nothing ever happens in Sweden, but it was a very impoverished country in the early twentieth century and 70–80 years later it became the world's greatest welfare society. When you take a look, though, it seems like nothing much ever happens. With us, there's a fantastic dynamism, but we can't solve the issue of *laïcité* or the Kurdish question. Sweden has become one of the richest countries with the greatest and most advanced democracies in the world, solving all its problems and leaving them behind. Accordingly, Turkey isn't dynamic. We have an unfaithful dynamism.

Do you think that this empty dynamism will continue after this?
Yes, I do. I teach a law and economics class at Strasbourg University. It's a law class. We view the law as an asset and study its relationship with the economy. Law is something that is produced. In that sense, it is a public asset, but there must be demands for a public asset to be produced, just like a shirt, jumper or watch. There are no demands for law

in Turkey. The lack of such demands does not stem from ignorance. It originates from a state of rational disinterest because people have no interest in having a relationship with the law. The law does not serve the interests of most citizens and voters. What does this mean? They engage in production in the underground economy, they don't pay taxes, they reside on public land, they steal electricity. So I make this claim: let's set up a political party in Turkey and have our platform be to establish the rule of law. It's a beautiful demand, is it not? We would never get more than 5 per cent of the vote. So what does this mean? The most fundamental element of the rule of law is that everyone has tax liabilities. But look, I'm not talking about paying taxes, I'm talking about tax liability. In Turkey, the government is removing the obligation to declare taxes for 850,000 tradespeople as if it's a good thing. This is the greatest treachery that could be done to Turkey. If those 850,000 tradespeople do not have the ability to pay taxes, still then help them make declarations, make that mandatory, but bring a limitation such that they don't actively pay taxes. You'll say that those residing on public property will pay this cost. Is there such a thing, to reside on public lands without cost? Is there such a thing in Britain, to live on public property without paying any money? When I criticise them for stealing electricity, they get mad. 'Those people don't have the ability to pay,' they say. Okay, I acknowledge that they don't have the ability to pay, so you remove them from illegal status and provide them with direct assistance, but don't let them steal electricity. If Turkey cannot get a toe in the door to the European Union, it will never have the rule of law.

Would you return to Turkey?
I would return to Istanbul. I'm not in love with Turkey, but I am in love with Istanbul.

Do you think that you'll return? Do you have any such hope?
God willing, but I'm not very hopeful in the short term. I'm sixty-eight. Maybe I won't be able to return at all. I miss Istanbul, I miss

Turkey. I am very fond of Istanbul in a special way. I have a considerable library in Istanbul which I can't access right now. I set up a thousand plaques in Istanbul with Murat Belge before coming here. We took all the important Byzantine, Republican and Ottoman buildings in Istanbul and wrote a brief history of each one right next to them. At the time, our relationship with Istanbul's mayor, Kadir Topbaş, wasn't too bad. But the conservatives have a problem in Turkey. One day, Murat and I came across the wedding ceremony of Hrant Dink's younger daughter at the Armenians' big church. The Grand Patriarchate is there. We had set up a little plaque there. Murat went and read the plaque and said, 'They completely changed what I wrote.' That's when I understood. They were probably uncomfortable with what Murat had written. Talat Pasha's old home is in Sultanahmet. Murat didn't write about this. We had a meeting one day with officials from the municipality, and they asked, 'Professor, why aren't you writing about Talat Pasha's home?' 'You won't print what I write, so why should I?' I said. 'If I write there that this was the man who was behind the Armenian genocide, would you print it?' They couldn't say anything. 'Then what should I write?' I asked.

I really want to return to Istanbul, I really miss Istanbul. I studied at Boğaziçi University. I spent my youth on the Bosporus, in Bebek and Arnavutköy. About ten years ago, I read a news article saying gangs were fighting in Arnavutköy. It seemed strange. Then I learned that a massive neighbourhood called Arnavutköy had been built behind the new airport in Istanbul. Of course, I had never in my life set foot there. I really miss Kalamış, I really miss Moda. I was born and raised in Moda. I miss the green plums. You can find them here, but it's very difficult. Plums and raki. They have raki here, but it's undrinkable. I don't know why. I don't know if there's a problem with the water they add to it or with the taste of the tomatoes and feta cheese. Because a *meyhane* probably has something called feta cheese. But there aren't any here, you see. I couldn't even find it to bring home. You can only find that cheese at a *meyhane*, not at a supermarket. They don't have that cheese here. And the cheeses that you can find in Germany don't go well with raki. I don't drink it here at all. Every alcohol has its geographic space. I'll drink wine, but I never would have drunk wine in Turkey.

Do you think that you are safe in France? Are you sure that the French state is able to protect you no matter what?

I don't know how the French state would protect me, but the Turkish state knows that I'm a French citizen. I went to the consulate to make a declaration. I mean, if something happens here, something will have happened to a French citizen.

Is that why you let Turkey know that you're a French citizen?

Yes, I declared it a little bit because of that. They could kidnap me, but it would be a big problem to kidnap a French citizen from France. I don't think they'll spend that much time fretting over me, I'm not that important. This is what I'm most upset about for Turkey. I am a person very close to the establishment, I'm a man of the establishment. What am I defending? I'm defending the rule of law. I'm defending a market economy. I'm defending freedom of expression. But the Turkish centre has shifted to such a place that the universal values of the establishment have become marginalised in Turkey. This is a frightening thing for Turkey. I'm not actually a leftist in the political smorgasbord, I don't look fondly upon a discriminatory movement, against religious movements. But I am marginalised in Turkey because I defended an establishment of universal values. There's nothing more upsetting for Turkey than this. Because the values of the centre in Turkey have completely shifted away from the universal establishment. They ask me what I did. And I say I truly don't know. They think that I'm hiding something. I defend the things that an average citizen in London, an average intellectual can defend. I defend a more open market economy, a social state and freedom of expression. But our dear president says he's making legal reforms and plunges the presumption of innocence and personality of the crime into the scope of reforms. The presumption of innocence is a rule originating from Justinian. The principle of the personality of the crime also originates from Justinian, perhaps even earlier. And these are being forced into the scope of legal reform in Turkey. It's truly a painful thing. I couldn't believe my ears when the president said this.

This is also a confession, of course.
Of course. I had been connected to someone, and I also said there that this was a written confession.

You were impacted by the statutory decree. There weren't any actions such as seizing your property, were there?
No, there weren't.

So were you fearful?
I was, but it didn't come to pass. I was able to sell what was handed down from my father. I had my own home, and I sold that. I was able to transfer that money here.

So you sold all your property? You don't have anything left in Turkey?
Yes, I sold it. I don't have much left at all. I have my pension. But I have a longing for Istanbul, though that's most important.

7

FATIH VURAL AND GÜLİZ VURAL

Fatih: We're sorry for those left behind . . . For example,
my mother's words bewildered me. A sixty-seven-year-old
woman tells her son, 'Don't stop, don't even look back. If I
were younger, I would go too!' This is said by a mother whose
two children are abroad.

Güliz: It's like we came out of a fire at the last moment!
I felt like, 'What I left behind continues to burn up.'
I still feel that way. It's like my country is on fire!

*Fatih Vural was born in Manisa in 1978. He graduated from the
Sociology Department of Ege University in 1999. In the same year,
he started his master's degree in general sociology and methodology
at the same university. He completed his master's degree in 2003 by*

presenting the first comprehensive sociological thesis on mentally disabled people in Turkey under the title 'Mentally Disabled People in Turkey in the Context of Social Illness: The Example of İzmir'. Between 1999 and 2004, he taught mentally disabled children. He settled in Istanbul in 2004 and started a journalism career. Until 2016, he worked at Zaman, Türkiye *and* Today *newspapers. He also worked as a reporter and interviewer for* Aksiyon, Aktüel *and* Nokta *magazines.*

In 2005, he undertook the editorship of a book titled 'My Father Should Not See: Prime Minister Erdoğan's Football Adventure' by Hacı Hasdemir. In 2013, he wrote a biography of Can Paker called 'No Looking Back'. In 2015, his interview with Mim Kemal Öke was published under the title of 'Wounded Gazelles Club', which tells about Dr Öke's mystical journey. In the same year, he undertook the editorship of the famous businessman Uğur Ekşioğlu's autobiography, 'Find Your Own Job'. In 2016, he wrote a biography of Caner Tunaman, 'The Master of Brands'. This book was followed by 'One Neyzen, Two Deryas: Şems and Mevlana', which he prepared with the world-famous ney player and mystic Kudsi Erguner. In 2017, he wrote 'The Man Who Lives Tomorrow', the first volume of his biography of Besim Tibuk. In 2019, he published the second volume, 'An Angry Liberal: The Liberal Democrat Party and Cyprus'.

Güliz Vural worked as a photojournalist and editor in multiple newspapers and magazines. Her first personal exhibition, 'Sade(ce) Beyoglu' ('Only Beyoglu'), was held in 2011. 'Oy'un' ('Your Vote'), which she presented at Mimar Sinan University in 2014, satirised the election system. Her short documentary, called 'Kaderimizi Çöp Kutuları mı Belirleyecek?' ('Will Dustbins Determine Our Faith?'), received great attention from journalists as well as the public.

She started to work on immigration-related issues in 2014. In the same year she took daily photographs of migrants by going to their houses in Fatih and Sulukule in Istanbul. In October 2015 she managed to become the first photographer to take the tragic pictures of immigrants trying to pass to Lesbos from Çanakkale. To do so she got into the boat that was carrying the immigrants. She was arrested the moment the boat arrived in Lesbos and was held in custody for five days. Her trial took two and a half years. In November 2015 'Ranza', another project which included a photo exhibition of immigrants in Sulukule, was exhibited at Bursa Photo Fest. In September 2016 she won an award at one of the biggest photo festivals in the world, 'Upcoming Masters of Photography', which was held in Cologne. In 2017 she attended the TUYAP art exhibition (Istanbul) with her work called 'Mültecilerden Geride Kalanlar' ('The Remnants of the Immigrants'). In November 2021, she presented an exhibition of photos of immigrants at Coventry University's RISING Global Forum. She is currently working on independent documentaries and photo shoots.

Dear Fatih and Güliz, thank you so much for this interview. Can you briefly tell us when and how you came to England?
Güliz Vural: We arrived on 23 June 2021. The Ankara Agreement between Turkey and the UK was continuing and we wanted to go abroad. This seemed the easiest method to us. Our application was accepted upon my starting a company in the field of photography. Six to eight weeks after the admission, we took a plane and came to England.
Fatih Vural: We came to England for a week's holiday in 2009 and toured London from top to bottom. England was not a country we did not know. This was also effective in our choice.
Güliz: It couldn't be Germany. Language would be a big problem. We have a language problem here too, but at least we have a background.

How did you make this immigration decision? Even if you came under the Ankara Agreement, there is a serious cost to living here when you compare sterling with the Turkish lira. And you have a fourteen-year-old daughter. What kind of motivation

**did you have for a new country, a new life after the age of 40?
What did you experience internally, in your relationship?**

Fatih: The idea of leaving was more dominant in Güliz. It was our cousins who really motivated us. They had gone abroad by finding work. My cousin working in IT went to Poland, and my cousin working in transport went to Hungary. My brother settled in Canada. So we were the only ones in the family who hadn't 'left'! They were constantly putting pressure on us, saying 'You have to go now, too'! These pressures, my wife's request and the departure of many of my journalist friends from Turkey motivated me. Especially when journalist friends leave the country, people feel a serious sense of loneliness: 'Why did I stay when everyone else left?' That feeling is a bad thing! I experienced this a lot, especially with one friend of mine. I was so demoralised.

The direction of Turkey also reinforced our idea of leaving. We have a fourteen-year-old daughter who will start high school this year. Why should we believe in and deliver our child into an education system where even the governing minister understands that he cannot change the system and asks for pardon? We sent Mina to a private college for eight years. Because we wanted her to learn a foreign language. It was more important for us that she had a good command of English rather than her other classes. When we came to England, we realised that we had made the right decision.

As you said, forty and beyond is an important threshold. I am forty-two years old. Yes, it was quite difficult for me. I was leaving my comfort zone. My wife Güliz has constantly been saying, 'Let's get out of our comfort zone. See, we will encounter much more beautiful things,' she said. Our three months in England have proved her right. Glad we came!

After I came, I saw this: even my friends who are close to the government or who are supporters of the government seemed to want to leave the country! After we came, they started to ask 'How did you go, how can we come?' but the Ankara Agreement ended as of 31 December 2020. We got rewarded for our courage.

Güliz: My motivations were different. I felt chained. It's like they locked that chain and threw the key into the sea! That key was at the bottom of the sea. It was impossible to remove it.

I had a problem not only with power, but also with people. I wanted to get rid of them and live as we deserve, humanely. I wanted to show this to my child. I was very scared when there was a knock on our door at night in Turkey. One night, at two o'clock, there was a knock on the door and I said, 'Fatih, which of us have they come for?'

I want to intervene here . . . You are two people who worked in the media of that community without being a member of the Gülen Movement . . .
Fatih: I worked in the Movement media, not Güliz.
Güliz: Such a thing was attributed to *Nokta* magazine and therefore it was closed, but [the allegation] could not go beyond a claim that it was the media of the Movement.

Between 2006 and 2012, the AKP and the Gülen Movement were very close. They embarked on a struggle between 2013 and 2016. After 2016, a process began in which the Gülen Movement lost this war, and 'the one who touched it burned'. You decided to come in 2021, not in 2016. Güliz just mentioned her 'chains' and you mentioned your 'comfort zone'. What is the reason for the paradox you two are experiencing, Fatih?
Fatih: My comfort zone was my biography writing. I was dealing with businessmen. I was working from home and earning much better than in journalism. This inevitably creates a comfort zone. I made my own order.

I had such a comfort zone, but we could not do journalism from 2016 until the day we left Turkey. I still had an escape route, I was writing celebrity biographies. But Güliz never had one! Güliz was the photo editor of the latest *Nokta* magazine. Before that, she was the photo editor of the newspaper *Türkiye*. But after the coup attempt in 2016, Güliz was cut off! She couldn't do anything. I was still able to produce. I wrote three books from 2016 to 2021.

As for the part about the community media, I worked for the newspaper *Zaman* from 2004 to 2012. I got there purely with my talents. During my special education teaching, I interviewed them externally, and they invited me to work together with them. In other words, there was no 'my brother' whom I knew from the Movement! I resigned voluntarily in 2012, even when the relationship between AKP and Movement was still good. Because I wanted to open a new lane for myself and write a biography. The reason for the fear that Güliz refers to by 'the fear of knocking on our door in the middle of the night' is the political interviews I did in the *Bugün* newspaper in 2015. Especially in my interviews with former AKP members, their criticisms of the government had serious repercussions in the government media. I was targeted. I even encountered indecent proposals. They made very attractive transfer offers. I refused. Because they were looking for hitmen, not journalists!

Because I rejected their offer, we were targeted by the person who brought that offer to me from the *Sabah* newspaper, but nothing happened to us. Because there was no concrete evidence to show that we had any ties to the Gülen Movement. Neither ByLock nor Bank Asya accounts, nor scholarships, nor participation in the Digiturk closure campaign, which are the criteria set by the government! In fact, during the Movement's campaign to shut down Digiturk, completely independent of that campaign, Güliz said, 'What if we close our account? We pay the earth for Digiturk.' I remember saying to her, 'No, I'll never get rid of it! Then how will I watch Fenerbahce matches?'

Güliz: Before 15 July, we were experiencing fear, but with 15 July, we had a serious mental shock. I was so scared because it would wear me out to go in for a crime I didn't deserve. I wanted to live in a place where I was not afraid when the doorbell rang at night.

Can you tell us the story of that door knocking?

Güliz: One night, at about two o'clock, our doorbell rang. I said to Fatih, 'Stop, let me change. Have they come for you or me?' That was the first thing that came to my mind. They reflected that fear so seriously on us! Fatih immediately opened the door and it was some-one from a kebab shop. He had come with a delivery and pressed the wrong bell. I was so angry with the kebab shop! I even accidentally said, 'People have fears.' The next day, we went to our neighbour across the street and I said, 'If one day the doorbell rings and the police take us away, the child is entrusted to you!'

Fatih: There is another traumatic event related to this! We had to throw away the books in our library.

Güliz: In a night operation, we shredded them, divided them into bags and threw them away. Fatih waited for me in the place where we threw them away, and I looked to see if there was a camera. We may have travelled to ten different skips like this!

Fatih: What we threw in the trash were not Gülen books either. At that moment, silly ideas such as 'They can relate me to this author through something' run through your head. Unfortunately, the fate of Turkey does not change, in the country where the books of Nazım Hikmet were banned since yesterday, years later people are arrested because of the books in their library. This cycle is so bad! Let me tell you a painful memory . . . The word 'Hero' was banned at that time! Yes, the word 'Hero' was banned in Turkey because one of the putschist soldiers used that word in a correspondence! Just like a dollar bill![1] We went to Karaburun, a town in Istanbul province on the Black Sea coast. 'Hero' had been written in graf-fiti on an electrical transformer before the ban, and afterwards, that

---

[1] One-dollar bills were used as a token of communication among the soldiers who were involved in the 15 July putsch. See Tulay Cetingulec, 'Why are Turks dispos-ing of $1 bills?' *Al-Monitor*, 18 August 2016, https://www.al-monitor.com/origi-nals/2016/08/turkey-gulen-movement-one-dollar-fear.html, accessed 4 April 2023.

word was covered with whitewash! This example describes the traumatic state of Turkey and us so well! A time when words and even money were banned!

Güliz: For example, we had a lot of problems with our downstairs neighbour. He was obsessed with noise and was constantly complaining as if it was from us, even though it wasn't us. It had reached harassment. One day I had something to do at the Police Department. I also wanted to report him for these harassments. The cops said, 'We can start proceedings immediately.' Then I came home. I thought, This is a man close to power. If he said 'They are Fetöists!' anyone would believe it! I was so scared that I couldn't report that man!

Fatih: At the time when my journalist friends were being arrested one by one, we were going to Cyprus for a holiday and to meet with my boss. In fact, Nazlı Ilıcak was arrested that day and when we arrived at the airport, we said, 'Is there anything wrong with us? Will they take us?' I can't forget our anxiety.

Güliz: I even said to Fatih, 'Whichever of us they take, the other will continue to Cyprus without looking back.'

How did you suddenly take this migration decision? Did you have a breaking point like 'This incident happened and I said one cannot live here anymore'?

Güliz: I love Turkey with everything. Migration is a traumatic concept for me! But we couldn't live like that. That troubled mood couldn't continue any longer. The breaking point was 15 July. After 15 July, our ties, our memories no longer mattered.

You got approval from the Ankara Agreement, shut up the house, passed the passport check and the plane took off . . . How did you feel at that moment?

Güliz: I couldn't say, like, 'Oh! We are saved!' frankly. It's not like that for me!

Fatih: That didn't happen to me either. Maybe it is because of this: we came to England under the Ankara Agreement. We did not seek asylum. So we can go back any time we want. However, we're sorry for those left behind . . . For example, my mother's words bewildered me. A sixty-seven-year-old woman tells her son, 'Don't stop, don't even look back. If I were younger, I would go too!' This is said by a mother whose two children are abroad.

When you look back, what kind of Turkey did you leave behind?
Güliz: It's like we came out of a fire at the last moment! I felt like 'What I left behind continues to burn up'. I still feel that way. It's like my country is on fire!
Fatih: Going with a fish metaphor, you get a better view of what it's like when you step out of the aquarium. We started to look at Turkey from a wider perspective. Things started to get worse there after we arrived here. The unquenchable forest fires, the growing economic crisis, the increasing desperation of the people . . . So much has happened in the past three months! We are in purgatory right now. We are in a culture we do not know, but our roots are outside. We want to be able to establish a system where we can live in Turkey for 3–4 months in five, ten years from now. It's our country! It is not the country of any power or group!

One of our motivations for coming was the English language. We are middle-class people who have intellectual activities and our networks revolve around such activities. In this sense, the poorness of our English was a big disadvantage. We had to fix this problem now. However, we could overcome this by coming to England. My biggest ideal is to be able to write a biography in English, for example. Güliz is a world-class photographer. The only journalist and photographer in the world to get on the refugee boat and travel with them from Turkey to Greece! We couldn't market such a big event to the world, so to speak, because our English is not good! It was a serious wound inside us. We couldn't carry this wound any longer.

You came here. There are approximately 400,000 Turks in England. 200,000–250,000 of them emigrated long ago. The rest are from the last thirty years. When you meet the Turks here, do you experience any reservations about seeing reactions like 'You wrote for *Zaman*, you worked at *Nokta*!'? In short, have you seen the polarisation in Turkey here as well?

Fatih: Let me very frankly admit, I am censoring myself! For example, when I feel that the people in front of me are thinking with mental templates, I do not say, 'I worked at *Zaman*, at *Bugün*'. But I haven't seen many people in the UK yet to practise this self-censorship with.

Güliz: I don't think self-censorship is right. At least I want to be comfortable here. I am also selective about the Turks here. Because the man who comes with his nationalism and mentality there, he doesn't change anything about himself. Just as we escaped from those people in Turkey, we will continue our lives by escaping from them and being selective here.

Fatih: And the common identity of all of us is exclusion! Academics for Peace, Kurds, members of the Gülen community . . . This is a very large cycle. It has a common denominator. You are not an 'acceptable citizen' for power or the state. You are 'dangerous', troublesome people! Because you do not obey them. You oppose them. You oppose what is being imposed on you. The government does not accept this objection and has been labelling you as a 'traitor' or 'terrorist' since 2016.

The time we feared was the time when people were being killed in the confusion! People whose names you do not know or cannot know could turn your life into a mess by reporting you. Thousands of people's lives have been made miserable by secret witness statements. I have friends who were imprisoned for a year and a half to prove that there was no alleged crime but were eventually released by the judge, almost apologetically, as no crime was discovered. Who will give back the stolen lives of those people and their families, who will pay the price? After seeing all this hell you think there's no point in staying.

Güliz: For example, when I came here, I said to Fatih, 'I want to be known as a Kurdish photographer in England. I don't want to be known as a Turkish photographer!' I didn't want to hide my identity, I wanted to be more transparent here. I wanted to open a cleaner, more real page where we are who we are. The state's assimilation policy has worked so well that I have become an 'acceptable citizen'! I want to get away from that. I want to be myself now!

What would happen if you stayed?
Fatih: We would rot! The depression in Güliz caused by not being able to produce anything was more than I experienced. Time flows like water and you can't do anything. This is the greatest torment for people who are productive. We've both been productive throughout our lives.
Güliz: We didn't want to be spectators to life anymore!

How did you explain this decision to your daughter?
Güliz: I think my daughter felt it. We were talking a lot. Our fear was probably reflected in her. We even talked to our family therapist while explaining our decision. He said, 'You must not say anything before the decision is made'. At first, we weren't going to say anything, but then, while the conversations and correspondence were going on, we didn't want the child to hear it from somewhere else and wanted to be the ones who would explain it. Mina always had the idea to go. She likes to live in different places. If we moved to Büyükada, she would be happy there too. In fact, we were moving to Bodrum last year, it didn't happen at the last moment. Mina's future played a big role in the England decision. You are forty years old and reset everything. Maybe I'll make money by washing dishes, I don't know, three months from now. But I can agree even to that.
Fatih: For example, I am currently experiencing this contradiction. A lot of people here do 'delivery'. I will resist that. I consider it as the last bullet because I want to run my own business and grow my wife's photography company. This is what we came here for. Many of those

who came with the Ankara Agreement do not or cannot do their job. They have to make a living. But despite everything, we have ideals.

I have to add something about Mina . . . Last year was Mina's exam year. From the moment we applied for the Ankara Agreement, she lost her motivation for the exam. She was conditioned to go and was happy that she wasn't going to take the exam. She, on the other hand, gave us a great surprise with her English. We didn't expect it to be this good.

You have been in England for three months. Do you plan to be politically active and a part of diaspora activism for the future? Did you come here with your political baggage from Turkey? Or do you say 'The important thing for me from now on is the decision that will come out of Boris Johnson's meeting next week'?
Fatih: Those bags are your identity! I consider myself a liberal person. Liberalism as an ideology brings with it a universalist perspective. I have a human-centred approach to life. I see the reward for this from my English neighbours. Today, a parking ticket was issued to my car, my next-door neighbour saw that fine, he gave me a parking permit so that I will not be fined again. When we moved in, he said 'Welcome' with chocolate and flowers. Our other next-door neighbour put a 'Welcome' card through my door. The perspective of the people here is also relevant to you. If you have a good education, if you are a conscientious, decent person and you get it noticed, they respect you.
Güliz: I am disturbed by the fact that people who come abroad from Turkey illegally or legally throw their weight about here! I am angry that they act here by putting their relatives' lives in danger by saying every word they couldn't say there. They constantly applaud the coup. Because they live off the fat of the land. I hate this!

Do you feel that you have suffered a serious loss of status with immigration?

Fatih: Absolutely! In fact, this is my biggest problem these days! I ask myself 'How can I join the working chain, the working ring?' I'm looking for a way out. We have much more important virtues than the West, with the problems we experience and the power to struggle with them, and the practical intelligence created by that power. This is also reflected in what we produce. It seems extraordinary to them. For example, when Güliz won first prize in Germany and Turkey with the photos she took on the refugee boat, they could not understand how she could do such a thing, how she was able to take these photos. They had no such problems! For them, the quantitative facts that are the subject of the news are a part of our daily life. The page 3 news that they read in a British newspaper is very likely to happen to you in Turkey! I also believe that the power to tackle those problems and the practical intelligence it creates can be an advantage abroad.

Güliz, are you resentful towards or angry with Turkey?
Güliz: Maybe both! But I think these feelings are temporary. I have not given up.
Fatih: I also want to answer this question. I am greatly disappointed. Despite such a bad administration, the fact that there are 30–40 per cent of people who approve of this situation even when everything has hit such a low, makes me feel hopeless on behalf of Turkey. This human resource of Turkey makes me very pessimistic. As they say, 'A misfortune is worth a thousand pieces of advice'; people in Turkey do not want to understand the evil of something that exists until it touches them! When it touches them, it's already too late.
Güliz: I think you didn't know the society! I have no disappointment.

Do you see yourself 'in exile'?
Güliz: No, I never see it like that.
Fatih: I never see it that way either.

How do you define yourselves then?

Güliz: I see myself as 'someone who will get to know the culture, language and people of England for a while and then come back'. Being here for me is like a 'gift wrap'!

Fatih: I think we turned a disadvantage into an opportunity for ourselves. We turned it into an opportunity that we postponed for years. What appeared to be evil turned out to be good fortune! What I'm really wondering is, will we be able to come back as the same 'we' when we return there? In my opinion, we will not fit in there. Therefore, we will have a 'double', go-and-return life.

Those who left Turkey in the 1980s are very important in our migration history. Intellectual people in particular were stationed in countries like Sweden and Germany. What is your difference from them? What do you think has changed since then?

Fatih: I like Zülfü Livaneli's song 'Sürgün' ('Exile') very much. He wrote this song in exile, in Sweden. He sings together with Sezen Aksu. While surfing YouTube yesterday, I saw that he had shared the video from his own channel. A fan of his had collaged the clip, it includes Livaneli's exile photos . . . . While watching, I felt so close to Livaneli . . . I watched it over and over. At that moment I thought, 'I am in exile, not physically or mentally, but spiritually.' I can return to Turkey at any time, physically or mentally. I have my passport. But my soul says, 'No, you will not return now! You have to stay here.'

Güliz: Our difference from those who came in the '80s is that we can go back. We may not know what we will encounter, but we have the freedom to return. Also, the world has changed a lot since the '80s, especially in terms of communication. If they had come like us today, they would not have felt such exile. Everywhere is like everywhere now! We can video chat anywhere in the world . . .

After all these conversations, you've created a paradox in my head. You talked about the trauma of the kebab shop,

who accidentally rang the bell at midnight. 'We ran away,' said Güliz. You say, 'We'll be back later.' But while describing all this, Fatih talked about Turkey's recurring history while describing the books he threw in the trash. Then why are you thinking of returning?

Fatih: I think it will take at least five to six years for the idea of returning to become a reality. We say, 'We will live in Turkey for three to four months, and live here for eight to nine months.' This is the plan in the minds of everyone who has come here! Our sense of escapism was a sense of resistance to the inner decay we experienced. We would still live there, but we would die spiritually. It may seem like a paradox, but all the things we have experienced have separate realities in their own periodicities. The fear of being arrested after the coup attempt was a fear we experienced five years ago. Families were reporting each other at that time. A father reported his son, a brother his brother . . . A woman says she will shoot and kill her neighbour if necessary, and no criminal action is taken against her! What can you do in such a schizophrenic state? But the thought that prompted us to 'escape' was that we were rotting because we could not produce. It was the fact that our loved ones were gone. We were the only ones left.

Güliz: If we had stayed, we would have continued a way of life imposed by the government and blended with fear. I think that when this government changes, something will change with it. Because it is a rapidly changing country. So it won't always be like this.

Fatih: But I have no idea whether those who have left, especially young people who have gone, will return. Turkey is experiencing a serious brain drain. In surveys conducted in Turkey, more than 60 per cent of young people say that they can afford to be stripped of their citizenship in order to leave Turkey, if necessary. For example, a very important study called 'Leaving This Country' was recently published in a book. In this book, we see that the idea of leaving among young people started after the brutal intervention of the state in the Gezi events. After that time, they started to leave, thinking that they would not be left with a living space. In time, it became clear that they were not wrong. Moreover, these children are graduates of Turkey's best colleges and universities. What could be more dramatic for a country than that?

8

FAYSAL SARIYILDIZ

**A darkness is forming where the regime has amassed, where
authority is formed. The state has created a darkness in
Turkey. That's why the state must be weakened. Society
must be strengthened. Civil society must be strengthened.**

*Faysal Sarıyıldız was a politician of the Peoples' Democratic Party
(HDP) and a former member of parliament representing Şırnak. He
was elected to parliament in June 2011 as an independent supported by
the Labour, Democracy and Freedom Bloc parties but was not allowed
to assume his post as the court ruled that parliamentary immunity
did not apply in his case. In January 2014, after a court decided their
imprisonment violated their human rights, since they had been elected
as MPs, he was released from prison along with Selman Irmak, Gülser
Yıldırım and Kemal Aktas. They subsequently took their oaths in parliament. He was re-elected as an MP for Şırnak in the general elections*

of June 2015 and the snap elections of November 2015, representing the HDP. Sarıyıldız defended the wounded during the curfew in Cizre in the winter of 2015–16 and called on the UN for help. In April 2016 he left Turkey in exile and Turkey issued an arrest warrant for him. While in exile he continued to defend Kurdish rights. On 7 September 2017 he and Tuğba Hezer Öztürk were both relieved of their duties in parliament by a vote of the majority of parliamentarians. The next day the Constitutional Court confirmed their dismissal.

Mr Sarıyıldız, thank you for your interest in our book. Could you kindly share your story with us?

I left Turkey in May 2016. Coming to why I left, you know that extraordinary developments occurred in Turkey in 2015 and 2016.

You became an MP in 2011, no?

I was elected MP when I was in prison in 2011. If you want, I'll first explain about how I entered politics. I was born into a wealthy family in a village connected to Cizre. What's the measure of wealth for us there? If there is enough earth to cultivate and enough animals, you're considered wealthy. I was born in a village between Cizre and Nusaybin. I grew up in a semi-liberal environment. Cizre largely remained unaffected by assimilation policies because it is located in the middle of Kurdistan. As a result, it was a place interested in political debates. For example, while my father was previously interested in conservative movements, his interest shifted towards the more secular Kurdish political movements with us, and then a little to the PKK. When we were small, men and women with weapons began to come to the village. They were PKK militants and they were very sympathetic. One person from our village joined the PKK. There was a lot of pressure, especially during the 1980s. For example, I remember that immediately after the 1980 coup, all the villagers were lined up and forced to wait on their feet for hours. At no point was there a good perception among us towards the state. The state, to us, always appeared as dominant, tyrannical. That image always stayed with us. We never saw the other face of the state, because the language was different, and a language we didn't know was being imposed on us when we went to school.

Did you learn Turkish at school?

Of course. My first contact with Turkish happened at the age of six or seven. There weren't any opportunities to communicate at the time. Now, children begin to learn even earlier through television and other tools. At the time, Turkish wasn't spoken where we were. By the time I finished high school, my marks in all my mathematics classes were between 8 and 10, while they never passed a 6 or 7 for Turkish. I still can't speak Turkish very well. Many of my friends joined the PKK, but I stayed behind. This was because I grew up in a bit of a liberal environment. I started to gain awareness when I went to university.

Where did you go to university?

I studied at Harran and Dicle. I started higher education in 1993, but when I went, half of the university wasn't there because in 1992, almost half of some of the cohorts left and joined the PKK. Western students were scared to come to Kurdistan. We continued school as a class hung out to dry. After two years, I was accepted into the Harran University Department of Engineering. While I was at university, my father was serving as the HEP [Halkın Emek Partisi, People's Labour Party] district leader. It was 1991. He was frequently arrested. When he was arrested, he and my brother were tortured sometimes for forty days, sometimes thirty days. We didn't recognise them when they returned. They were covered in bruises, and their beards had grown long. I saw, for example, that my father's beard had turned white after he was released for the first time and came home. I had never seen his beard when it was long. He must have been in his forties at the time. They talked about unimaginable torture. And that caused a constant flow of fury to build up among us. But you say, I should still study a bit, be useful in a different way to society, to my people, to myself. You go to university, but my political life bothers you because you're embedded within it. There was a group called Patriot Youth at Harran University. We studied and grew up in that environment. I was able to finish school in six years, although it is normally supposed to take four years, because I was expelled for a year because I participated in a commemoration of the Halabja massacre, if I'm not mistaken. There were raids on 16 March, and we were detained. Then there were investigations, and I wasn't thrown in prison, but I was detained for two or three days. I was suspended for a year. In school, there was an opposition Turkish newspaper called *Gündem*. Of course, the newspaper was changing its name two or three times a year at that point. At one time it was 'Free Look', and then 'New Agenda'. I tried to help this newspaper as a correspondent. At the time, during the 1999 process when Öcalan was extradited to Turkey – the Kurdish people refer to that as the Rome process – two of my friends from university said goodbye and joined the PKK. I mean, can you imagine such a fragmentation occurring among you? Some say, 'I'm going, it's like there's nothing left here, nothing to stay for in this system.' They go, and I hear a few years later that they have died. And when life continued like this, I went to Cizre after 2000, after finishing university.

Did you ever consider joining the PKK?
I never considered it because I knew that joining was a path I couldn't turn back from and I had a bit of a religious identity back then. When we were little, almost everyone was sent to the village imam for Quran-reading courses. We came to see that our village imam was a political individual. When the villagers left for Cizre during Newroz in 1992, they were mown down and flattened by a Turkish military vehicle. More than ten people were killed. And one of those who was killed was our imam. I was quite studious and remained so until high school. When I began engaging with political issues during my final year of high school, my level of studiousness

dropped a little, and I started to stumble. By the time I finished high school, first, there was a reaction against the state that was based on more than just being a Kurd, and second, I also had a religious identity. My religious identity prevented me from joining the PKK, because when you join, there aren't any circumstances where you can pray, and it is a sin to kill a person. These partially prevented me from joining. Also, the liberal environment in which I lived spared me from a choice that would have completely separated me from my life. But my uncle's son on my father's side joined the PKK while he was at university, then my uncle's daughter on my mother's side and other children followed. Maybe five, ten people with the last name Sarıyıldız joined and lost their lives. After the year 2000, I opened an engineering firm in Cizre. At the time, I was the only mechanical engineer in Şırnak. I began offering my expertise at state institutions. After 2007, old friends and journalists began to come and go a bit too much to Cizre. And I began to get affiliated again with political work. At their insistence, I became a candidate for the municipal legislature in Cizre in 2009, because there was the possibility at any moment that the friend who had become the mayor would be dismissed as a punishment. We needed someone who would replace them if they were dismissed. I was the only person to have graduated from university, and they recognised me. They insisted quite a bit, and I accepted. In 2009, I became a candidate to join the Cizre municipal legislature. We achieved a level of success incomparable to the previous election and we won a number of municipalities. We began to receive word at the time about the operations against the Kurdistan Communities Union (Koma Civakên Kurdistanê, KCK). A month after the election, I was detained with more than fifty others in Şırnak as part of those operations. I was detained, but it was something else that actually shocked me. I appeared before the court a few months later, my bill of indictment had been prepared and they were asking for a twenty-eight-year prison sentence. That was the first time I experienced that shock.

This was the operation you think the Gülen Movement and the AKP coordinated on – or which is known as such – correct?
Yes. At the time, the leader of the court was a Gülenist named Menderes. Then, I said, 'Look, you say twenty-eight years in a cruel, a very nonchalant way. This is a human life. I've never laid a finger on a weapon thus far – even a toy. This is frightening and unjust. Tomorrow or the next day, you could be struck by this injustice.' Right now, that man is serving three consecutive life sentences. I refuse to use the word 'FETÖ' (Fettullahist Terrorist Organisation) because it's a discourse that works in favour of the regime. The Gülen Movement is a reality. It had truly functioned as the mentor to the AKP until that point and conducted all the operations. I was in prison for five years. The elections were held in 2011. Friends made a recommendation – it was weird to me – and I was nominated while in prison.

So you were in prison for close to two years?
Yes. I was elected in 2011, but I wasn't released even though I was elected. I had three and a half years left. Because we had finished our five years on 24 January 2014, I was released with two other CHP MPs. I was out of prison for two years, but I experienced some frightening things. I served as an MP for two years – three terms (the twenty-fourth, twenty-fifth and twenty-sixth terms) – while things such as Kobane were happening. I was forced to leave the country in early 2016.

Why?
I'm from Cizre, and I was an MP for Şırnak in 2015. In 2017, my MP status was revoked because I had been absent.

Why did you decide to go to Germany when it wasn't clear that your MP status would be removed?
I witnessed many horrible war crimes from a close distance. The state persistently tried to cover up its crimes. In fact, there was something

truly horrible I witnessed, and it needed to be announced to the world. This was a humanitarian and political challenge for me. I could have been arrested at any moment. While all these things were happening, I was staring down the barrel of a gun as someone who was announcing these crimes to the world as both an MP and a former journalist. For example, I went to a neighbourhood that was under siege to bring out three injured and a number of deceased individuals about whom the European Court of Human Rights (ECHR) had issued a precautionary decision to remove them from the streets and take them to hospital. I shared this with the world, with the religious community. Everything was occurring out in the open. The next day, a written allegation was prepared saying, 'A HDP MP was surrounded while trying to rescue sixteen terrorists. He tried to smuggle terrorist weapons past the blockade while rescuing them.' When the human remains were brought to the hospital, the police planted weapons in there, and because the weapons were brought to the hospital wrapped in a body bag, they were left there afterwards. There were already dozens of weapons in the neighbourhood. But how was this reflected in the press? How was this reflected in Erdoğan's words? 'A HDP MP tried to smuggle terrorist weapons past the blockade.' This time, the administration files a lawsuit against you. The lawsuit is opened and you could be arrested at any time.

Did you make the decision to leave yourself, or did the party advise you to do so?

Selahattin [Demirtaş] called me while I was still in Cizre prison. The blockade in Cizre started on 14 December 2015 and ended on 2 March 2016. It lasted for a total of seventy-nine days. After the fiftieth day, the people stuck in the basements began to be collectively burned. Very horrible things happened. Coming to the sixtieth day, not a single living thing was left on the streets. Even stray cats, animals and sheep in barns were killed. Terrible war crimes were committed, and a twenty-day curfew was implemented to allow evidence to be removed. They took down the buildings that were burned and bombed and under which people had been killed using dozens of machines, bulldozers and trucks and dumped them in the Dicle River. Such dreadful war crimes were committed that human limbs appeared out of all the wreckage that was excavated. I tried to share this with the public while in Cizre. It wasn't possible for an adult to reach the rubble. Children aged six and seven were going and seeing the human body parts among the wreckage. They would come back and tell their families. A family sent me a message. I gave them my phone and showed them how to take pictures. 'Get them to take pictures and bring them back to me,' I said. Really, children aged seven and eight took pictures of the human limbs in the debris, and we published them immediately. They shared the names and information about the people stuck together in the basements. There were students and journalists among them. For example, the people in the first basement were saying, 'There are thirty-one of us, and they are going to kill us.' There were injured people there. You apply to the ECHR to take them to hospital. The ECHR makes the decision to adopt precautionary measures necessary to ensure security in the neighbourhood to take the people to hospital. Based on this, the conflict there must stop, and the injured must be taken to the hospital, but the state insisted, 'There is a conflict there, terrorists there; the conflict cannot be stopped because there are terrorists there.' However, an affiliate said, 'There is no conflict here; we are under siege, and they have surrounded us.' Of course, we immediately stopped this. And this made me furious at the government and Erdoğan.

So there's a sort of personal grudge?

Yes. During the Kobane process, for example, we faced an allegation saying, 'Faysal Sarıyıldız possessed a weapon in his car.' If there had been such an allegation, Co-chairman Selahattin would have showed it to them a few times. Nothing like that happened; no weapon was found in a vehicle. We were on our guard at the border for up to three months because ISIS members were being transferred across the border. We were trying to prevent this and to let Kobane breathe. At the time, a case of mine that hadn't been mentioned previously and which had lain dormant for more than a year was being revisited. Then, while I was still in Cizre, Co-chairman Selahattin called our group leader, called İdris Baluken. He said, 'I'm in Efkan Ala's room right now.' Efkan Ala was the interior minister at the time. 'He's saying you need to leave, because he's saying he can't influence the militant forces in Cizre,' he told me.

So the interior minister at the time told you to leave?
Yes, and I'll tell you another thing; I believed the interior minister's sincerity. We were once again surrounded. We took the wounded and brought them to hospital. We were surrounded by armoured vehicles, so we took refuge under a building and were being searched for. We were about to be killed. I got in contact with our friend İdris Baluken again. He immediately went to the interior minister's office and I personally heard his voice as the interior minister called the governor of Şırnak, and he said, 'There's a co-mayor in the municipality, a member of parliament, we'll be stuck if something happens to them.' The governor said, 'That place is a warzone. We cannot intervene, Minister.' I think the governor received instructions from Erdoğan personally or a clique that makes decisions on such matters. Efkan Ala had once before served as governor in Kurdistan. If I'm not mistaken, he was educated internationally. He was someone who knew about the state's function and how frightening this was and who saw that they could be accused of war crimes tomorrow or the next day and that they could be tried for this. And he got mixed up in that. Efkan Ala was removed from his position immediately after this process and was replaced by Süleyman Soylu.

One branch of the state told you to leave while another was trying to put you in jail. Do you think that different branches of the state are in conflict?

Actually, the state arrived at a consensus regarding that issue. While not a single bullet had yet been fired in Turkey in 2014, the two parties had silenced their weapons, and hope had formed throughout society, a round table meeting was held immediately after what had happened in Kobane with the General Staff, the National Intelligence Organisation, the government and Erdoğan. In my opinion, cliques with a century of unionist mentalities were at that table. And they produced a consensus. Later this was constructed as the Overthrow Plan. In 2019, the original version of this was broadcast on Egyptian state television. But a journalist mentioned this plan in 2015.

There was an issue lasting close to a year while you were a member of parliament, as far as I understand. What was your legal status during this process?
I actually didn't want to leave because I was a member of parliament there, I was from there and horrible things were happening. My departure would mean the continuation of those terrible things. A significant majority of the people who were killed were people whom I knew closely. As such, your life no longer has value. I grew up in this environment, and I had major fears. Despite that, I didn't want to make this trip after these horrible things occurred. I later wanted to meet Co-chairman Selahattin Demirtaş personally. I went to see him, and we met in Diyarbakır. He said to me, 'You have witnessed a lot of important things, but their intention is to incapacitate you, to shut you out and to direct you to different things. We think it would be helpful for you to leave. You'll conduct your diplomatic work and share what happened with the global public.' That's why I left.

Why Germany?
Germany is a country where a significant population of Turkish nationals live in Europe. German is also a key determinant European politics. Germany is also a country that keeps Turkey on its toes. That's why I chose it. I was going to be exactly in the centre of

society in our diaspora; I was going to continue my work there. We were going to engage in politics and diplomacy to influence Germany's politics about Turkey and to pull Turkey back from the position it's in right now. That's why I went to Germany.

You came as an attorney. You probably didn't request political asylum directly? How was the process for you?
I kept my MP status after I arrived and maintained it until 2017 – almost a year. In 2017, my MP status was revoked because I had been absent from parliament. This was the first time in republican history that an individual's MP status was revoked due to absence, but I was sick and was sending reports about that to the country. Legally, my MP status was not supposed to be revoked. No report that I sent had been processed, and my MP status was revoked in 2017. But I had left for Europe in 2016 and remained an MP for a year while I was there. I had a diplomatic passport. I travelled to almost every European country with that passport, including the UK. I had meetings with international circles.

As you operated in Europe without going to the Turkish parliament with your diplomatic passport, did the Turkish state follow you?
Immediately after my status was removed, two or three plainclothes intelligence officers from Germany wanted to meet with me.

German?
German. We met at my lawyers' office. They politely told me, 'Turkey wants you from us. We won't send you. According to our laws, an individual in your position must be protected. We can provide protection, but we see that you're going to other countries, that there may be a situation of repatriation in other countries and that you could be at risk, and we want to make this clear.' I live in a small town in Germany. As a refugee, you get state assistance from the bank. Every

once in a while they sent me letters saying, 'We are unilaterally dissolving our agreements with you.' I showed one of these letters to an attorney and said the agreement was being dissolved for political reasons. There was the signature of a Turk named Mehmet Ali, who is the chief of the bank, located at the bottom of the letter. He actually isn't a Turk; it's more accurate to say he's a rightist conservative – it's clear he's a regime supporter. I sent a letter telling [the lawyers] to write to the bank asking why it sent me that letter and saying that I will expose them if they don't do this. In the letter I mentioned the possibility that this person was a rightist-conservative and said, 'This person is undermining your laws.' The bank's regional manager wanted to meet with me about this and host me. They said it was a serious misunderstanding and that they would correct this. They drove that person out of the bank.

It's clear that Turkey is following you in Germany, but you are a well-known face. Do you encounter any reactions in the street?
I have never walked alone in the street.

Is that an intentional security choice, or has that just never happened?
I have never walked alone for security reasons. Sometimes I try to enjoy walking around when I go to new places, but I don't go out alone where I can be seen or where I live, because it's known that there are structures in Germany that Turkey – Erdoğan's government, more specifically – has created by spending significant amounts of money. Istanbul MP Metin Külünk was directing this personally. Metin Külünk organised meetings with the pro-government Turkish authoritarians in the region where I live. An organisation called the Ottoman Hearths was created. He organised meetings with them and gathered intelligence. It appeared in the German press that meetings were held about how to approach certain segments of the opposition here. As such, I don't walk around alone for security reasons.

Do friends from the party or the German state protect you?

The German state asked whether I required protection when I first arrived. I said, 'Rather than protect me, [make Germany safe]. You're a big state, you have power. There are 6,000 people appearing in your intelligence reports who have organised around the Diyanet here and who are gathering intelligence. Stop this. Make Germany a safe place for those in my position. I am constantly in the press and I don't want the police all around me. I'm not alone in this; there are others in the same position as me.' I refused. Generally what happens is that individuals come with me when I attend a programme. We go to events, meet with them, and they help me board a plane or train afterwards. I can manage to not be alone like this for a while.

Are you happy about being in Germany?

Having to leave the country is inherently a bad feeling. If it was under different circumstances, maybe I would have wanted to come and live here, but my story is constantly challenging me. I mean, you are forced to leave while you have experienced those things and while you have a mission. That weighs on me. I'll say this: it's not unique to Germany, I'm talking about the challenges of being in the diaspora. Even if you are burdened with a certain tyranny, your chest can expand when you take a breath because you feel like you belong, like you have ownership, like you are the subject of where you are. You can be satisfied. But there is a psychology of being a freeloader while you're here. I didn't know many languages when I came here.

And now there's German too, right?

Yes, a little but not a lot. Germany is the most sensitive community in relations with foreigners. Germany's past has a significant effect on this. Although it is a place where xenophobia has been castigated, you still keenly feel that orientalist, elitist attitude that views you as someone who must be shaped. An elderly person with good intentions approaches you on the street or while boarding a train and tries to teach you something. But you feel that even the desire to teach relates to the desire to assimilate you. It wears on people even though it's done politely. So you start to consider that you're not yourself here. That psychology worries me a little bit. You give meaning to everything that happens. I'm a person who has adopted a political consciousness. I was in prison for five years. I studied social sciences for five years, I studied psychology and social sciences. I studied rational movements, revolutionary movements around the world. I can give meaning to all sorts of social reactions. I can give meaning to my own position. I know that this is the result of being here, and I can't make sense of it. I still work as the co-spokesperson for the HDP in Germany. So I continue my struggle here, but being forced to remain here is rather tedious. I would probably be a little more comfortable if I was in a different country. Germany really resembles Turkey. There is a rightist conservative regime party in Germany – the CDU – and it has a lot in common with Turkey. There's Die Linke, which resembles the HDP. There's the Greens, but there isn't a comparable mass party in Turkey. The Greens are somewhere between the CHP and HDP. There's the SPD, which is the same as the CHP in Turkey. It exhibits the same reflexes as the CHP when the social democrats appear, and the interests of the state come into question. For example, Erdoğan went to Afrin and occupied a portion of Rojava. He committed horrible war crimes there and opened a space there for Salafis to live and settled them there. The CHP's signature is behind all this. Germany is willing to maintain trade relations with Turkey, with a man like Erdoğan, but the small coalition of the regime and the SPD, which is Germany's social democratic party, also approves of this. The foreign minister is an SPD member. Consider that the CHP and AKP have a shared regime in Turkey. In the past, for example, Germany made a statement and said how satisfied it was that Turkey had managed to retain 3–4 million refugees, how much it valued this and that it was a measure of the healthy continuation of its relations with Turkey. In parallel to this, the SPD foreign minister said Turkey had closed the HDP but that the HDP must break off its relationship with the PKK. Do you know what this looks like? For example, a bigger child and a smaller child are fighting and the bigger child constantly beats up the smaller child. Then the father comes and grabs each of them by the ear. He tells the bigger child not to take on the smaller child and says the bigger child acts like this because the smaller child has misbehaved. This approach cannot influence the end of the anti-democratic climate there. Unfortunately, this is the approach in Europe. So wherever I am in Europe, I constantly have problems with the states. I have meetings with members of the regime, but they don't invoke any excitement in us anymore, because they all act with statist codes and pragmatist emotions.

Your identity and political views are clear. There are many different diasporas that have come from Turkey after 2010. There are new arrivals and those meeting with the old arrivals. Islamists are coming, the Gülen Movement. The Alevis are coming, the Academics for Peace are coming, white-collar seculars are coming . . . all sorts of colours of Turkey are here. How is your relationship with different groups? Do you meet with different groups? Do you have contact with them? Do you try to understand them? Do you have contact with the Gülenists, for example, or do you still fight?

There is no conflict. Everyone forced to come to Europe, without exception, is part of a community forced to abandon their country because of the oppressive policies of the current political regime. Apart from the HDP and its electorate, there is a segment of academics. Our relationships with those we have met are very good. We have pretty good relationships with people here who were previously CHP supporters. At the start, I said that I refuse to use the word 'FETÖ' because it is a discourse Erdoğan needs to try to ingrain and institutionalise fascism in Turkey and which many people don't deserve.

I'll briefly say this about the Gülen Movement; it is a structure that has sinned in the institutionalisation of the political regime in Turkey and which, over time, colluded with it. But there is a senior level and a public level of the structure we call the Gülen Movement. Tens of thousands of people in Turkey can study and graduate with opportunities from the Gülen Movement. But there is a certain morality in this segment. We see news about advisors getting rich and driving vehicles worth hundreds of thousands of euros. I don't think that there is this kind of corruption in the Gülen Movement outside a certain segment. There are tens of thousands of members of the Gülen Movement in Europe. In particular, we haven't had a search like 'Let's find one another and start a relationship'. They haven't, and neither have I. There have been Gülenists whom I have met in some settings. They are the type of people we call Anatolians. A significant portion of them are truly like this. But I know that the Gülen Movement was a structure that mentored Erdoğan until 2015. I know that the Gülen Movement is a structure that America supported in Turkey and offered all sorts of support to while seeking to encircle the Soviet system. I know that it's also a nationalist, conservative structure consistent with the global system. I know that this is why it has had its fingers in many terrible developments in Turkey over the past twenty to thirty years. But you can't categorise everyone in the Gülen Movement the same way. I believe that a significant portion of them, a foundation, are from the general public and are sincere. There are the people I speak with. For example, they have diplomatic work in Europe opposed to Erdoğan's displays of fascism. We prefer not to appear together with them too often, because we don't find it very helpful. It's not appropriate. There are tens of thousands of people called Gülenists who are imprisoned or forced to leave the country. If I see them, I'll go to their homes, drink tea with them and invite them. We don't only have or try to form an institutional relationship.

Selahattin Demirtaş has been imprisoned for a while, former MPs from the HDP are imprisoned. There is word that a party closure lawsuit will be launched and 687 old and new HDP

administrators will be banned from political activity. When things like this happened before, there were mass protests in Europe. They haven't been able to happen in the past year because of the impact of the pandemic, but there is also a clarification for this. Does the new Kurdish generation in the diaspora not view the events in Turkey as their own primary agenda as much as before?

This is a pointed and wonderful sociological discovery. I have nothing to say about it.

Or are some clashes between the PKK and HDP affecting this situation?

No. This is a discourse that the dominant system produced. I witnessed terrifying things in the 2015–16 process. A segment of society thinks that the events described as the Trench Incidents,[1] which were autonomous revolts by the public, were terrifying things that happened in the aftermath of the peace process. It is known how brutal the Turkish state is. 'The PKK could have prevented this but didn't.' There's a reaction and reproach like this against the PKK. There is an indescribable fury directed at the state. The point you made relates to the sociology of the diaspora in Europe. The Kurds first came here in waves during the Ağar–Çiller period in the 1990s. Another wave came after 2015. There were workers long before then. That worker segment is largely assimilated here. Those coming in the 1990s were generally political exiles. They were able to survive with a fury to a certain point, but they integrated into life here afterwards by necessity of the nature of life here. They're now in their fifties and sixties and their children grew up in Europe. They were entirely shaped by the curriculum of liberal civilisation. As such, their sensitivities regarding what

---

[1] For further information on trench warfare in Turkey, see Noah Blaser, 'Trench warfare in Turkey', *Foreign Policy*, 29 January 2015, https://foreignpolicy. com/2015/01/29/trench-warfare-in-turkey-kurds-pkk/, accessed 1 March 2023.

happened in Turkey were rubbed down and extinguished. You were able to gather hundreds of thousands of people here in the 1990s. But it's not like that right now, and there's a reason for this. Another reason is whatever event you organise, passers-by immediately pull out their cameras and take pictures. These are believed to be intelligence officers hired by Turkey. It is thought that these people won't be able to go to Turkey anymore if their photographs are taken. Right now, between 80 and 90 per cent of those living in Europe have investments in Turkey. Some have built homes, some have opened a business, some have bought land and want to visit their spouses, friends and family.

Would you ever return? Do you think you'll ever be able to return to Turkey? Will the order change? What do you predict?
Do I think this is a sustainable situation? The social circumstances in the country are frightening because there are millions of hungry people. It's a very painful thing that this economic crisis is almost something to be pleased about for some dissidents without any other opportunities to fight – and I am included in this group. Because a devastating crisis can overthrow this system of tyranny, this authoritarian system. Erdoğan has seized and obtained all the institutions of the state. The opposition has been suffocated. There are similar situations. As such, the crisis is growing deeper in these situations, reaching an unsustainable point, breaking relations with the world because of the method adopted; the crisis grows deeper when isolated from the world. Capital is already being withdrawn from Turkey, but Turkey's geostrategic position maintains its importance for Europe and America. Undoubtedly, we don't want Turkey to collapse or to be like Syria. But this oppressive, despotic political regime must go, because they have made life hell for everyone except for themselves. There is an unpredictable situation because of this. I'm very comfortable on this issue; whatever happens to the Kurdish political movement, if the pressure increases a hundred-fold, it will increase in size and will continue to bother the state and make the chaos deeper.

I am convinced of this, because the Kurds are not in a position where they will be pinned to a specific place and suffocated. A consciousness has formed, and they are everywhere now. I have no hesitations about this. The state is finding a slew of new war techniques. It can do this. Nonetheless, I trust the Kurdish consciousness that has formed. More than a third of those who voted for us are not Kurdish. There are people who are keeping us on our feet. There's a sociology in Turkey which has saved itself from the rhetorical nationalism and religionism the nation-state uses while consolidating its power. This is very important for us. It is constantly trying to establish a relationship between the HDP and Kurdishness. I think the HDP is something else. This is attacked as soon as it is mentioned: 'The HDP used Öcalan's views when creating its party platform.' Öcalan defines authority as evil. A darkness is forming where the regime has amassed, and capital is accumulated. I saw this with live examples. Numan Kurtulmuş, for example, was conservative but led a liberal party before coming together with the AKP. I actually met with him. But when he moved to the AKP and became its spokesperson, he became the sharpest AKP member. A darkness is forming where the regime has amassed, where authority is formed. The state has created a darkness in Turkey. That's why the state must be weakened. Society must be strengthened. Civil society must be strengthened. Otherwise, what is dividing Turkey, what is drawing this border, what is on our agenda are not things that we have thought about or hope will help. There's chaos right now, and I can't predict it, but I can say that it won't be good for sovereignty. The problems for us perhaps will continue for a while.

9

GÖKHAN BACIK

I'll say this first, these processes are not rational. You live with a survival instinct. I don't even know why I did some of the things I did. Think about it like this: my family came with me to Brussels. I lived in a room with them for a while. For a long time the four of us slept in the same bed. There are those Hollywood films that symbolise transcendence, with four spoons, four forks; that's how you live, because you have nothing. So you become a whole other person in the process. You don't act like an academic making rational decisions.

Gökhan Bacık was born in 1974 in Bursa, Turkey. He graduated from Ankara University's Faculty of Political Science. He got his PhD at Middle East Technical University (METU) in 2005. Bacık worked at several Turkish universities including Fatih University and Zirve

University. He was published in various leading Turkish media outlets such as Today's Zaman, Milliyet, Radikal, Zaman, Bugün, Yeni Şafak *and others. Bacik has also been published in leading scholarly journals such as* Middle Eastern Studies, Middle East Policy, Terrorism and Political Violence, Nationalism and Ethnic Politics *and* Studies in Conflict and Terrorism. *Bacık became an associate member of the Turkish Academy of Sciences in 2012. He left Turkey in 2016 due to political circumstances. When the government closed down Ipek University as part of the ongoing purge of academics, he was the dean of the School of Government there. Various investigations and lawsuits were opened against him. His passport was cancelled. In 2021, the Turkish government froze his assets. He is frequently targeted by the pro-government media. He was also a former fellow of the International Institute of Education Scholar Rescue Fund (SRF). He is a regular contributor to* Ahval, *an online outlet that reports on Turkey in Turkish, Arabic and English. Abroad, Bacık has published* Islam and Muslim Resistance to Modernity in Turkey *(2020) and* Contemporary Rationalist Islam in Turkey: A Religious Opposition to Sunni Revival *(2021), two books which have tried to explain the problematic relationship between Islam and politics in Turkey. He now teaches at Palacký University Olomouc, Czechia.*

When and how did you leave Turkey?

I left close to the 15 July incident. Why did I leave? Because my personal and professional life had become unliveable. I was going to school, for example, and the police were pressuring me. I went to school one day, and the door was locked and sealed. The newspapers where I worked were constantly being pressured. Second, my family life had begun to be affected. I was thinking that this process, this fight in Turkey would last for a long time. So I left Turkey close to 15 July. I left and came back when I first left; I had thought that I would observe the situation in Turkey. Because I couldn't figure out exactly where the events in Turkey were heading. But there were constant problems in my inner circle. There were problems with my family. My costs for them were increasing. I live in Czechia. Kafka has a famous story here: Gregor Samsa wakes one day as a beetle. I experienced that in Turkey. We were fairly respected people – and when I say respected, I mean we were people who had a decent dialogue with the community. But after a while, we awoke as beetles, and this impacts your relationships, your lease agreements. Academic isolation had also begun. People are scared; they don't answer their phones. So I decided to leave then.

Did you quit as you left? Did you think you would go and come back? With what kind of prediction did you leave?
I needed to leave quickly. I brought very few belongings along with me. Although 15 July hadn't happened yet, you got a feeling from Turkey. There were some operations against the university, for example, against the newspaper. Your name was constantly in tweets, your close friends were constantly warning you about things. So I left with few belongings and left my family behind. My family – my wife and two daughters – were forced to leave by more difficult, different means after 15 July. My new car is sitting, completely unused, in my father's garage right now in Turkey. I left all my belongings. Think about it like this: the political conjuncture is incredibly difficult, you're worried, you have concerns about your circle and you want to leave first to see the situation. How many belongings can you bring? I remember that I had two bags and as many clothes as possible inside. Many of my things remain in Turkey. This is a very challenging experience, not like moving, for instance. You give away your remaining belongings, selling some, and it's not clear what happened to the rest. I was forced to start everything again here. There are very few belongings I brought with me from Turkey that are still with me, my mouse, my pen and so forth . . . but everything else remained in Turkey. When the university was closed, I had a jacket, belongings and books in my office. I don't know what happened to them.

Did you go directly to Czechia?
No, first I went to Brussels.

If we look back on all we've talked about so far, three countries stand out in Europe as places people preferred to go to: Britain, Germany and Greece. And with America, it becomes four. But Czechia is an exception. Why Czechia?
I'll say this first, these processes are not rational. You live with a survival instinct. I don't even know why I did some of the things I did. Think about it like this: my family came with me to Brussels. I lived in a room with them for a while. For a long time the four of us slept in the same bed. There are those Hollywood films that symbolise transcendence, with four spoons, four forks; that's how you live, because you have nothing. So you become a whole other person in the process. You don't act like an academic making rational decisions because there are two huge problems. First, your money is limited, your money is running out. Second, your documents expire. Your documents are very important, especially in exile. They say, for example, 'How will we prove that this is your daughter? Prove how old she is.' What will you do when the consulate won't serve you? I submitted applications quickly there. Meanwhile, I heard that the Czech foreign minister said, 'We don't agree with the purging of academics. Our country is open to victimised academics.' There are foundations like the Scholars at Risk Fund and Scholars at Risk that protect and support academics around the world who have been victimised. I wrote to both of them, and the SRF immediately decided to support me. They even recommended a university or two in America. They were pretty good universities. I was corresponding with many universities at the time. Upon that statement from the foreign minister, I began researching the websites of universities in Czechia. I don't know how what I'm describing is being perceived but think about it in this psychology. I heard a university chancellor mention multiculturalism, victimisation, the struggle against populism in Europe.

Professor Jaroslav Miller, a history professor, was the chancellor of Palacký University at the time. I wrote to him directly. These are things that came together completely by coincidence. I didn't know these people, I didn't know these institutions, I didn't know this university. I wrote to other places – other places in Germany, for example. They began to respond to me. I was in Brussels at the time, and there are many Turks in Brussels. There are certain psychological problems which this invoked for me. Attacks began on the street. I wasn't sure whether they would know me, but there were some incidents. They were bothering me. Two factors guided me here. The first was that the university made a quick decision and said they would do what they could to resolve my victimisation. Speed is very important. Because, as I said, you're in survival mode, and you can't say 'I'll wait'. There are two children, schools will start, and there are schools for children. You have many basic problems like laundry and household belongings. It was fast here. Second, Palacký University was helpful with things such as getting me a visa and residence permit. Because I was a citizen of the Turkish Republic, I was living in Belgium and it was normal for me to receive services from the Czech consulate. They made things easy for me on this issue.

You went to Belgium on a tourist visa, correct?
Yes, of course. My wife was a teacher. I was someone who had travelled a lot, but I was travelling with a visa. Because my wife was a teacher, she was able to get a green passport after a while. And my entire dream was to one day get a green passport, because as you can guess, it is very difficult to get a visa as a Turkish national. By a twist of fate, the green passport helped us quickly leave Turkey. Accordingly, even if you have residence or a passport, you normally can't receive services from a country's consulate in another country. Or if you are able to, what would happen? Why are you going to Czechia? Nothing is clear. You have no documents, only a few that you get from the internet, from the electronic state portal. Most of these aren't accepted, because they

must have an apostille.[1] A sample ID card is not accepted, because they don't know where it's been obtained. You have no opportunity to do these things. And within this chaos, this place treated me humanely, was very helpful and adjusted for me. I later notified SRF that this university was interested in me. They agreed to transfer a year-long scholarship they had given me to this university. So I used the scholarship support I had received from SRF here, and it was helpful for me.

What is your legal status and academic position right now?
Right now, I'm a professor here. I'm permanent here.

So you have a permanent position?
Yes. So as of now, my contract has been extended for three years, but I am in the process of becoming permanent. This is a process, and I am in the middle of it. Things are progressing a bit slowly because of the coronavirus, but I have no problem. How is my residence? I didn't apply for asylum, because the government gave me permanent residence with the support of the university and with the reference of the Ministry of National Education here. I obtained a Czech passport. The fact that I have an ongoing residence permit makes things such as exemption from language exams easier. I have met with many Czech officials while staying here, and I have received incredible attention. Czechia, you know, is where the 1968 Prague Spring took place. This country has such a tradition. The father of my daughter's friend is an academic who arrived from Venezuela. There are people who have come from Ukraine. This is a country with a small refugee population, but which maintains a political culture brought about by a rebellion against a sort of authoritarianism. That's why there is an interesting culture regarding support for victims, for providing them with opportunities. I wasn't aware of this before I arrived in the country.

---

[1] A certificate that authenticates the signature of a public official on a document for use in another country.

You know the concept of extraterritorial authoritarianism and its different channels of repression. One of these, as you said, is for the consulate not to provide services or to be blacklisted at a Diyanet mosque. But apart from this, there are many different practices, from being attacked on the street by supporters of the regime to a market not selling you cheese. Can you compare your experiences in Czechia and Brussels?

I was in Brussels until December 2015. There was a clear manhunt there. I wasn't a direct target, but people I knew were targeted. People who are attacked while at the market or whose cars are damaged are reported to the police. None of this happened to me, but I know that a group of people were organised at the behest of the government. This engenders a trauma in you. I was going to my office to work, for example. You look, and three or four people have gathered together and are looking at you. 'I wonder . . .' you say. You start to be careful. People I spoke with during that time would tell us that we must be careful on the metro and in other places. Because the population there lives according to Turkey. Second, I was very careful. I would never go to those places, for example. I wasn't going to those neighbourhoods or the mosques. I protected myself, but I was always in that psychological state. I had to be careful. We weren't going out at certain times of night; we were careful not to leave after eleven o'clock. Isolation. There was a sort of manhunt. It was on behalf of the consulate here, but there was never a social aspect, because there were no Turks where I live. I already know that there are maybe a thousand Turks in the whole of Czechia. As such, we were relieved of that social pressure in an instant. This social pressure is very important in two ways. It's not, for example, that they hit you, that they punish you. First, it creates a significant psychology in you. It starts to dictate your entire life; while going to the market, while going somewhere, while at the shops . . . Second, it turns your entire life into a war because they are constantly motivated. You go to a conference, someone there is shouting at you, and so forth. Honestly, I didn't come here thinking that there were no

Turks, but this has become a considerable advantage. The Turks who are here are in Prague. I'm far from Prague; I live in Moravia. This isn't close to Prague, it's closer to Vienna. So I don't experience the social pressure here.

And the consulate?

The consulate doesn't provide services for you. I went twice. I'll explain one of them. I went inside. The building I went to was like a mansion. Consulate services were provided downstairs in a place like a vault. There was a tall, tanned man there. His name was Ömer, if I'm not mistaken. I came to sort out documents. I did the first process normally, and he said, 'Wait.' Then it began to take longer. You're standing at a sort of tiny cashier's desk because it's in a place like a basement. There's nowhere to sit. You perch on the stairs; I sat there and waited. I felt something inside myself. Of course I was worried. Then Ömer went upstairs. I waited there for a while, I would guess another twenty minutes. Then a woman came and said they wouldn't be able to provide services for me. I asked the reason, saying, 'Is there a legal problem?' She said, 'I can't say there is and I can't say there isn't.' She persistently asked me for my address. I said I was staying at a hotel. I didn't give her my passport, because what I was trying to do was something that could be done with an ID card. That's why I didn't bring my passport, because I was worried I wouldn't be able to get it back if I brought it. A passport was very important at that moment. We had no documents. The most important aspect of this process is our documents. You don't have the luxury of losing your passport. Lose everything, but the story ends if you lose your passport. I didn't bring my passport. The documents I wanted to get were actually documents I could get with an ID card. They didn't do it despite that. She insistently asked me for my passport. I told her I hadn't brought my passport with me. She wanted me to bring my passport. I asked again whether it was something related to me. Again, she said, 'I can't say it is and I can't say it isn't.' The woman was incredibly nervous. Then I left. I later learned from the system that my passport had been revoked.

When did this happen? Probably not right after 15 July?
I don't remember exactly, but yes, a while after. There are two points there. First, something like a passport inquiry was added to the electronic state portal then removed. I immediately took a screenshot, because there wasn't anything else. There are still very few international rules on issues like passports and residence. One is the Hague apostille law. You can use your passport even if it has been revoked, interestingly, if you aren't under an extraordinary international investigation. When you give your passport to a local authority and extend your residence, they accept that. I mean when an authority here looks at your passport through the system, they don't consider that your passport has been revoked in Turkey. But the system revoked the passport. So the consulate didn't provide the documents I asked for.

This extraterritorial repression is utilised against not only you but indirectly against your relatives and property in Turkey. At the start of our conversation, you mentioned that you left a new car in your father's garage. Was any of your property seized?
My father-in-law is still in prison. I have no property in Turkey. I had no home, I was renting my home. I was an academic – middle class, I mean. We were men who spent the money we earned on our children's education, on reading books. So I honestly don't have any property to be seized. What is left? My car. Why? Because my family was forced to leave under extraordinary conditions. It was a complicated process. We left our car there. We can't do certain things for the car. I would have needed to send a power of attorney for us to do that. The car isn't registered now, because the consulate didn't do that. My father had the car worked on for a while, on the side. But he grew tired of it after a while. They thought that this process would be temporary, that we could return after a while. When it continued on, as far as I

know, my father had put tyres on the car and placed them on wedges, and it's sitting like that. If you want to sell it, you can't sell it. If you really want, you can break it down and sell it for parts. There's nobody to do that. But our pension rights, for example, our social rights were left behind. All my belongings, my clothes, my personal belongings were left behind. But none of my things were seized because I don't have any property.

I don't think your wife's father was imprisoned because of you, right?
Of course. He was working at a low position in a company. In fact that was why he was someone who did additional work. Right now he's in prison. But we haven't been able to learn what crime he's in prison for, to be honest. But there are legal processes going on about me. I can guess what they are. Because as far as I understand, the state has produced categories based on whatever it wants – A, B, C and D. These are fixed; C is 6 years, A . . . And then there's the main trial. They're placing the people into that algorithm based on that.

While being subjected to practices we call extraterritorial authoritarianism, there are also solidarity networks. Even if you had not engaged entirely there, you're someone who is known in Turkey for being close to the Gülen Movement, who at the very least worked at one of its universities and wrote articles in its newspapers. As far as I can see, there's a category in Turkey's new diaspora where there are Kurds, Alevis, signatories for peace and a sort of solidarity among them. On the other side is the Gülen Movement, which everyone has excluded and opposes. There is as much conflict as there is solidarity in the Gülen Movement. What are your experiences on the issue of solidarity?
Primarily, context is very important. I live in a Czech city. I'm already alone geographically because there are no Turks close to me.

But you have experience in Brussels?

Of course, I was working at İpek University. I was writing in the movement's newspaper. I certainly don't have an orthodox religious perspective on issues such as individuality, but I was close to the movement. But these incidents changed all of us. First, they started an internal debate. This internal debate is on a website called Mavi Yorum and began before 15 July. In this debate, a group of people like me began to voice reservations about the movement's position within the state, the relationships it had with society and, most importantly, its religious interpretation. A portion of these were discussed in the media. I discussed them in my own opinion pieces, responses were given, some academics participated. But the political tension in Turkey forced us to postpone these. Because it had devolved into a fight. For example, I went to university, and the students were gathered together. 'Why are you all gathered?' I asked. 'We've been branded,' my professor said. In that situation, you can't stand up and hold an intellectual conversation. But this became clear after 15 July happened, and as far as I saw, the Gülen Movement reached a point where it could no longer actively harbour this type of intellectual perspective. As far as I observed, I wasn't even sure what I had observed, since I didn't have much contact left, and intellectuals who had gained their economic independence had distanced themselves from the movement. Because I think the movement had shifted to a more Salafi – and by Salafi, I don't mean radical – a more middle-of-the-road, classic religious interpretation you would see from your parents. So my connection to the movement was no longer a point in question. But I can talk with Gülenists; if I have a humane relationship with them, of course it will continue. But as I said, there are two factors in this: geography and the coronavirus. Contact has already been cut off because of the coronavirus. For example, although I wouldn't often have gone to Brussels in the past just because there was a meeting, I would have drunk tea with someone close to the movement. But that's not the case anymore. Accordingly, I don't find the ideology of this structure – I'm not referring to 15 July or the fight with the AKP – to be persuasive or superior. Furthermore, I'll say something radical, I think there must be a religious paradigm in the world, that democracy must remain within the rule of law. Apart from that, I think that religion cannot be presented to the world as a theory. I mean, since I no longer find the idea of producing macro solutions for economic problems through religious means to be convincing, I have no intellectual relationship remaining apart from my personal relationships with such a structure.

Why is the movement demonised so much? Because people are scared. First, there's significant pressure. I saw it; in Brussels, for example, a nationalistic Kemalist doesn't get that angry at the movement but is scared. Because the consulate could cause problems. Coincidentally, I crossed paths with a businessman working in food at an unexpected place. This person normally has no relation to this work. The man was selling cheese, importing mineral water from Turkey, but his problem was that, as a businessman, he believed that if he were to be seen with me – the Gülen Movement – the government would obstruct him. So that ends relationships as well. Accordingly, this incredibly unethical isolation that the Gülen Movement is facing originates more from fear than willingness. People are scared. There was an internal debate after 15 July. In that debate, I saw that the problem was with me. It was wrong to expect the intellectual perspective that I had expected from the movement. It's an incredibly religious, traditional structure. So I no longer find the paradigm of that structure to be intellectually intriguing apart from 15 July, the fight with the AKP. But I'm moving beyond that too; the problem isn't in that structure either. Anyhow, as I said, I think religion is an important notion – religion is certainly important, I can't say anything about that, as I consider it as an area of freedom – but I don't find it as thrilling a notion as liberalism, as secularism.

You are actually experiencing both personal and familial trauma. You are separated from a place you became accustomed to, whose language you spoke, whose culture and streets you knew. You

also are separated from a group you were closer with but had looser connections. These two are compounding. Was there a reason you were ostracised and isolated in your own circle?

This is a difficult question, because I'm not a very social person. I'm someone who doesn't get bored of being alone. There aren't many Turks where I live. We socialise with the Czechs and live here. Second, what happened in Turkey naturally created a reaction, whether justified or not. We entered a cultural detox. This still makes me happy. We lived through such a traumatic experience in Turkey. The authoritarianism that emerged in Turkey, other events, what happened to the Kurds here and there, it has been helpful to stay far away from those things. You experience such problems with your own roots, but keeping your distance doesn't make you unhappy. I don't know how to say it, I don't want to be hurtful. I meet with people I know personally, whom I like in this environment as it relates to the structure. I would be sad not to meet with them, but they already meet with me. Because my relationship with them is personal; I like him because he's a businessman or an accountant. Apart from that, people who think like me already have no relationships left with many structures. As I said, I don't have any evidence that 'Don't meet with these men' has been said, because of the influence of the coronavirus and because of the distance. I don't know. Don't forget that it's been five years. I left Brussels in December. I met with a few people before the coronavirus pandemic, the number I was meeting with had gradually shrunk because time was passing. You establish a new life, there are new priorities. That story was already left behind for me. Compared to the past, I'm meeting with people with whom I've established friendships for personal reasons. I don't meet with anyone apart from them. I don't think there is any discrimination against me. I wrote a few articles three or four years ago to explain to the public what I thought about this topic. They may not have wanted their supporters to read them, they may have said, 'Don't read them.' This is fairly natural. I mean, it's illogical in my view, but this response is natural. So I don't think I'm in any kind of isolation. But I'll say this openly: I cannot exaggerate my own story. We write normal things. Read Hermann Hesse's *Journey to the East*; life is like that, every generation tries something, becomes educated somewhere. We are learning, by the way. I learned two things while learning this. First, I learned that I don't know Turkey very well. The circles which set out to solve Turkey's problems actually have problems themselves. Accordingly, the intellectual trauma I actually experienced was when society didn't criticise the problems in Turkey in the way that I wanted, and that upset me. Society could say to me, 'What did you do?' But at the same time, I was upset when I considered that the people to whom I went to ask about these problems had similar problems. And ultimately, I became someone who angered my former friends who angered the government. Strange things happen sometimes; there are cases against you claiming that you're a terrorist. The people in the warrant in which you were accused claimed to the government that you were a freeloader. This didn't cause me any trauma, but honestly, I was upset. When 17 December[2] happened in Turkey, my close circle reacted, saying, 'Doesn't society see this corruption? Why don't they see it?' I responded in that way. But now, they act like the AKP whom they criticised when the corruption of the people reacting in this way emerges. So this is what I want to say: I didn't experience such a significant trauma, but I think that I am actually very naive and don't know the incidents very well. Of course, it is important not to forget that my advantage is being geographically far away. If I had lived in Brussels for five years and five people to whom I said hello on the street didn't say the same back to me, maybe I would think differently.

---

[2] 17 December 2013 is an important date in the Gülen vs AKP rivalry. To know more, see Hendrik Müller, 'Turkey's December 17 Process: A Timeline of the Graft Investigation and the Government's Response', Institute for Security & Development Policy, 1 June 2014, https://www.isdp.eu/publication/turkeys-december-17-process-timeline-graft-investigation-governments-response/, accessed 1 March 2023.

Every group, every person has a separate Turkey in their imagination. What are Turkey's turning points, the critical junctures that brought you to where you are today? And, as far as I know, this is your longest international experience. What kind of difference is there between how you interpreted Turkey five years ago and how you interpret it right now? What kind of critical juncture brought you here?

This is impossible to answer theoretically, because there's a political culture here, a state tradition, and this tradition inherently and constantly produces people like us. The current package in which we were produced could be 17 December. For instance, there's a product – let's say butter. It continually changes its packaging, but the product is the same. We are shaped in certain contexts, because the Turkey that produced us has these structural issues. We are shaped in the context of 12 September, of 17–25 December, of the AKP–Gülen Movement, of Ergenekon. This is a natural thing in my view. I think that the situation in Turkey will continue as long as this structure exists. This is like a great transatlantic liner; you get riled up when you fall, people shout at you. Then you continue on your way. Your psychology at the moment you fell, those who were looking at you, that fight, perhaps that was 17 December, 12 September. For example, I encountered Assyrian Catholic Maronites, whom I had never heard about, in Europe. They had left Turkey. Their story was completely different, and I had never heard it, for example. I didn't even know that they were kicked out. Whatever the discussion is at the moment we fall from the ship, we repeat that to whoever asks. For example, I didn't leave Turkey on 12 September, so I can't explain that to you. If I had been an academic who left on 12 September, I would have mentioned Kenan Evren, the persecution and Dev-Yol. But as far as I see it, Turkey's state tradition will inevitably produce these, so it's impossible for me to connect this to somewhere. I could connect it to 17 December and what happened before, but what do I know? I could connect it to the AKP's rise to power. This is a difficult question. I honestly don't know where I'm going to connect it to. The incidents that brought me here . . . I refer to them because they were between 2000 and 2014. But there were previous events that caused these incidents. So I'll say 17 December or Ergenekon because I'm referring to the period when I left. İhsan Yılmaz and I tried as much as possible to meet with many people, local and foreign, about the absurd place these arrests had reached.

When you say 'arrests' . . .?
Ergenekon started in 2007–8. I was a doctoral candidate at the time. When I started writing op-ed pieces and articles, this Ergenekon business went off the rails. We tried to talk with a number of people to end this absurdity with whomever we spoke to. You have to engage in this sort of neighbourhood solidarity if you're going to live in Turkey. That's why I view this neighbourhood solidarity as normal. There has been no successful nation project, being a citizen is useless, a passport is useless. That's why I'm looking for a clan. If the passport you gave me and which I put in my pocket isn't going to work, if we are not equal in our citizenship, I'm going to go and hunt in the Ice Age. Which clan will come with me on the hunt? I consider those clans normal.

In 2003, Hakan Yavuz wrote, 'Turkey is actually a product of religious organisations,' meaning everyone has a group.
Yes. I see this as normal. That's why the Kemalists today are forced to stay in this neighbourhood. The man who wins the fight beats the others – that's the rule. Don't leave your neighbourhood, win the fight and destroy the other. This is how the order is, unfortunately. I haven't specified the fight of these clans. The other neighbourhoods are not very much like this; they're problems are separate. So the critical point is the incidents there because I left during that period. I was in a place like that in the incidents there. I don't know in that regard, what's the threshold? Has my perception of Turkey changed? I'll

say this: my perception of Turkey began to change in 2009 or 2010. I made a radical decision and went to Gaziantep. I told my friends there, 'If I was to stay in Gaziantep three more years, I would become a Kemalist.' I was born in Bursa. I'm someone whose entire family lives to the west of Eskişehir, who perceives Turkey in a certain cultural basin, right of centre, who has no one in his circle who isn't Kurdish. When I lived in Gaziantep, I saw that Turkish sociology is challenging. I saw issues of smuggling, Kurdish issues, femicide. I saw that the job is challenging and convoluted. I saw that Turkey is a difficult country. But that relates a little bit to age. You could win the Nobel Prize for Physics at age twenty, but the social sciences relate to personal maturity. You need to mature a little bit. I began to look at things somewhat differently. But of course, you compare things when looking from outside the country. I'm someone who has travelled a lot, but now I live in Europe, in the villages and towns of Europe. Seeing this difference on this level isn't like travelling as a tourist or travelling as an academic. Accordingly, I have an entirely different view of Turkey, and unfortunately, this comparison has not changed my love for Turkey but has made my view of it more negative. I told one of my friends in exile, 'The film ended 400 years before we were born.' So yes, my view has changed, I have a more negative view. So my ideas have changed, that is true. But life is like that. You don't say, 'If only it had changed earlier.'

You mentioned being in constant exile. How do you define yourself? And if this is exile, what kind of psychology is being in exile?

I'm an academic, and I must make something clear first. If a person cannot return to their country, it is exile. Someone who cannot return to their country, who cannot carry a passport for their country, who is living here because they cannot return to their country is technically in exile. In a strange twist of fate, I wrote an article in 1999 in the *Muslim World* entitled 'Exile and Turkish Politics'. In that article,

I addressed Esat Coşan, who died in Australia, Ahmet Kaya, Üzeyir Garih and Fethullah Gülen as a case study. We are technically in exile, but you may not feel that way; you may be happy. I can't say anything about that. My forefathers migrated to Turkey in the 1860s due to pressure from Czarist Russia in the Caucasus. We're a family which has migrated from the Caucasus. And now I've come here. So I consider it like we came and lived for a while in Turkey, and then we came here from there. So how is your psychology? It has been five years. I've grown very accustomed to this place. It's a beautiful country, the countryside is beautiful, the architecture is beautiful, the people are polite. We're calm. It's important to differentiate between saying I'm in exile and the psychology of exile. I'm technically in exile, but I don't experience that psychology of exile. While in Brussels, I visited the home of an individual who was forced to leave Turkey and about whom there were lawsuits in Turkey. I saw a massive Turkish flag on the wall when I first entered. I was shocked. It's important to differentiate between an intellectual exile and an expatriate. There's a psychology unique to expatriates. To be in a foreign land, to long for something, and so forth. There's nothing like that. Coming to my children, my younger daughter is twelve years old, she has completely become a Czech-Turk, she's becoming a Czech, because that's what her environment is like, the dialogues she has, her lifestyle. My older daughter was born in 2005. She has changed a lot as well. They are not a piece of this story. For them, this story no longer has any meaning. When they reach a certain age, maybe they will consider what this story means for them. Maybe they'll be interested, maybe they'll study history. So they have no place in this story. For them, Turkey means the aunt speaking on social media or a screen. But yes, we are technically in exile. Of course, it's not that people don't consider what happened or how a man such as myself became unable to go to Turkey. This evokes something interesting in people. Am I able to explain what I mean? I think this is a personal, philosophical question. What kind of political culture is it that means you have reached such a point on this issue? On the other hand, there's an intellectual side. When I was young, I read a lot about German academics who came to Istanbul University, about who came here and there. I always heard good things about them. We've become like that now. We entered Czech history as 'the academics who came from Turkey'. It's very small, but there's a historical discourse like that in Turkey regarding the German academics: they came and founded that, and so forth. We haven't established anything here, but we came and entered that footnote of history. So yes, we are in exile, but I'm not experiencing that exile psychology. I went to Iran. Someone I spoke with while I was there told me that the people who left Iran after the Islamic Revolution understood their situation ten to eleven years afterwards. There was an excitement, they thought it wouldn't last, it would change, it would collapse, it definitely couldn't sustain itself. But at that point, this person said that those who had left Iran accepted, after ten or eleven years, that the situation wouldn't change. I don't have anything like this for Turkey. I want the people there to be happy. I left the picture, but the transatlantic liner continues; it doesn't consider you. I won't say Turkey is horrible, or Turkey be damned. I'm trying to observe Turkey from afar and understand it. But I'm not categorising it.

Would you return to Turkey one day? Do you think that you'll return?

There are two questions here; I honestly don't know whether I'm considering it. I don't know if I would return; it won't be me who determines this. Would I return? I won't say 'Yes, I'd return', but I also wouldn't say that I'd never go back. A group of people are rightfully saying, 'I won't ever go back to that country.' I respect these people's ideas. I won't say that. What I experienced was a major occurrence for me. How many years has it been since I saw my sister? These are important things in a person's life. Theory does not shape our everyday lives. What we love, our environments do. So if the conditions in Turkey improve one day and I have the opportunity to return, I'll sit for a day, consider it, and I may return. But will these conditions arise? I have no idea. A certain psychology has been formed in this process: our views about Turkey, like a weather report. Some days you think affairs will be fixed rather quickly in Turkey, and some days you say they never will. I have no opinion about whether the conditions will help people like me return to Turkey. But I will say that if you call me tomorrow, if the environment in Turkey changes, we can return. I'll consider, then, what I can do there. I'm not categorically saying that I will never return to Turkey. I may return. I would like to go to my village tomorrow; I would like to walk in my village. I don't miss every aspect of Turkey, but I would like to talk with my friends. I haven't made a prediction in the past five years about whether the academics and journalists who have left Turkey will return. But I may return if those conditions arise. I wouldn't want to disrespect the pain of people who have suffered more than me, but that's life. What we experience is, in a sense, normal, and life continues as such. We must not transform these experiences into binding memories.

10

HASİP KAPLAN

My greatest goal is to introduce our country to peace, tranquillity and democracy . . . That's why we want to be on the side of our fellow citizens against those selling our country's harbours, forests and minerals, parcel by parcel. We have a great amount of debt. We can work to fulfil that [ideal], and we want to return for that. I wouldn't stay one more hour in Europe if my goal were achieved. It's that clear.

Hasip Kaplan is a former member of the Grand National Assembly of Turkey for several parties. In 2015 he represented the Peoples' Democratic Party (HDP) in the Turkish parliament. He was one of the lawyers who represented Abdullah Ocalan in his trial on Imrali Island in 1999 and also in his appeal before the European Court of Human Rights (ECHR) in 2003. Between 1994 and 2002, he represented politicians from the banned Democracy Party (DEP) before the ECHR, including Ahmet Türk, Leyla Zana, Orhan Doğan and

Hatip Dicle. The court's verdict was that there was a violation of the European Convention on Human Rights and Turkey was ordered to pay compensation to each of the applicants in the case. Kaplan also represented the Freedom and Democracy Party (ÖZDEP) in their appeal to the ECHR against their closure by the Turkish Constitutional Court. In July 2021, the German authorities informed him that he was on an execution list of fifty-five critics of the Turkish government.

Mr Kaplan, we are grateful that you agreed to give us an interview. Could you kindly tell us your story? When and why did you leave Turkey?

I left on 24 January 2018. I wasn't a candidate in the 7 June 2015 elections because of the two-term limit. There were more than 100 police inquiry reports about us. When our MP status ended and our immunity disappeared, trials began based on these police inquiries. We were continually going to the courts to give statements. I started working as a lawyer a year later because the immunity status of MPs was voided starting in 2016. Selahattin Demirtaş and Figen Yüksekdağ were arrested, and lawsuits were filed against them. As a lawyer, I joined the trials of Figen Yüksekdağ first and then Selahattin Demirtaş. There were numerous arrests once immunity was lifted. Almost my entire life was spent between Silivri, Edirne, Kandıra, Diyarbakır and Ankara Sincan prisons. The lawyer friends working at our office would join the trials of our friends in prison, international trials. I was mostly going to visit them. I would see if they needed anything. If you want the truth, I knew that the ruling party would follow this path after ending parliamentary immunity and, especially, that it would be directed at designated Kurdish politicians and opposition politicians who side with democracy.

It was Friday, 19 January. Selahattin Demirtaş wanted to meet. I went to Edirne prison. We had a long meeting. In fact, a congress was going to be held in early February. He said he was going to be a co-chairman candidate and, if necessary, would send a motion with his original signature from there to Divan. There was a weekend in the meantime. On Monday, I learned that I had been sentenced at the Gaziantep Court of Appeals to three years, one month and fifteen days in prison. Two things were required of me. First was that I would be prevented from practising law. Because you cannot practise law when you receive such a sentence. Second was that I automatically fell into a state of a political ban. But to my surprise, the decision to call early elections in June 2018 was on the AKP's agenda. The fact of the matter is that it was preparing to do this. It had begun investigations, arrests, detentions and punishments against all key figures in Kurdish politics for this. One night, the homes of seven MPs, from Demirtaş to İdris Baluken, were raided. It was interesting. It was clear which prison these friends would be sent to even prior to their court appearances. The tickets for the planes they would board, the helicopters allocated to take them from the airport to where they were going were all clear. The regime prepared all of this without a court order. And the regime told the court to arrest these friends with a political order. They were arrested, unfortunately.

The AKP regime officially turned the 15 July coup attempt of the Fethullah Gülen Movement into a conspiracy against its opposition. It primarily attacked the HDP, the Education Labour Union (Eğitim-Sen), DİSK, the labour unions, NGOs – the dynamics of society. They closed organisations, they closed law bureaus, and they arrested hundreds of lawyers. They assumed a position conflating lawyers with their clients just because of the cases they worked on. They called Öcalan's lawyer and Fethullah Gülen's lawyers. The Modern Lawyers Association president, Selçuk Kozağaçlı, who throughout his life was a part of the fight for human rights, hastily received a terrible sentence. Coming to my situation, I'm a criminal lawyer, actually. I started working in criminal law after the 12 September coup [in 1980]. I was a lawyer who filed the first cases in Strasbourg for human rights and the first to enter the hearings. I have over 100 police inquiry reports. They issued Law No. 6352 in the third judicial package. According to that package, postponement decisions were given regarding crimes with certain punishments. It later affected elements of violence and force in propaganda crimes. Then, Law No. 6459 helped close investigations into thought and freedom of expression. There was the solution process [*cozum sureci*] at the time – in 2013. Despite these, I think there were more than twenty investigations into me. These were delayed.

In June 2010, we were going to make a statement to the press in Silopi. As the Şırnak MPs, Sevahir Bayındır and I were there together with our other MP friends. During the statement to the press, armoured trucks suddenly attacked and targeted us – MPs. They shot pressurised water at us and three gas bombs and canisters. Sevahir Bayındır was badly injured and was later unable to come to parliament for months. Our lawyers filed a complaint about these officials, but it was decided that there were no grounds for legal action. Think about it, there's the Habur process; we presided over this process, met with the regime, and the regime made requests of us. During the solution process, we tried to be effective there as well with peace groups coming from Habur. But police inquiries were written against us unceasingly. We said 'Şevbaş, good evening' when I first became an MP, and a police inquiry was filed. I mean, there were no good intentions in this incident. When this postponed ruling was finalised, delays on twenty other files were lifted. Besides that, I have files waiting in the Court of Cassation. They wanted me to serve 100 to 200 years in prison like the sentences given to Selahattin Demirtaş when we convened. It's truly a period of lawlessness and injustice. On 24 January, I immediately warned my lawyers in Gaziantep. I was expecting something at any moment, because they had given the date for the hearings very soon. It was clear they were working to issue a sentence very quickly. But in the appeal, it didn't surprise me that they finalised the ruling at lightning speed in between a month and six weeks. After I came here, they filed a case in Diyarbakır High Criminal Court and filed another case in Cizre High Criminal Court. I have arrest warrants now.

The 2nd High Criminal Court of Cizre issued the red notice. For what crime? Because we held a night pitching tents with the participation of municipal mayors, provincial leaders, party assembly members and MPs in the Şırnak Kasrik Boğazı between 6 and 7 February 2008 and for statements we made saying 'Stop the operations, peace now'. Approximately 15,000 people went to that. What were we going to do to do this? I went as an MP, and I brought the current Istanbul governor, Ali Yerlikaya, then Şırnak governor, a security official, a gendarme regiment commander and municipal mayors. I brought the entire press along with us. We first arrived and scouted around for a place to set up our tents at the Kasrik Boğazı. There was a coalfield where cars would be parked, we specified that. Officials were going to be members of our group to prevent traffic congestion. Ahmet Türk, Sırrı Sakık, Aysel Tuğluk, Nuri Yaman and I were there. We had to go to the assembly that night. Co-chairwoman Emine Ayna stayed there, and Co-chairman Ahmet Türk came with us to Ankara, because the hijab vote was the next day, 7 February, in the assembly. I was a speaker there on behalf of the party group. There are official assembly reports. I say, 'I returned to Ankara on this date, I spoke in the assembly, here are the official reports. Why are you issuing an arrest warrant for me? Why are you issuing a red notice? My lawyer presented these official reports, I presented them.' Despite this, they issued a red notice. Strangely, no investigation or case had been opened against anyone because of this event in 2008; those that were opened were postponed or thrown out. This is the situation we were faced with, and there were two options before us: either go to prison and fight this injustice and lawlessness until we die or leave the country and, if we have the resources, fight more. So I jumped in my car thirty minutes after I learned about the ruling on 24 January.

Was a ban on leaving the country immediately implemented?
No, it was not implemented. The appeal ruling was handed down, the sentence was affirmed. They implement two methods in these types of

things: sometimes they claim crimes of terrorism and tell you to come to prison by letter. Then you can be taken immediately and put in prison. Second, as in the Gergerlioğlu incident, they write a letter, tell you to come and surrender yourself. I'm a notable figure. The police will recognise me if I go to the airport. When the Anadolu Agency's news began to be reported repeatedly on social media, on television, I thought the best outcome would be to try my luck at the border and leave immediately. There is no ban on leaving the country in the ruling. I had a green passport. I went and crossed into Greece through the Edirne Pazarkule border crossing. The next day, I flew to Germany, to Frankfurt, through Thessaloniki.

Why Germany?
The Şırnak Botan region witnessed a load of significant investigations and village burnings – unsolved cases in the 1990s. Many of my relatives emigrated to Germany during that period. We're a very big family. I have eight siblings right now in Germany. I have maybe more than 200 nieces and nephews. I have maybe one, two thousand relatives here. My actual goal was to do different work, but you tend to gravitate towards writing in periodicals or newspapers as you grow older. There are news channels and television programmes that broadcast on YouTube here. We participate in programmes there. As soon as I got here, the June 2018 elections were held, and we contributed to work here related to that.

Did you seek political asylum in Germany?
People in our position are forced to apply for political asylum. It was later accepted through bureaucratic procedures. It wasn't like the 12 September coup or the 12 March coup; there's a major group of political migrants, refugees. Because party leaders have spoken, tweeted, written articles, and an investigation is immediately launched against them. Of course, I have more comfortable opportunities here because my family is here.

Did your immediate family come with you?

My immediate family comes and goes. I have two children: one works alongside me, and the other works in Turkey.

Have there been any demands or pressure from Turkey on Germany to send you back?

They haven't informed me about anything like that so far, but there are many people about whom such notifications are sent and who are political refugees. Regardless, Germany doesn't take these requests seriously.

You have a lot of relatives abroad. You're also a prominent figure in the party, in the media. There are many people who know you and approach you with sympathy – Kurds, Turks, HDP members . . . Do you have any contact with liberals, leftists, Gülenists or other groups except for your own relatives or party members who were forced to leave Turkey?

During the June 2018 elections when I first arrived, we held conferences both individually and collectively in about ten to fifteen cities with Alevis, Kurds and Yazidis. I was indiscriminately coming together with everyone who could. I have a unique trait that makes me act in solidarity with people from every segment, especially people who have been mistreated. The reason we bothered the regime in Turkey was not only that we were influential HDP MPs or MPs from Şırnak. There's another reason. We set up a group after the 7 June elections with former Social Democrat Party members, MP Ziya Halis, Hüsnü Okçuoğlu, members of the Republican People's Party such as Binnaz Toprak, Süleyman Çelebi, Zülfü Livaneli, Rıza Türmen, Altan Öymen and Gülseren Onanç, and others including Akın Birdal, Levent Tüzel, Ufuk Uras and Nesrin Nas, and we called it the Dialogue Group. During those challenging days, we would gather in my office once every ten to fifteen days. Our first spokesman was Altan Öymen, then Rıza Türmen, then Zülfü Livaneli, then

Binnaz Toprak and Süleyman Çelebi. We had a situation of rotating spokespeople. We were fighting for democracy together with friends with whom we had come together and who were from various segments. Then Rıza Türmen made a call under the name Union for Democracy (Demokrasi İçin Birlik). We organised two massive meetings to add all political parties, institutions and civil society to this. We coordinated this. I assumed a role there. Our meetings and conferences continue with the Dialogue Group online. We make statements every once in a while.

These are things that make the regime incredibly uncomfortable, because our network has expanded significantly. Hüsamettin Cindoruk's office, for example, is close to me, and we participated in a press conference together. We created a committee from our group and sent it to Kılıçdaroğlu. A group of ten of us visited former president Abdullah Gül. We also visited the HDP. A good fight for democracy is something that disturbs the current racist, far-right regime keen on totalitarianism. They were already silencing everyone. They silenced the media, they closed newspapers, they closed radio stations, newspapers were closed together with television stations, they seized property, officials and their colleagues were punished, and the regime created a press that we call the mass media. A certain situation emerged when we look back: you know the 2010 constitutional referendum was approved by the Council of Judges and Prosecutors, but the referendum in April 2017 completely eliminated the separation of powers and checks and balances. While I was in the assembly, we had two important commissions. The first was the Constitution Reconciliation Commission, which comprised three members from the four political parties in 2013. Serious work was done in this commission. I was deputy group chairman at the time for the Peace and Democracy Party. They met with thousands of people, experts, academics and scientists. They met and had conferences with institutions. They went to the provinces in groups. The AKP later said, 'We're gone if there's no presidential system,' and turned the tables.

The second was the Internal Regulation Reconciliation Commission, which did more technical work. We first went to Washington in four groups. We examined the presidential system there. But the presidential system there has a fantastic checks and balances system. The executive, legislature and judiciary do not mix. The judiciary can call presidents to make statements whenever it wants. After seeing this, we said, 'Friends, there are checks and balances here. They want a presidential system in Turkey without checks and balances. That's a type of regime called Caudillo, a one-man regime, it more closely resembles that.' They said, 'Then let's look at a semi-presidential system. Let's go to France.' We went and monitored the work there. In fact, we monitored the National Assembly on a day when attendance was at its highest. Most importantly, there's a mechanism there called question-answer, it lasts for an hour, there are twenty-four speakers and everyone speaks for two minutes each. They ask their questions directly to the ministers, and the ministers respond directly. The senate in France functions somewhat like a constitutional court – the laws that come from the parliament are reviewed. Someone said to me, 'Do you see that man sitting there?' He had a sandwich in his hand that he was eating. 'That's a minister. He'll be up all night here so his own law is passed, he'll listen to us, and he'll try to influence the passage of his law,' they said. 'Our ministers don't eat sandwiches, they give orders, and they do it,' I said. Then we came to London. We did a fairly long study in London. For example, that thing called the sword's length in the House of Commons is a fantastic thing. No one has crossed this in a hundred years. 'Whenever we defend our rights, a hundred people attack us,' I said. I counted individually so I wouldn't be mistaken. Of course, the work of a commission in a settled democracy is hierarchical, orderly. We are very far from this, but nevertheless, we reconciled over 90 per cent of the articles as friends from four parties on the Internal Regulation Commission. Only six or seven items were left that we couldn't agree upon. They wanted us to submit the Internal Regulation by the end of December. But when the AKP insisted that it wouldn't give up on the omnibus bill, that study of which we had agreed on 90 per cent in the Internal Regulation Commission was thrown out. Now we've come from a period like that to today. What is the leader of our presidential system, our president, doing? He withdrew from the Istanbul Convention[1] by presidential decree. He seizes legislative authority. The executive has replaced the legislature. The speaker of the assembly can also withdraw from the Montreux Convention if he wants. The opposition must speak out here. Gergerlioğlu was punished for being an active defender of human rights, and his sentence was immediately finalised. We saw the AKP Congress. One person is elected as both party leader and president. This regime is a one-party state. The first article of the AKP's 2023 vision document was that parties cannot be closed, saying they'll eliminate that completely. But now they are closing the HDP because Bahçeli wanted to, and he did so such that the chief prosecutor of the Court of Cassation wants a political ban for three dead MPs. Who are these 687 people for whom political bans have been requested? All former MPs, all municipal mayors, all directors of the party.

And you are among them?
I am, of course. Would I not be? They added me, and they added people who have left the party. They're doing this indiscriminately. They individually added the activities of 687 people to the bill of indictment and said, 'Close the party, cut off the treasury support, pass cautionary judgments on their property, ban them from politics.' They've thrown everyone into a bag and called it a bill of indictment without doing any research.

---

[1] For more information on the Istanbul Convention see Özlem Altan-Olcay and Bertil Emrah Oder, 'Why Turkey's withdrawal from the Istanbul Convention is a global problem', OpenDemocracy, 2 June 2021, https://www.opendemocracy.net/en/can-europe-make-it/why-turkeys-withdrawal-from-the-istanbul-convention-is-a-global-problem/, accessed 1 March 2023.

You're a very popular figure. Everyone who watched a little bit of television between 2010 and 2016 knows you. At the very worst, people would be reminded of when you broke a glass at the parliamentary lectern.

I had done this in meetings against violence in sport. We presented the law against violence in sport together, but later, the other three parties decided the fines were too much and agreed among themselves to lower the fines. Amedspor and Cizrespor were being attacked in Bursa, in Ankara, and there were racist attacks against them. I wanted to speak out against this. As these debates were ongoing, we were notified about a bill of indictment for a match-fixing case. Former AKP minister Canikli's relations with the federation president appeared in this bill of indictment. I stood up and said, 'You're involved in this.' All hell broke loose from there. I swore and broke the glass.

Yes, there are those who love you, but there are also Turkey's transnational institutions such as the Diyanet, MİT, TİKA and the consulates as well as the supporters of the parties that make up the People's Alliance attacking figures such as Can Dündar and Eser Karakaş. Does this happen to you too? In Germany, do you feel the reaction of the state or Turkish nationals who oppose you?

I didn't even experience anything like this in Turkey. There are always people with me whenever I go anywhere. I mean, I'm never alone, but I have never encountered disrespect like that from anybody here. I know that in the past, MİT would monitor the friends of MPs and association leaders and that plans were made for an assassination team.

But nothing like this has happened to you, as far as I understand.

There's something against us where when we share something on social media, they sometimes mobilise paid trolls and swear and insult us. I block a portion of them, and my lawyers deal with the more prominent ones.

Are you happy with the German government's behaviour towards you?
The security and intelligence here are more responsive compared to other countries. But I'll say this: I think that the European Union, European Parliament and European Council protect their commercial profits and interests, particularly those of Germany, and that they must move beyond the diplomacy of condemnation. The biggest diaspora here is the Turkish diaspora. Kurds are second; there are more than 1 million Kurds, and that is an underestimate, it's not a simple figure. But it is true that there is a threat emanating from Turkey – including ISIS, for example. The German government is opposed to this threat, of course, and we must be careful. It's not like there's security everywhere. It turned out that networks which include intelligence operatives killed three Kurdish female politicians in Paris. There's no foolproof security anywhere, but some countries are more careful with political refugees. Germany is among these countries. It doesn't take most of the red notices seriously and drops them.

It's true that a transnational community of Turkish intellectuals emerged on the other side of Kapıkule, especially after 2016. You're one of them. They all have a different breaking point when it comes to Turkey. Some mention the coup, some go back to the 2010 referendum, a portion say the end of the peace process, some say 16 April 2017. What is Turkey's breaking point for you? What was the breaking point in the process that forced you to remain in Turkey, either willingly or unwillingly, in your view?
First, thousands of leftists, Gülenists, Alevis and Kurds were indiscriminately targeted with thousands of decrees issued during the state of emergency declared after the 15 July coup. Consider that an academic fired by decree can't find work anywhere else. The only thing that thousands of people they arrested or fired from the Gülen Movement did was deposit money in Bank Asya, stay in their rooms or read their

newspapers. The fact that a military coup was staged didn't even cross the minds of most of these people. The AKP regime that led to their former ten-year partnership said the Ergenekon and Balyoz cases were a Gülen Movement conspiracy and began to mingle with Eurasianists and Perinçekists. The regime is creating an alliance. This alliance is largely being created strategically over Kurdish animosity in the Middle East. Attacks not only on Rojava but on all Kurds in the region are in question. ISIS is crossing the 900-kilometre border, waving its hands. All of them are occupiers and neo-Ottomanists and are the product of a racist regime mixed together with a Turkish synthesis of Islam. There is no justice left here, the press is not free, and all rights and freedoms have been eliminated.

I think you're in the diaspora for the first time – that is to say, you haven't experienced this before, have you?

Because I worked in the Association of European Lawyers and came to Strasbourg in particular, I travelled around a lot for work. But my experience of exile in the diaspora is new. I will have been here for three years in January. And the conditions in Turkey are gradually getting worse. There are no signs of improvement.

Has your perspective on Turkey changed in this process?

My perspective of the opposition has changed a lot. I'm furious with the opposition and its passivity. I'm furious it hasn't done anything despite all the regime's blunders. Think about it, the central bank fires its president, empties out $123 billion, the rapture happens, but our opposition is just minding its own business. Think about how the legislative duties of the parliament regarding the Istanbul Convention have been seized. But the opposition party, Kılıçdaroğlu, pins a decree on the door of the speaker of the assembly, saying, 'You cannot use this authority.' Were they able to do it? No. Where is the central bank's money? It's been smuggled out; it's gone. Who stole it? No answer. And now the issue of midnight decisions has begun, you know, they'll make subsequent appointments based on this. When such a clear erosion of power is taking place, the powers of democracy must come together under certain principles. You'll say, 'We support not the unification but the separation of powers. We support an independent judiciary. We support freedom. We support equality. We are opposed to the presidential regime.' Five points. Tayyip [Erdoğan] knows very well that the Kurdish votes will determine the upcoming elections. That's why he's trying to divide the Nation Alliance. He's leaning towards a centre-right party such as the Good Party or the former DYP, but he's unable to do this because of some elements in the party. Right now, apparently, the main opposition party is the HDP even though the CHP is still here. Meral Akşener sometimes makes noise, but her biggest mistake pertains to the HDP. There are seven rulings the ECHR has handed down regarding the HDP, and all of them have condemned the state. Go and say, 'Why are you scared of the parties?' She hasn't made any noise regarding the state-appointed trustees, who are now being appointed one by one in major cities. They most recently took Gezi Park and turned it over to a foundation. This tyrannical regime has become integrated with the mafia, with the deep state, with the intelligence of the deep state. They clearly and shamelessly talk about international operations and assassinations. If this regime is still talking about war everywhere from Libya to Armenia and taking money for military expenditures, nothing remains for it to provide the public in sickness or in health or in the future.

Would you ever return? Do you hope to return?
I would undoubtedly return to our country because I can still come and go abroad while in our country. Certainly nobody wants to remain far away from their own land. You'll find few people in exile who wouldn't return to their country when given the opportunity. They went, made a new life, but they come and go to their country, their relatives come and go. We would also certainly come and go, because our family is very large. There are many of them here, but

many of them are there as well. I was one of twenty-seven siblings. Could I be politically active? I don't really have that kind of enthusiasm. They want to ban us from politics; I'm one of the 687 people. When a political ban is imposed, you are prohibited as a party but can still be an independent candidate. I was already elected as an independent candidate in Şırnak in the 2007 elections. I was elected as an independent candidate in the 2011 elections. I could be stubborn and be an independent *muhtar* candidate; there's nothing preventing this. Closing this party is a step that will end the AKP. I hope the Constitutional Court doesn't make such an error. Right now, we want peace in our country, that's why we are opposed to war. We want there to be democracy in our country, that's why we are opposed to a one-man regime, to the presidential regime. We are opposed to racism, discrimination and the discourse of hatred because we defend equality. There are Assyrians, Yazidis, Kurds and Turks where I have lived – different languages, cultures and religions. I want all of them to live as free Turkish citizens. We are opposed to the regime's ownership of all the assets of such a rich country, to everything going to five holding companies participating in the public tenders. We support the equal and fair distribution of the economy for all citizens. I really value schools and education, because a country's ability to survive is dependent on neither its military nor its money. A country without educated power cannot survive, regardless of its military or whether it has as much money as it wants. Turkey rests on a historic geography compared to the rest of the world. While developing relations of peace and friendship with our Middle Eastern neighbours, why are we fighting with the Syrian regime, fighting with the Kurds in Iraq, fighting with the Kurds in Syria, building a 900-kilometre wall? They built a 900-kilometre wall between Rojava and Turkey that's taller than the Berlin Wall. They want to do what they can to build the same wall on the border with Iraq and Iran. I would go if only just to strike the first hammer blow against the walls of this mentality. Regardless of how old I am, I want to share my ideas there.

My greatest goal is to introduce our country to peace and democracy because we have a very beautiful country. We live in a country with a strong history and people, where it's always summer and winter and spring together in all its regions, where there are all climates. We don't know the value or the worth of our country. That's why we want to be on the side of our fellow citizens against those selling our country's harbours, forests and minerals, parcel by parcel. We have a great amount of debt. We can work to fulfil that, and we want to return for that. I wouldn't stay one more hour in Europe if my goal were achieved. It's that clear.

11

HAYKO BAĞDAT

**We're at the point where we can't sit around doing nothing.
Each of us are rebelling in our own space. It's not bad, by the
way, Turkey's rebellion, despite this oppression. I hope we
win, otherwise the situation will be bad. What we win
won't be heaven, but the alternative is quite terrible.**

*Hayko Bağdat was born in Istanbul in 1976 to a Greek mother and
Armenian father, attending Armenian schools for primary and sec-
ondary education, and later Istanbul University. He began a career
in journalism in 2002, when he produced and presented the radio
programme* Sözde Kalanlar *('The Remnants'), focusing on minority
issues in Turkey. The next year, he started writing for the Armenian
newspaper* Marmara *as well as the liberal daily newspaper* Taraf. *He
is also one of the founders of the civil society initiative Friends of Hrant
Dink, established in 2007 after the assassination of the journalist and*

free-speech advocate. In 2015, Bağdat was fined by a Turkish court for 'insulting' Melih Gökçek, the mayor of Ankara, and exposing his slanderous remarks about Armenians. A year later, he moved to Berlin after surviving an assassination attempt in Turkey, enduring numerous death threats and a Turkish arrest warrant issued for his detention. In 2017, he co-founded the news site Özgürüz ('Liberty') with Turkish journalist Can Dündar to provide impartial coverage on censored issues in Turkey.

You were one of the intellectuals who left Turkey in the wave starting after 2010. We would like to know more about your story. When did you leave Turkey?

I am actually the most senior individual on the matter of leaving Turkey, because of my Armenian identity. [It feels like] we left a century ago. I left in 2016 – after 15 July. I first went to Thessaloniki.

How did you leave?

I went by road with my normal passport. I stayed for twenty days – maybe more, close to one month – in Thessaloniki. At the time, my name was on the list of journalists who were being detained and arrested in Turkey. I later returned. When I returned, they took my passport. It was quite an event because I was the first media figure whose passport they confiscated. Our Armenian friends like Garo Paylan and Selina Doğan, who was a CHP MP at the time, asked interior minister Efkan Ala about my case. At the time, I was doing a television programme on Bugün TV with Nazlı Ilıcak. Then Efkan Ala said that extensive lists had been prepared, that my name was not within the scope of the Gülenists and that my passport would be returned. And then I actually got my passport, but getting that passport back was also a message from the Turkish state telling me to leave. We know that. I was already living in Turkey with protection. There were threats and one assassination attempt. I went on a tour of London and Vienna in December, and then I came to Berlin.

Can [Dündar], at the time, was setting up Özgürüz.[1] I received a job offer. And I never went back.

After this process, was your passport revoked again? Or were any rulings issued for your capture or detention?
There can't be an arrest ruling because I'm not in Turkey. There are rulings for my capture. I have enough dossiers – dozens – for which I can be tried for several lifetimes, from which I could receive numerous sentences if we count the upper limits.

Are all of these related to the coup?
They don't have anything to do with the coup.

So what do your punishments or warrants relate to?
Terrorist organisation propaganda. They mention the PKK probably, or other leftist organisations. I'm not sure if they've added the Gülen Movement. I know of 301 dossiers for my trial waiting for me at the Ministry of Justice. A few of them are for insulting the president, public malice and sedition. So all of the files have to do with what we wrote and filmed.

As far as I understand, the reason you chose Germany had more to do with work than because your friends or a lot of Turkish nationals are here. Why Germany?
Exile is not a choice, it's up to chance, generally. Some people stayed in the country because their passports were seized. A portion of those intellectuals you mentioned are in Greece, a portion of them are here. Why? Because some went wherever they could seek refuge. People are really lucky when they can choose where to be. But we had a few reasons. My wife, Belma, was working at the Nauman Foundation while

---

[1] See Özgürüz's YouTube channel at https://www.youtube.com/c/%C3%96ZG% C3%9CR%C3%9CZ/video .

in Turkey, and the foundation has a centre here. Can Dündar was setting up a newspaper, and I got a job offer from him. We have a few relatives here, so it was here.

Your family came with you in that process, no?
Belma took the children and came after a while.

So the passport revocations and lawsuits against you didn't reach your immediate family, correct?
No. Can Dündar – his wife was taken hostage in Turkey, you know – explained the situation in those days to Belma. A decision was made very quickly, and Belma took the children and came here within fifteen days. Then the children's passports expired. But because I had a warrant, passports weren't given to my children. They don't perform that task at the consulate. My passport expired too.

There's a concept we use at the academy known as extraterritorial authoritarianism. This concept refers to certain practices such as being unable to use a passport; having a passport taken when visiting a consulate; a witch hunt by the Diyanet, TİKA and the YTB; being followed by people or Turkish citizens in the diaspora; and lynching certain groups by assuming that role independently. Has anything like this happened to you? There have probably been situations while in Germany in which the state threatened you directly or indirectly. Could you explain this process a little bit? As far as I know, you appeared on stage with body armour while performing *Salyangoz*.
I had already been living with protection since Turkey, and this still continues. And there's a reason for this: there was a notice. They were going to attack me; I was on a list. There was a notice that hitmen had been dispatched. Garo announced this notice in parliament. Then the German authorities – the Berlin State Interior Ministry and the federal government – confirmed this notice. I lived

with the highest level of protection for up to eight months. This changed not only my life here but a lot of things. Germany formed a diplomatic relationship with Turkey on this issue. There were meetings between intelligence units. The precautions here increased. As a result, this isn't a case within this wave of migration you mentioned, this only relates to me. My name is meaningful because my name was mentioned, because I was one of the targets. Otherwise, the matter is much bigger. Turkey had previously executed three female Kurdish politicians in Paris. There were experts on CNN saying explicitly that action must be taken in Europe. Had Turkey never conducted an international operation before? It had! This is a place where the consulate functions like a criminal headquarters because there are so many Turkish nationals and the area of operations is so expansive. So the Turkish nationals here continue their lives facing crises on a number of issues, like the notices you mentioned before and having their passports seized. I'm one of the people who's had the biggest share of this.

So how long did this last? It's ongoing, as I understand, the protection and so forth.
There has been protection in my life since Turkey, so that's ongoing. But I really did go out on stage with body armour. I called Hasan Cemal that night, saying, 'Hasan, I've got something to say. I'm going around here with body armour, fifteen police officers, armoured vehicles because you Turks committed genocide and didn't acknowledge that. God damn you. I'm an Armenian living in Europe in the twenty-first century, and the Turks are going to attack me. I called first and foremost to say this,' I said. 'Second, I'm calling Cemal Pasha's grandson to find some morale as an Armenian in this situation. God damn me as well.' I explained this to show both the Turkish state's view of Armenians and how the state chases after the dissidents it lets escape from the country. This is a more recent case.

When you went to the city where you live, especially in the past, did you receive support from the members of the diaspora who had migrated there? Did you encounter any kind of solidarity? Or did you look after yourself? Ranging from finding a home to finding a job, from finding a job to sending your children to school, what was your daily life like?

This forced migration changed me, my family, my children, our lives and our life plans at a great cost. The weight of everything we experience, like it is for everything that happens to people who are forced to leave their country, is burdensome. This is a truly challenging period for us, materially and morally. People's children are drowning in Maritsa. I acted sincerely when I struggled for rights in Turkey. And I received appreciation for this; they rolled out the red carpet. Our Alevi friends prepared meat for us when we couldn't find a butcher. They found a home. They searched for even the smallest things. Our Kurdish friends didn't leave my side until the protection arrived. You don't call those kids to your side with money. They were volunteers. They didn't ask for money from me anywhere I went. I saw a great deal of solidarity. I travelled the world for my play. I went to Canada and America. I received invitations from Turkish institutions. I went to London four times. I sold books there, gave out autographs and sold tickets. Thank God my profession suited this. I am able to work in a few areas. I have a play that I can stage, I can make television programmes, and I can write books and scripts. It wasn't very comfortable, but these opened up a lot of doors. I lived through the toughest moment of my life in terms of having enough money for food. I have no savings. But we have pulled through so far. So, yes, we would have crumbled if it wasn't for that network. Those without networks didn't pull through. And I opened up this network, again with all my sincerity and all my strength, to others in my situation. I never asked anyone what they did. This exchange continues more beautifully in my life than it did in Turkey.

Apart from these professional teams of assassins, did you encounter anything negative on the street?

Little things happen. I went to Rojava. I filmed a segment with the beleaguered Kobane. I was talking about this while sitting in a pizza restaurant. The waiter acted crossly, so we got up and left. I am always careful about matters of security. I'm never comfortable enough to give up the security measures. I'm always tense, especially when there are Turkish nationals around. But nothing too perilous has happened.

There are two views. The first is that a new hand will be dealt in Turkey and that the current regime will disappear, though perhaps not too quickly, and that a new Turkey will be established. This is a view I don't consider too realistic. And then there's the view that Yavuz Baydar articulated and which we have written about extensively in which a diaspora much like the Iranian diaspora will begin to form for Turkey and that those who left, especially after 2016, will remain permanently. What do you think as it relates to your own fate?

There's a geographic space for the Turkish diaspora. This diaspora has already been around for more than a hundred years and has been constantly growing stronger, re-harmonising and connecting with different identities. But if we look at the Armenians, Greeks, Kurds, Alevis and other migrants from Anatolia, it isn't terribly powerful in society. Now a new era of intellectuals is being added to it. Is a new diaspora emerging together with them? I mean, something more is happening to the diaspora, or we can say that it is transforming into something else, yes, but nothing new is emerging.

Do you consider yourself a part of this transformation, or are you saying something will change tomorrow or the next day and you'll return to Turkey?

Yavuz Baydar and our friends like him are done with Turkey, in their own minds, and they want everyone else to be done with it too. But in fact, a twenty-two-year-old engineer who has come here doesn't think like that. He or she may think that the country will be fixed, and they can return. I mean, when did Turkey end, should it end with the AKP? It has always been bad, it has always experienced winding turns. Of course, when Turkey is rescued from this regime and there is an acceptable country with more civilised and international standards, everyone will return. Those who can stay will stay; some have created two-sided lives. But the view that nothing will come of Turkey after this late hour. So it depends where that person has ended up. Let's not do that. Turkey of course will transform and change, and it could be worse. Maybe it'll be better. And if it is better, of course we'll come and go.

Do you want to set up your children's future in Germany or in another Western country, or do you want it to be in Turkey?
This depends entirely on time. It requires more than taking a simple decision as it depends on the quality of one's network of relationships in one's country. The kids have just started school here. Should we not let them finish? We've already made them change schools once. What I'm saying is that if there was an opportunity today to return, the most serious issue would be my kids' education. Second, the work relationships I've established here. If we return to Turkey, what would we do? How would we live? We don't have anything left. Life is changing. My children are growing older, the economic situation is changing and we're all growing older. So the answer to this question isn't left to acquiescence. This is entirely based on how much time we will spend here. There are a lot of other things here. Families fall apart, people get divorced here, children are born here and marriages happen here. So almost three out of every five people naturally don't return. We can't return right now. Children can't be raised there right now. So if we look ahead from today, I'm not making any plans based on that – they can't be made. You have to consider things realistically.

Twice now you've mentioned the economic situation, how it was difficult to get by when you arrived here with nothing. I want to circle back to that a little.

I didn't come with nothing. I sold my house, I sold whatever I had.

My question relates to that. Did the state seize any of your property in Turkey, if you had any?

Nothing was seized; we sold it after we came here. This is a really expensive place, so selling everything in Turkey and exchanging that money for euros can't save your life. I have no savings. I spend my money each month. Everything is gone, I lost it. We had some things, but not after this time.

Do you believe you live in a safe country? Or do you worry that if things change tomorrow or the next day Germany will repatriate you to Turkey?

I'm in the best country in terms of police precautions, intelligence and preventing my assassination or protecting my life. Would they keep us here? Would they repatriate us? I mean, anything could happen to us at any time, of course. I know this deep inside, historically and contemporarily. But under the current circumstances, Germany's sending me or Can [Dündar] back to Turkey would mean a whole other world. And it isn't only me or Can who would be in trouble in that world. You would be in trouble too. There's another Europe.

There's another world, probably.

By the way, there's a different set of tactics they use against the Gülenists, you know, like kidnapping and such. These aren't talked about much in Turkey unfortunately, because they are done against the Gülenists. I'm talking about practices such as extra treatment against the Gülenists, extra forms of torture, revoking passports for seven degrees of their extended family. If we look at it statistically, it means the Turkish state is doing these things. Let's not look at who they are doing them to. Let's not assume that the Turkish state is standing idle. There could be new developments we can't predict, or political assassinations come election time. This isn't only related to my personal situation. I think that in the coming era, this diaspora will be subjected to new circumstances.

And I understand you think these will be more negative?
Definitely. We have already filled up our quota. From now on, half the asylum seekers are being rejected, you know. Even though a lot of people need not to be sent back, they are being sent back in a very risky way. There won't be such a welcoming situation in Europe after this. They got the intellectuals they could. Now this migration has slowed – has been slowed – a bit. Also, Turkey won't leave Europe alone in the election processes. The process ahead of us is chock full of new circumstances.

I don't fully know your life story, but as far as I can guess, this is the first time you have been this far away from the city, the country where you were born for this long, no?
Yes.

What has changed? Are there any differences in how you interpret Turkey?
In my view, I can't move an inch from where I stopped in the fight. I would have done the same if I had done it a hundred times. Rebelling against death in every historical period, during every era of repression, is the responsibility of anyone who holds a pen. We love those people in history, and being one of those people is a gift. I can't move an inch from where I have stopped. To the contrary, I'm more radical. I have greater freedom to speak the truth more directly because I'm not in Turkey.

I understand, it's more freedom than bravery. So do you interpret Turkey any differently now?

Leaving the country means looking not only at Turkey but also else-where. This, for me, was a very pleasant experience. I toured around for a year and a half with conferences. To turn around and look at Turkey from afar is important, yes. I saw again more comfortably that the things I considered to be normal while I was in Turkey are savage under universal standards. There is truly a very big difference between the standard where fascism and repression are the norm and the stan-dard where the police come and arrest you if you say something rac-ist to someone here. I can say that this led me to see the real state of Turkey. Apart from that, I'm in my work, in my strength. I am not so much a part of the German community, nor in the diaspora. I write, I draw. I've returned more to creating.

Final question: what are your short-, medium- and long-term predictions for Turkey?

First of all, the issue will be shaped through the Kurdish question. Because the Turkish state has decided to resolve the Kurdish question similarly to the Armenian question. This is a situation that many branches of the state have approved. The violent oppression of the Kurds will increase significantly in the coming period. It's already increasing. The Turkish state has a dictatorial Turkish-Islamist intention to expand, to grow the *Misak-ı Milli* (National Pact), to decimate the Kurds, as you know, not like being embarrassed or ashamed towards Europe. This is very clear. Very serious massacres, a harsh repressive regime and a regime that perhaps has henceforth been categorised differently by the rest of the world. We'll see whether this can stop us in the near future. This is the intention of the other side, I'm sure of that. Nevertheless, we're at the point where we can't sit around doing nothing. Each of us are rebelling in our own space. It's not bad, by the way, Turkey's rebellion, despite this oppression. I hope we win, otherwise the situation will be bad. What we win won't be heaven, but the alternative is quite terrible.

12

JÎNDA ZEKİOĞLU

My asylum interview lasted for six hours. At the end, the woman interviewing me said, 'I'm never supposed to do this, but I want to hug you. Because my grandmother migrated here from Seferihisar by boat a hundred years ago. My grandmother, grandfather and dozens of their relatives were dumped into the sea in Izmir.'

Jînda Zekioğlu was born in June 1987 in Istanbul. She started her journalism career on the Hürriyet *newspaper during her high school years. She studied photography at university, specialising in documentary photography. Her works for newspapers have been included in three solo and more than ten group exhibitions. She also worked for several magazines in Turkey before she worked for IMC TV. She presented the first feminist TV programme, called* Mor Bülten *('Purple Bulletin'). She also produced the* Gender of the Media *programme on Nor Radyo for two seasons. She prepared special files for ANF News Agency, and prepared interview series for Artı Gerçek and* Gazete Duvar. *She currently works for* Le Monde Diplomatique Kûrdî.

Jînda, thank you so much for sharing your story with us. What was your motivation to leave Turkey and when did that happen?
I gave birth in June 2017. I had a daughter. While pregnant, I didn't want my daughter to grow up in Turkey if she was born there. Part of this was influenced by my own personal history. I didn't want my daughter to grow up in that country not only because of the violence of the state but also because she's a girl. That's why my husband and I have always had the idea of leaving. I haven't been able to work as a journalist for a long time. Starting on 7 June 2015 we couldn't even tweet because an investigation was being opened into everything I wrote, even my retweets. So I had stopped doing journalism, and I wasn't opening my mouth. How was I maintaining my life? I was running two projects. I was a fine arts photography graduate. I was taking pictures, writing various guidebooks and I was coming and going to Europe for this. It's impossible for someone in our field working in independent media to return to the mainstream and do that job there. So I gravitated towards my husband's work, gastronomy, but a lawsuit was filed against him.

Actually more than me, it was his lawsuits that compelled us not to stay in Turkey. I reached a fork in the road where my daughter and her father would have absolutely left if I had wanted to stay in Turkey. Either my husband was going to prison and would be separated from his daughter or my husband would leave and he would be separated from us. There was no situation that would have compelled me to leave; I had my visas and my passport. When the idea of going to another country becomes a topic of conversation, what places pop into people's minds? Germany, central Europe, England. My husband's entire family already lives in England. So we thought of those places first, of course, but that passed because we wanted to change our lives completely. If a war had started, if that spring air in 2013 had lingered, we would have set up a life in the home of my husband's family in Şırnak, which is no longer there. That was what we wanted. But we understood that we wouldn't be able to do this there. I was a journalist at ANF in Şırnak between 2013 and 2014, working as a regional correspondent. I came across a story during that time, and I wanted to write that story. But I knew that if I wrote it, I wouldn't be able to live in the country.

Can you tell us more about that story?
It's actually the story of a family. This was certainly a political family, and they wanted me to write their story. It was the story of seven women. I had partially written it, but I knew that it couldn't be published. But truly – I mean, there are turning points in people's lives – I told myself that I would write this even if the cost was me having to leave the country. When lawsuits were opened against my husband and prison sentences emerged, we decided to leave. Where would we go? We had gone to the Greek islands many times before on holiday. We had friends and relationships there. Because my husband's profession was in tourism and gastronomy, it was easy for him in terms of his field of work. I, on the other hand, could do my job anywhere in the world. So we decided to migrate to the Greek island of Samos, which we already were quite familiar with.

Did you leave using your passport and getting on a ferry or did you leave by different means?
I didn't have any lawsuits against me, but Zana did, and that was reflected in the general information-gathering (Genel Bilgi Toplama, GBT) system, so he left before us. He left legally. He had visas. He was in a partnership with Osman Kavala. Zana was a close friend of Selahattin Demirtaş and had supported Selahattin Demirtaş during the presidential election as a businessman. We already know from our

history what happens to Kurdish businessmen. Zana was heading that way too. In the end, a punishment was handed down for something absurd. Zana had allegedly said 'I'm in the PKK and I'll kill you' to another business partner. There was no evidence. Lawsuits were filed against him like this with absolutely no evidence. Normally, if he were to have a fair trial, in no way would he have been punished, but the situation wasn't like that. So he was definitely going to be punished. That's why Zana went to Samos by boat from Kuşadası before the search for him appeared in the GBT. My daughter and I travelled legally from Kuşadası a week after Zana. I actually hadn't considered myself a political refugee or an asylum seeker. We went to Samos. My husband had rented a hotel at the time and had started working. He hadn't applied for asylum either. We were thinking that there was a chance the situation would resolve itself, and why should we force ourselves into a place where we can't return to Turkey? We were hoping that it would get better. But it didn't. Raids occurred after we left. We had a home that we left behind in Istanbul, in Kurtuluş. They raided it. They searched through all of our things. They had already planned several raids at our home before. They don't open investigations, but they constantly raid our home. They constantly call my family.

Do the raids continue even though you are abroad now?
Yes. The reason they didn't open an investigation is because if they did, I would see this in the system, so they don't want to do it like that. They want me to go and then they can grab me directly from the airport or from customs. They want to stick me in a cage without scaring me off. That's why they aren't opening an investigation, but they are searching for me. This is something caused by the war on terror. That's why we applied for asylum one month later in Greece, Zara first and then my daughter and I. There are different classes of asylum in Greece. For example, you have meetings based on whether you want to go to a another European country. But we wanted to apply directly to Greece, because we didn't want to go elsewhere in Europe. We liked

this climate, we were living on an island, and this was the best for our daughter. We were able to create a life for ourselves here earning even less money than in Turkey. Because we could form a team – animals, this and that – and we set up a life like this.

There are policies in Turkey such as where people like yourself who are members of groups that after 2013 have continuously challenged, have struggled to challenge or are accused of challenging the current regime are having their property in Turkey seized. Was any of your property in Turkey seized?
We really had to plan all of this, and we did transfer the property holdings that belonged to Zana to his mother. His mother was in Turkey. We were honestly saved by doing that. But if we hadn't done something like this, our property probably would have been seized.

Did you do this transfer process before or after you left for Samos?
Before, but it was two months beforehand because we had understood what was going to happen. Even if there hadn't been a search for Zana and an investigation for me, we knew which direction this road was taking us. Osman Kavala's imprisonment, Selahattin Demirtaş's situation, the situation of dozens of our friends gave us the feeling that we had to leave the country and take certain precautions. Because we didn't want to make the same mistakes that our fathers and mothers had made. Zana is a man who has worked since he was eleven years old. I had worked too. We gained and sold some things. Yes, the state was going to take these from us. But because we had experienced this before and knew how the Turkish state could act, we didn't want to make this mistake, and we took that precaution two months beforehand and transferred them to his mother.

Many people are migrating to Germany, the Netherlands, France, Sweden, the United Kingdom, more exceptionally to the United States and Canada and recently even to Japan. Greece

is being used in two ways. The first is as a place to which very exceptional people such as yourself are migrating. The second – and we know this from EU data – is as a place where numerous Gülenists have requested asylum. There is a new generation of Turkish migrants, refugees and asylum seekers in Greece. What is your approach to Greece? Are you safe in your home?

This is actually related both to understanding what kind of country Greece is and to what you said. We had idealised this country a lot when we first arrived. What had we idealised it with? We had idealised it with its nature, and its pastoral beauty. These are permanent. I'm truly amazed at the nature here. We saw a truly friendly, welcoming and understanding demeanour from the Greeks. The island where we live is a place where the Greek Communist Party is influential. And Samos has a unique history; it's an island that was under Ottoman patronage. There were no mosques. There is a very intimate, affectionate, internationalist atmosphere. For example, Nâzım Hikmet's poems are read at opening ceremonies for new buildings. The people here really love Nâzım Hikmet, Can Yücel and Zülfü Livaneli. When they listened, became familiar with who we were or when they heard our names, they understood that we weren't typical, classical Turks. Nowadays there's something on social media where you can see who someone is from their social media. They saw from my social media that I was previously a speaker and a journalist. So I saw positive discrimination from being Kurdish here. But if we had been typical Turks, we really wouldn't have encountered a negative reaction, because I have many Turkish friends here. But there is a common issue against which Kurds and Greeks fight: the Turkish state. And this creates a sort of partnership here between us.

But over time, this loses importance. I mean if you're a migrant, you're a migrant. Your class, your position and your gender are unimportant. If you're a migrant, you're a migrant. Because you're exposed to bureaucracy here from a place that they aren't exposed to. You have no identity. Everything began to fall apart and disappear after asylum.

My asylum interview lasted for six hours. At the end of those six hours, the woman who was conducting my interview said, 'I'm never supposed to do this, but I want to hug you. Because my grandmother migrated here from Seferihisar by boat a hundred years ago. My grandmother, grandfather and dozens of their relatives were dumped into the sea in Izmir.' There are Greeks on this island who migrated from Anatolia in the late 1800s, early 1900s.

It's one of the closest islands, as far as I know.
It is the closest island. Only 700 metres separate Kuşadası and Samos. It has been the most used route since the 1980s. Many people have gone to Europe via Samos since the 1980s. I understood that we shared something in that interview. I trusted this and still do. When our friendship with a Greek progresses, they begin to tell you all of a sudden the story of their grandfather or grandmother. And then they say, 'Gosh, forget that now, everything's in the past.' Ultimately, I come from a Muslim family. No matter how atheist I am, I'm a Muslim here, culturally, because I come from Turkey. So the distinction here is not between Turks and Kurds but between Muslims and Christians. So regardless, even if a Muslim had impaled their grandfather on a sword, they can stop and say, 'Forget it, that's our grandfathers' business.' I realised that I couldn't leave it alone. I realised I couldn't leave behind what they already had. When I went on holiday here seven years ago, I saw dozens of people dancing to songs together at a Virgin Mary festival at a village tavern, and although I had no idea what would happen in the future, I remember that my eyes welled up with tears.

Europe is now saturated with migrants leaving Turkey. Acceptance rates have now dropped to less than half of the levels seen in 2017 and 2018. In fact, only one in ten applicants are accepted now. There are a few reasons for this, the first of them being that the population has really filled up. So do you trust

the Greek government? I mean, do you trust that the Greek
government won't repatriate you if Turkey asks that you be
sent back tomorrow or the next day?

No, I will never trust it. I don't trust any state in that sense, because
we have seen many examples of this. We still see them. Our first asylum interview was held on 25 February three years ago. At the time,
they had given a date to decide on our application three years in the
future, meaning they said it would be decided in three years whether
to send us back. The procedure advances a bit like this: even if they
say they'll send us back, you can appeal, and if by that time you finish out that three-year period in Greece, Greece can no longer return
you. After five years, you have the right to apply for citizenship. This
is a procedure they won't obstruct. The fifteenth of April marked
three years that I had spent in the country. But nevertheless, there
are two states here. What if they say 'We're sending you to Iraqi
Kurdistan, not Turkey'? I have no connection with Iraqi Kurdistan.
I'm not someone who belongs to Turkey, I don't consider myself as
having belonged there. But of course, this is ultimately a relationship
between two states. The fact that the relationship is poor today does
not provide me with trust in the Greek state. I mean, I won't trust
any state. So I don't trust this one, of course. Of course, they could
send us back – I mean, I wouldn't be surprised.

**You mentioned that there were a few Turkish nationals in
Samos. How is your relationship with the new arrivals? There
were people who had arrived previously – there were Kurds.
As far as I know there are a few Turkish nationals there who
aren't Kurdish. How are the relationships between earlier and
newer arrivals? Also, how are the relationships between different groups – Kurds, Alevis, Gülenists?**

There have been quite a few people coming and going from this island
since it's a reception island, but nobody before us had planned on
settling here. There's Sevan Nişanyan, who is in the same situation as

us, but we don't have a relationship. There have also been quite a few Kurds who have come and gone. We tried to help them in the asylum process, for example on how to get to Athens and with whatever else they needed since we were the first ones here. I just moved to another town on the island. This is a place occupied entirely by urban locals. It's a place where more upper-class, wealthier people live. There isn't anyone from Turkey here apart from one person. We met her later. Her name is Hilal. She's a Turk from Burdur. A young woman and a graduate of Boğaziçi University. She married a Greek here. They introduced us. At first when I was about to meet a Turk, I would think, 'I'm Jînda, this is my husband Zana, would they like us? Would they see us as terrorists?' But I haven't cared much; if that's how they see us then so be it. Because we're at a point of independence now, we're on a level playing field. If someone had told me that I would see the greatest degree of solidarity in my life from someone from Burdur, I never would have believed them as a Kurd. But she's become my sister. That state of being in a different home . . . because she's not next to your safe zone, or your mother. We overcame such hardship together and now I have a sister for the rest of my life. I really believe that women have a shared language. Who are my closest friends? There's Hilal from Burdur, Natalie from Argentina. This is something that reveals the ineptitude of people. Someone asked, for example, 'Have you met Hilal?' I said, 'We haven't met yet, but I would really like to.' 'But she's a Turk, and you're a Kurd. You won't get along,' they said. 'Maybe, we'll see,' I said. I later met Hilal. I think the fact that she had studied at Boğaziçi University had a significant impact, because she's a well-read woman, an academic, teaches classes here out in the world, she's very young – younger than me – and married to a Greek. Sometimes I want to complain about something related to Greece, for example, but I remember that she's married to a Greek. So I don't think I can complain about this here. But later when I can't stand it anymore and do complain, she complains even more than me. Yeah, that shared discontent is something that really keeps people together.

Turkey has practised extraterritorial authoritarianism for a long time, doing things such as not allowing certain processes to be conducted at consulates, blacklisting certain individuals and so forth. Have you experienced anything like this? Is the Turkish state still after you?

This island is very close to Turkey, so the Greek state told us not to stay here and to go to Athens, Thessaloniki or somewhere further away. I can say that we have lost dozens of agents in the past three years.

How?

You tend to come across a lot of police if you're a refugee. If you don't make it known there that you're a Turkish national, you can hear a [Greek] civilian police officer inside or just outside the door speaking Turkish. You see that a lot of people who have come here as if on holiday and run into you are actually agents. This network of agents is truly an intangible thing. But you understand after a while why so many people have got close to you. I'm already a very distant individual during these encounters. I don't really prolong conversation, I'll cut it off right away. We learned Greek during this time. We know Turkish. We know English. Zana knows Spanish. As such, [the Greek police] began to seek us out when he arrived to help the Gülenists seek asylum. Then you become friends because you drink with the police officers in the same tavern at night, you swim in the sea with their wives, your children play together, and you're friends. For someone who won't be friends with a police officer in Turkey, the police are your closest friends in Greece. It's truly bizarre for us. Of course, we immediately understand when we go to the police station whether someone is a Gülenist.

How does it feel as a Kurd to translate for the Gülenists?

I'm more professional on this issue as a journalist, but Zana isn't, to be honest. One Gülenist arrived on his father's yacht. They called Zana to conduct an interview and understand how he arrived. The goal here is actually to attain information about human trafficking. They were forced to get Zana out of there, because the man was terrified because he thought Zana was a civilian police officer from Turkey. Yeah, I mean you have a reaction, but I can approach this more professionally than Zana.

Do you view Turkey any differently now that you are far away? Do you believe it has changed much?
It's so bizarre that just a week ago no party closure lawsuit had been filed against the HDP, and Turkey had not left the Istanbul Convention. So a great deal of terrible things happen rather quickly in Turkey. That's why I never think it's in the same place. Even the country I left was a better country. But when I look at the overall picture, I say, 'Turkey is Turkey.' Turkey is bad, I mean. So it's never in the same place. Okay, so Kurds don't defecate in a ditch or dump it in a well anymore, but there are new age malfeasances that exist today. That's why I think it's getting worse.

Would you return one day, or do you ever think about returning?
Of course. Two days ago, my father had surgery on his aortic valve. My father suffered an aortic aneurysm a year ago. My brother had a son. My sister had a son, and I wasn't there for any of it. I thought there was a possibility that my father wouldn't leave the operating room. I thought, when would I see my father's grave if I lost him now? So I certainly want to go. I was born and raised in Istanbul. I occasionally feel like I belong to a place, and the place that I again feel like I belong is Istanbul. The other day, I asked a friend of mine who has been in Europe for twenty-five years, 'Does anyone know Istanbul better than me?' I mean, it's quite an assertion, I know, but I am truly that much of an Istanbulite. I feel like I belong to each of Istanbul's streets, each of its neighbourhoods. By the way, I don't find Istanbul beautiful at all, I don't love Istanbul, I just feel like I belong there. So I certainly want to walk again on the streets where I experienced all my pain and

all my happiness in the place where I belong. I want my daughter to walk there too.

But of course, this probably isn't a complete return?

No, I don't think I could entirely move again. I won't completely relocate to Turkey, no, it's not possible. Because I've mentally become very detached. Greek is a very difficult language. The fastest learners pick it up in about three or four years. I'm learning Greek, and I've been here for three years. Anyway, I'm living with a new language. Whichever language you speak, it belongs to you a little bit. Anyway, I am Greek. By the way, I want to add one more important thing. I have been a journalist since I was fifteen years old. I'm thirty-four, so I've been a journalist for many years. I have worked in many places, organisations from *Hürriyet* to İMC TV. I have worked in every field of journalism: photography, newspapers, magazines and television. In fifteen years, I couldn't get a single piece of paper in Turkey saying that I was a journalist. Forget a press pass, because it isn't possible for us to get a document like that. A few months ago, I applied to the Greek Ministry of Foreign Affairs to be a foreign correspondent. They sent my press pass twenty days later. And I'm a refugee without residence. If I were to stay in Turkey for another fifteen years, I still wouldn't be a journalist, but I would be put on trial for journalism. But I find Greece's respect and contribution in this regard to be very valuable. This tells me that it's definitely good that I migrated. It's good that I migrated because I was able to have my book published. Yes, there is profit to be had from migrating. I'm alive, I'm free, I can breathe, I can write what I want, and I can do my job.

13

MELTEM ARIKAN

Turkey is being divided. And saying, 'Let's be open, yes, let's share freely' and telling similar lies. On the contrary, everyone becomes engrossed in their own truths and wants others to live according to those truths. As long as we look around like this, I don't think anything will change.

Meltem Arıkan is a Turkish-Welsh author who has dedicated twenty-five years to writing against the patriarchal system and to fighting for freedom of speech and expression. She is known for her sharp critiques of society and fearless and outspoken voice in her novels, plays, poems and articles. Arıkan's first short stories and essays were published between 1992 to 1995 in various literary journals. Her first novel was published in 1999. Unfortunately, her fourth novel, Yeter Tenimi Acıtmayın *('Stop Hurting My Flesh') was banned in early 2004 by the*

Committee to Protect Minors from Obscene Publications. However, the ban was lifted after an appeal and Arıkan was awarded the Freedom of Thought and Speech Award 2004 by the Turkish Publishers' Association. Arıkan has written eleven books including nine novels and five plays. She wrote the libretto for the short opera Die Verführung Europas, *which was staged as part of Theatre Freiburg's large-scale multidisciplinary project Eurotopia in 2017. She has received several awards and was short-listed for the Freedom of Expression Award in 2014 by the Index on Censorship for her play* Mi Minör, *which the Turkish authorities claimed was a rehearsal for the 2013 Gezi Park demonstrations. The government's subsequent hate campaign, fuelled by state-sponsored media, forced her to leave Turkey for Wales. In 2019, a Turkish court accepted the Gezi indictment, seeking life sentences for sixteen people, including Arıkan. She was diagnosed with autism/Asperger's at the age of fifty-two as an exile in Wales. This diagnosis was liberating for her and many of the questions she had about herself were answered. She realises that her condition makes it harder for her to do many things that come naturally to other people, but it is important to be aware that Asperger's gives her many magical perceptions that many neurotypicals lack. She decided to come out because there is still not enough autism spectrum awareness even today.*

Thank you so much for your time, Ms Arıkan. It is a great pleasure to meet you. We are looking forward to hearing your story. When and why did you leave Turkey? How did you make this decision?

I actually didn't make that decision. It wasn't something that I planned. I could say that I was forced to leave. Briefly, I wrote an absurd play in Turkey called *Mi Minör*, but my life later became more absurd than the play. This was actually the first play in the world that featured social media, that people could watch from Ustream like Occupy Wall Street, that brought together the digital world and analogue world. They asked me, 'Why are you doing this?' while I was doing the play.

I replied, 'I'm doing this for the young.' I have no hope for Turkey. Nothing will happen in Turkey. Who could care about this place? I mean, we're having fun with young people. Adults already wouldn't understand this play. For many people, it will be 'Hey, what's this?' And I truly wrote it for the young because I had long lost hope for Turkey, to be honest. The play was exactly as I said it was. The young went crazy. There was a group coming to every showing. They began to do the play with us. How? They began to come to the play prepared. The play comprises various other plays. But at the same time, various problems emerged at the venues where we staged this play. 'What's happened?' I thought. But we understood after a while that we were being given a polite warning: 'Stop, end the play.' And we said okay, because we were getting reactions from the audience, like 'Man, what have you done? Are you crazy? How brave is this!' but I had never thought about it like that, to be honest. In my mind, it was an absurd play. Anyway, we stopped the play. Gezi started while we were debating whether to do a tour. But after Gezi started, those coming to the play began to send messages: 'Are you Nostradamus?' How? It was a dream come true'; 'We've already experienced this'; 'We already knew what we would do'; and '*Mi Minör* is coming true'. Some things I wrote in my play began to come true. In fact, some actor friends in the play joked around, saying, 'For the love of God, do you work for MİT, where did you come from? How does this happen?' But it was really small things like that, and we laughed and moved on. But when Gezi started, they said, 'What if we staged *Mi Minör* here?' We discussed whether we could do it, but no, it was too risky, and how we would protect the actors? For the first time then, I participated in a protest because it really related to nature. Until Gezi Park started, I had no hope for Turkey. Hope emerged for the first time when Gezi started, a sort of 'I wonder . . .' One night a few days after Gezi, Osman Coşkunoğlu, who was a CHP MP, sent me a message at three o'clock, saying, 'Did you see the newspaper?' And as I said, 'Ah, what newspaper? It's three o'clock in the morning, what's happening?' I looked and saw a *Yeni Akit* headline that said, 'Coincidence?' And when I looked from there, yes, what a coincidence. There are a lot of similarities in the play, but I had written the play a while ago. Tayyip's clothes, for example, are very similar. But how could I control that? How could I be guilty here? I had made the costumes for the play, I had chosen them. And it was like a joke. The woman in red, there was a woman in red in our play. But how could I be responsible for these? Anyway, they reported this with the headline 'Coincidence?' I didn't take it very seriously at first, but Melih Gökçek assumed this duty and did a programme for four or five hours every Friday on *Mi Minör*. This gradually began to move to other channels. A slew of threats made on social media began targeting at this point. We hadn't got married at that point, but my late husband was the former owner of the Çağdaş Stage in Ankara. He had been arrested during the 12 September era. He saw everything very differently to us. He was twenty years older than me. He made us prepare a bag. In fact, he said, 'Get some books out of the house.' But they were novels and such. 'What are you saying?' I said. I was writing a novel at the time, *Erospa*. In the novel *Erospa*, God was a teenage hacker. He made me delete my novel. It was the most difficult, most painful moment in my life. I deleted it, because 'you can't have something like this on your computer', he said. I thought to myself, 'He's exaggerating.' In my view, he was exaggerating everything. But his fears were warranted. The threats were initially weak, but death threats ensued. Then threats of rape were made against us. At that time, Melih Gökçek said, 'Now, I will tell you who is the brains of this operation.' Because at the time it was going through his mind because *Mi Minör*, Mehmet Ali [Alabora] were a bit more famous. And he was constantly saying things like 'You will learn'. We're saying, 'Oh my God, who is the brains of the operation?' Anyway, we were in sitting in front of the television one day, all irritated and so forth, and to our surprise, the brains of the operation was me: 'Here you go! The brains of the operation.' They found a speech I had given on television when the

AKP first came to power. And I'm saying in the speech, 'I don't agree to be a servant as a woman.' Yes, I said it, but they changed it. 'Look, this woman is against religion!' 'Look, this woman doesn't agree to be a vassal!' 'Look, she's already defending incest!' But the most critical thing here was that they portrayed me as an enemy of religion.

At the time, my husband said, 'Meltem, this is very dangerous. They have placed a target on your head, and they're saying "Kill her",' because when someone in this country is targeted, they're killed. We weren't leaving home, people coming to visit began to be uneasy, because things like 'enemy of the nation' began to appear in the neighbourhood where we were living. I needed to go to the bank one day. The bank was really close to home. We went in our friends' car. When we left, 'You're dead' was written on the car. The bank had security cameras. Of course, we went to the police, but the police couldn't find anything. My husband said, 'Start packing a bag, if you want.' 'It's a joke probably,' I said. 'I'm quite serious, pack a bag,' he said. Why? 'You may have to leave the country.' But before that period, I was always in love with Wales. My son wanted to study in Wales. We registered him at a university. Ege was going to go to Wales. At first there was a plan: I'll go and take a look first, maybe I'll rent a home, stay in Wales for a few months. He said, 'Look, it's already clear for Ege. You go and look for a home there. You may have to go.' Melih Gökçek then uploaded this 'enemy of religion' thing to YouTube. Do you know how it was? They were sharing it to YouTube maybe twenty or thirty times a day. They were constantly showing it on television. One Sunday, we were sitting at home. The weather was beautiful, and we were in the garden. Someone said to me, 'Meltem, would you take a look at Twitter?' I opened Twitter, and Melih Gökçek's son had set up a new account and for five hours selected sentences from my books. Five hours! 'See for yourselves, this faithless, ungodly [woman], know your worth.' Things like that. When I saw that my husband said, 'Yes, you're leaving. You're leaving the country right away, tonight.' 'How?' I said. 'You're getting your bag now and going,' he said. And like in

World War II, I got my bag. 'Do not use your credit card. When you get there, do not use your Turkish mobile. Nobody will know where you are,' he said. I told him directly, 'I'm going to Wales.' 'Okay, find a hotel there,' he said. 'Let's look, but I don't think you'll be able to return in the short term.' And I got my bag, in a state of shock, a sort of disbelief, and that night I left the country with a single bag. That was how I left. I went back every once in a while, but that's it.

Are you able to return to Turkey right now, or is there a case against you?

How should I return? I'm one of the sixteen people faced with a life sentence. I'm being tried right now with the same status as Abdullah Öcalan. It's like this: I never returned to the country, but the man I lived with was in Turkey. He was a businessman. He couldn't move here. And so we made a decision; he said, 'Meltem, everything is dangerous, let's get married, whatever happens. After that I'll come to the UK, but this is a process. I can't just close my business tomorrow and come. Let's get married.' We were married in April, and we learned in May that he had brain cancer. I think this part of my life was a bit more difficult. When he learned this, my first reaction of course was 'I'm coming to Turkey'. Everyone said 'Are you crazy?' 'No,' I said. 'I'm going to Turkey. To hell with it, whatever happens I'm going to Turkey.' And I went to Turkey. I stayed in Turkey during his surgery. But my lawyer in Wales said, 'You have to come here every two months. You're taking a huge risk.' I applied through the Ankara Agreement. 'You can't stay there, Meltem,' they said. People in Turkey were telling me, 'Meltem, you're at risk here. What you're doing is very stupid.' Anyway, I came and went like this, sometimes bringing him along. The doctors gave him two months to live, but he lived much longer than that. But he gradually got worse. I was coming and going from Turkey. The coup happened at the time. I was in Turkey during the coup. But my lawyer in Wales said, 'Come here. It isn't clear what will happen to you there.' My husband had already begun not to recognise me. They were using violence at the time. That was a horrible nightmare. I laid him down somewhere to rest. And his family said, 'Okay, we're here.' And I came here for a month. I was later going to return to Turkey. But unfortunately, I couldn't go back to Turkey. I couldn't go to his funeral.

It emerged too that my husband had told me a number of lies while I was in Turkey. It came to light that he had spent all my savings. That came as another shock to me, and I was forced into a situation in which I was in another country with no money, no security. That was a little difficult. I was in a position that could have driven me crazy. I really considered committing suicide. If I didn't have my son, I probably would have committed suicide. It couldn't be said that I was someone at peace with life. Anyway, I started to walk then. And I walked. I walked throughout all of Wales. I walked for six hours a day along the hilltops. Those walks really helped me. They helped me create a new connection with life. I started to pull myself together. I had already staged two plays in Wales. Those took up a lot of my time, and they were good for me. So I began to earn more money. I was living in Cardiff at the time, but city life didn't really suit me. I went to the doctor for menopause during that time and left with an autism diagnosis. Receiving that diagnosis changed my entire life and led me to rediscover myself from a whole new perspective. Two fellowships opened up for me. You'll live for six months in a cottage in a place in the middle of Wales. No internet, no heating. I went crazy the moment I saw it and immediately applied. And I won. That caused the second biggest change in my life. Being far removed from everything really changed everything for me. I told myself at the time that I had to set up a new life here. You can't live in this country writing like that. In Turkey, I'm Meltem Arıkan, but in the UK, there's nobody called Meltem Arıkan. Yes, the Welsh know me from my plays, but writing an English novel was difficult for me at the time. I'm still not sure, but I began to trust myself more. I asked myself what I should do. So I started a course at the time. I finished twenty-eight different courses. Being autistic is useful in that way. And as a result, I earned the title of complementary health practitioner in the country. I can work in psychological counselling, coaching. And I also discovered a method called groove dance. It was incredibly helpful for me. It was so helpful that I told myself it would be best if I was trained in it. Nobody does it in Turkey. Nobody teaches it in Turkish. There are some in England but none in Wales. I told myself I'll start doing it in Wales and in Turkey. It was the hardest course I have ever taken. I mean, I finished the counselling course and I didn't really struggle with it. Groove was very difficult. Anyway, I did that, and I'm now gradually starting a new business. But I understood in the meantime that, one, I'm not a city person, and two, I'm not a diaspora person. The Turkish community, Kurdish community are too much for me. The artificial relationships there are a lot for me. I don't find it very safe or healthy. I don't think there's any difference between those people and Tayyip. In whatever way you submit to Tayyip's truths, you become one of them, and the diasporas here are unfortunately the same. If you believe in those truths, they accept you. If you don't believe their truths, they judge you as the same sort of religious person. So I have no relationships with anyone as much as possible. I cut off my relationships with everyone. I moved here in January. I haven't met anyone here because of Covid. I only have a few female friends who are sugar farmers I met in the process. I met a few of their friends. But the state's autism support in mid-Wales is very limited. Since I enrolled in a number of educational courses, I have volunteered for a year at an organisation. That's really good for me. And I live in mid-Wales in my own cottage.

Do you want to return to Turkey?
When I first came to Wales fifteen years ago, I felt for the first time in my life that I belonged to a place. I had never felt like I belonged when I was in Turkey. But for some reason, I have a strange connection to this place, and I'll never forget the day when I stepped off the first train: 'I'm home.' I can lie out in the park, I feel so peaceful and

happy. No, I don't want to return to Turkey at all. But . . . What kind of but? You never know what life will show you. However much I've boasted until now, I've had to swallow my words. So I won't make any grand statements about that. But, for example, I have kept my health insurance going there. Why? Because I don't know what I'll feel when I grow older. You know how health works here. So I'll want to come and go. I will want to go and visit my loved ones. There are some places I want to see, so I'll want to go for that. But the place I want to die isn't Turkey. This is where I want to die. This is where I want to live. But I want to come and go every once in a while. But I never want to return to Turkey. I mean, I won't boast, but it's not in any of my plans right now. I don't feel like I belong to Turkey. I never felt like that, and I don't feel like that now. I feel more like I belong here. I'm happier here. I consider myself closer to the people here. That's my type. Nobody here calls me a Turk.

Is there anything you miss a lot about Turkey?
What I had missed most was *kokoreç*. But then someone discovered it and brought *kokoreç* here. And I couldn't believe it when I saw it. There were two things that I missed a lot: *kokoreç* and *midye dolma*. Now there's someone in London who makes *midye dolma*. They don't send it here, but my son will bring me some when he goes to London. I've missed these two things. If you're asking if I missed a place, I really love the Kaz Mountains in Turkey. But I don't have any sort of longing. Nothing like 'Ah, Turkey . . .'

What kind of Turkey did you leave behind when you came here?
The Turkey I left was a more normal Turkey. When I say normal, of course, everything was regressive. I can give you one example about the Turkey I returned to two or two and a half years later. I have always been a very stubborn person. So I always wore what I wanted. For the first time in my life – right before the coup – I wore a very small dress one day when I went to Turkey and thought, 'Oh, I really

won't be able to work together with anyone,' and took the dress off. I later thought, 'I really did this. Wow!' I had gone to Dubai and Abu Dhabi for work once. When I went to Istanbul and once to Ankara when Aydın was sick, I thought, 'Oh, this is Dubai.' I mean, I had left Ankara. But now it's pretty much become Dubai. I went to a shopping centre one day in Istanbul. I didn't know at the time that I was autistic. I got a few things. And then I got stuck. I couldn't find the exit. I began to cry. I called a friend. He's an architect. 'I'm in Syria,' I told him. 'Meltem, what are you saying?' he said. 'This is Syria.' 'Meltem, where are you?' 'I don't know, I'm at a shopping mall, and this is Syria.' I went to Syria. I really felt that I was in Syria. And my brain seized up. Crowds and such really affect me. My friend found a map of the shopping centre and sent it to me. I couldn't compose myself for a while after I left. That's why I don't remember its name, because that shopping centre, for me, is Syria. I saw that people had changed. People's essence had changed. That's why it was like a nightmare. I won't want to go to Istanbul if I go to Turkey. I won't want to go to Ankara either. I would like to see a few exotic places I love. I think I want to go to places where tourists go, like a tourist. It was awful. It's changed a lot, regressed and become jaded. I found Turkey to be very common, unfortunately.

Do you feel like you're in exile, or do you feel like you've been reborn?

I actually don't feel like I'm in exile. I feel like I'm at home. So in a sense, I'm actually thankful to Melih Gökçek. No, I don't feel like I'm in exile here. The reality of exile really hits you in moments when you understand that your pension won't mean anything here and that you're in exile. While enrolled in groove training, for instance, everything is in English, and you can't use terms used in dance in your normal speaking language. That's why this, for me, means memorising everything again. Memorise this, memorise the dance figures, memorise where the music changes – it wasn't very easy.

That's when you understand that you're in exile. Or when I first started doing groove dance, for example, my first preference was to do it with Turks. Because you don't forget the words in Turkish. Writing in Turkish, of course, is very easy for me. I only feel like that in those situations.

You've received support from various art groups since you arrived, as far as I gather. You were called to speak, received fellowships, and there was interest in your theatrical plays. I see you as satisfied with your life here. Is that the case?

I suppose I'm happier with my life here. When I cut off my relationships with everyone, and when Turkey and the Meltem who is connected to Turkey – Meltem the writer – died, we all became much more comfortable. And perhaps a woman more at peace with herself, who is freer and cares less about other people, is defining herself right now. In that sense, yes, I have been happier in the past year, but I approached the edge of suicide twice and received serious therapy for that. I had mental health crisis meetings. Coming here wasn't that easy. I can say that I returned from the edge of suicide twice.

Thank you for sharing this with me. I hope you've left those thoughts behind.

I have left those thoughts far behind. I had already done those courses and already re-created myself to put those thoughts behind me. I think this should be widely known. I'm sharing this with you openly because I trust you. Because yes, people sometimes think from the outside that everything is easy. There's also something where people have types. Some people know how to arouse sympathy for their own pain. Or become great victims. I don't know how to do this. Even during times when I was a victim, I didn't know how to play that game. That's why, I think, it's not obvious from the outside. So I think being alone and on my own and not doing things with others anymore was really helpful in finding myself.

Many people leaving the country have the inclination to remove themselves from the Turkish diaspora. What do you think the reason is for this? Have we separated ourselves from one another?
I'll try to explain it more clearly. When I first came here, I had no interest in these Turkish groups. I warm up very quickly to people, but not to everyone. I don't know how to play that game. I'll say it suddenly, I'll say I like you or I don't like you. I can't really succeed at those social norms, those games. That's why I maintained a distance, but during these games that we play, you become intertwined with the Turkish and Kurdish community, out of necessity. And I said to myself, 'Be open, try to understand. You're quite annoying, Meltem.' But my experience there is exactly as I said it is. I don't think they are any different to Tayyip. However Tayyip hangs two or three people up on a lie, they do the same. I don't see any differences, not in the slightest. And I say this through things I've experienced. They are incredibly closed off. They are incredibly narrow-minded. You're either one of them or you're not. If you support human rights, things like 'let's love people' and so forth, if you are a part of their truths and the values they aggrandise, it's valid. If not, they can toss you away very quickly. I think this is a very cruel and arrogant position.

Do you think this is a result of polarisation in Turkey or something that came about from being here?
It's a consequence of the polarisation in Turkey. I was a woman in Turkey who was dependent, who couldn't test my own limits. But there were people who would join my conversations. I would speak with them, but my prejudice was excessive. Because I was fighting over this with everyone from where I stood; I was telling people who defended the headscarf that if a person wants to be a slave, let them be a slave. I was a very rigid woman. I wouldn't even say hello to anyone who was connected to Fethullah. Throughout this process of change, and especially when I saw the attitudes of these people in the diaspora, I said, 'What am I doing? What is it to me? Am I going to decide

whether someone who's tied down is a slave?' I understood that these were very big words. And I was no different from those arrogant people I just criticised. I was an incredibly prejudiced, pedantic and rigid woman. There were times in the diaspora when I said, 'Don't you dare meet with them.' Someone wanted to interview me, and I did the interview. I later received a reaction from the diaspora where they said, 'How could you do an interview with them!' Why? 'They're Gülenists!' But I knew [the interviewer was] a Gülenist. But they said, 'They're interviewing you, because they want to vindicate themselves through you.' Through me how? I don't know or understand these games. They're very big for me. It's not the clothes I can wear. I can't comprehend them. Maybe they're more intelligent. I've grown very tired of this. Don't do an interview with them, be careful about who you do interviews with. What are we becoming? And who is being vindicated through whom? Vindicated for whom? My world is much more simple, so I decided to live in my simple world. At that time, *Gazete Davul* contacted me and asked if I would write an article. I told them I would. The owner of *Gazete Davul* is a covered woman who had to flee because of the Fethullah Gülen case. Right now, for example, I have a close friend called Deniz with whom I don't have any problems. What's it to me! I've grown very tired. They're a Gülenist, they're a member of I don't know what organisation, if you support them . . . And I understand how that clear divisiveness in Turkey came to be. We're all just as cavalier! We're all just as arrogant! We all say such grandiose things but inside are actually creatures who are just as pathetic! And those grandiose words protect us. I myself was like that, and I say this quite naturally. I think now that you can't change people with politics like that. You can't change the system with politics. People can change only when they themselves want to change, and the system changes or doesn't change as people change. I had a lofty desire to volunteer to help people like this before. I believed that I could help. Life has taught me that you can't help anyone, that people only change if they want to change. That's why sentences like

'I am training people for this and that' or 'this organisation trains the youth' do not make sense. I think this is arrogant and masturbatory. That's why this seems like a lot to me. Turkey is being divided. And saying 'Let's be open, yes, let's share freely' and so forth are lies. On the contrary, everyone becomes engrossed in their own truths and wants others to live according to those truths. As long as we look around like this, I don't think anything will change.

If dissidents living abroad can't talk among themselves and if there will be a period of restoration in Turkey, how will the opposition, which is unable to speak among itself, be able to speak with the other side and build something in the new Turkey?
It won't happen; between Kurds and Turks, peace won't happen. Do you know why it won't happen? Because I discovered that all these barriers are actually things that we project externally due to various problems within ourselves. Nothing actually relates to them. Everything relates to us. Nobody is actually taking responsibility. I love Atatürk, I think he really was a great man. But Atatürk is dead. There's no need for me to protect him. He did what he did and left. He did the right thing and the wrong thing, but what use is there in discussing this? I mean, he understood it, she misunderstood it, I understood correctly, you understood it incorrectly. I wonder in life what we both understand the same: should we agree on Atatürk, or on the headscarf or on religion? Let's watch this movie together; you'll understand one thing and I'll understand another. I'm writing a book, I'm delivering a book, and people later say 'You explained this in the book'. I then say 'That's what I explained?' I mean, I never explained anything like that in the book. When we are more honest with ourselves, maybe about our fears, maybe about our helplessness, then maybe we'll understand that there's no such thing as the other. But we need the other so that we can be satisfied with our own helplessness.

With the development of technology, migrants can feel like they still live in the same country even if they are far away, and authoritarian states won't let go of them even if they have left the country and are in exile. Similarly, people in the diaspora, even if not given an official duty, don't let the people whom they call 'enemies of the state' or 'traitors' breathe, even when outside the country. You received a lot of threats in Turkey. So have you encountered practices like this in the UK? Do you feel entirely safe here?

I feel completely safe here in Wales, because I am the only foreigner in the village where I live. There are very few Turks around. And it's because I live far away that I don't feel something like that. But when I came here, I experienced something where I created a brand called Witchmark when I thought about what kind of work I should do. I make very delicious food. I said to myself, 'They don't know food; it would be best if I were to teach them about food.' One day, a reader from Turkey said, 'I'm going to call the Cardiff police.' 'What's going on?' I said. 'Would you look at Twitter?' they said. And moreover, the person who started this was a journalist from Turkey. And they said, 'Look, the woman behind Gezi revealed herself and is calling herself a witch. Of course, she wasn't saying she was a witch in Turkey. But she revealed herself there.' Another tweet was shared on that, saying, 'I know where you live. I'll tell you, you live in Cardiff.' Another tweet said, 'She feels safe because she's in the UK. Don't feel safe, we'll show you what the end is like for witches.' And my reader actually called the Cardiff police. When this happened, I asked someone whom I knew from Cardiff what I should do. 'You can go to the police,' they said. But the police already knew about my situation. That's why I didn't do anything. Then it emerged that the person who wrote this was related [niece/nephew, unspecified gender] to someone who knew us. I haven't experienced much apart from that, because I'm not out in the open. I mean, because I don't head out and make big speeches about Turkish or Kurdish issues, I may not be attracting much attention.

Some people want to take advantage of exile and speak out more, and they do.

Yes, but I really don't want to do this, and I think it's very tiresome.

You said that your husband had suffered similar pressures back in the 1980s. There was a generation that had left the country at the time. We represent a new generation of migrants. If you know anyone from that era, what do you think are the differences between you?

I know people from that time, of course. I see that generation as very romantic. I mean, they were believers. I think they really believed. But unfortunately, they adopted a sort of dictatorial mindset instead of reckoning with their romanticism. More accurately, a portion of them broke off, maintained their own lives and left the diaspora. A portion were still in the mindset in the diaspora of 'Yes, we will change things'. They live in a sort of headmaster temperament. I observe it in the new generation where yes, although people left for political reasons, they try to adapt to the society they come to. They learn the language, pursue careers and become more assimilated. They sustain their lives in different ways. But the older generation came, they came but were still living in Turkey. Even if they speak English, they still live in Turkey. I don't understand this at all. How does it happen that you try this hard not to assimilate? How can you manage to change this little? But the biggest difference in my view is that the newly arriving youth are more open and adapting to the country where they live, develop themselves more significantly, and live in a greater unison with that country. That's why I think they have developed more and view life differently. But those who arrived in the 1980s still view life the same.

So what will Meltem Arıkan do after this? I think you'll continue living in Wales with the life plan we talked about.

I'll keep living in Wales. I think I discovered something really important, I discovered how people can find inner peace. I start each day saying, 'Thankfully, I'm very happy.' This doesn't mean that this is an amazing life. I miss a lot of things, I cry, my mental state falls and rises, but where I am now is happy and at peace. I learned that there are a few different ways for me to reach this. I learned that I can't teach this to anyone, but I can share it, and people can find their own ways. That's why I want this counselling work, this groove dance. I'm considering preparing workshops in both Turkish and English. I think they can remind people about some things they've forgotten. We forgot that we are one with nature. We have grown so big-headed that we think we can control nature. We act like the whole world is our servant. So that's why we are stuck at home due to the coronavirus. I see that I've started to remember things we've forgotten. I see how life changes into something that could be called magical as I remember those things. And I want to share these. That's why I really value my new job.

Second, I want to write in Turkish and English of course. I honestly wonder what I'll write. I'll produce something, but I wonder what I'll produce. And the other most important thing for me right now is autism. Turkey is a horrible place to be autistic. People's knowledge about autism is probably a hundred years behind people's knowledge of it here. There are organisations working on autism issues, as there are on every issue, but those organisations can't move much beyond fighting. It's not possible for someone of my age to receive an autism diagnosis. Psychologists and psychiatrists don't know about this issue. I'm writing about this, and I want to continue writing about it. We've just applied for a project. I don't know if they'll accept it or not. The EU set aside a budget for a journalistic project, and we applied for that. My project was that as an autistic woman, you're always odd in society if you don't receive an autism diagnosis. But after you receive an autism diagnosis, then you're odd among other autistic individuals. Because all the criteria for autism are made according to men. They're now discovering that autism for women is different than it is for men. So many women have died in mental institutions, a number of women have received incorrect diagnoses. I mean, if you're a woman, medicine doesn't take you very seriously, even if you satisfy the criteria for diagnosis. That's why I'm planning a project about how autistic women need to make their voices heard and about conducting interviews with autistic individuals. I volunteer at a number of autism associations in Wales. Maybe I could later work on autism professionally. That teaches me a lot. Do you know what it teaches me? It teaches me to be flexible in my work. We judge people very easily. But when I look back, especially over the past year, at myself and my proximity to autistic individuals, I see very clearly – if you want to see it, you can – that everyone has at least one characteristic that you can love and accept. Yes, maybe there are eighty characteristics that you won't love or accept, but are you God? On what basis are you making this judgement? What's important is seeing one of them and establishing a relationship through that. I also saw that if you stir up trouble over that arrogance, your appearance, you learn a lot. Yes, they love me, they say they learn a lot, but they taught me so many things about life. That's why I think I want to do more community work here. While I was in Turkey or when I first came here, for example, I couldn't understand the community mindset because I thought of them like I think about our diaspora. I didn't understand it very much because I didn't engage with them. But I understood why these people are from the West when I worked as an official in these communities. They're from the West, because they really try to help. No one's competing with one another. No one's trying to be something. They really try to help one another or the community with the work they do wholeheartedly. And I learned many unbelievable things. The Welsh are a little bit different, a little bit more emotionally open than the English. They resemble us more in that sense. They're warmer people, like people from the Balkans. They wholeheartedly work for the community. There's nothing like wanting their names to be seen, or this or that, not by a long shot. There isn't any support for mid-Wales on autism issues, for example. And they did something where one woman said she hadn't been able to find support for her child, and they started speaking with mothers like me and finding support for one another. What started in that manner guides everything here right now. Of course the state is providing support now. It's become an enormous organisation. The position of the woman who started it is still the same. So I'll continue living here and sharing everything I learn here. I hope I'll write books, maybe a play, but right now I'm at a stage of building something rather than writing.

14

MİNE GENCEL BEK

I don't regret not initiating the asylum process because doing
so would prolong my return to Turkey. But my daughter and
I went to Turkey after forty-four months away. It was good
for our psychological state. It was good for our normalisation.
I mean that forty-four-month exile psychology ended then.
It ended, but as I said, it lasted for forty-four months,
and that was a very long period for us.

*Mine Gencel Bek currently works as a researcher and co-principal
investigator for the DFG-funded research group Transformationen
des Populären (2021–4) at the University of Siegen on a project
titled 'Fabricating "the People"; Negotiating Claims of Representa-
tion in Social Media in Post-Gezi Turkey'. She teaches at both the*

undergraduate and postgraduate levels in the Media Studies Depart-
ment at the University of Siegen. She completed her PhD at Lough-
borough University in 1999 with a thesis titled 'Communicating
Capitalism: A Study of the Contemporary Turkish Press', which ana-
lysed the structural elements of the changing industry, news as texts
and the role of journalists in the news production process. She was a vis-
iting lecturer at MIT Comparative Media Studies, Open Documen-
tary Lab and Civic Media Lab in 2013 and 2014. Her academic life
started in Ankara University in 1991 as a research assistant. During
2008–2010, she worked as vice chair of KASAUM, a women's studies
centre, at Ankara University. She was dismissed from her position as
a professor in the Department of Journalism, Faculty of Communica-
tion, Ankara University, Turkey, with the decree in February 2017 for
signing the petition for peace. After that, she was invited to the Univer-
sity of Siegen as a Georg Bollenbeck fellow and later worked as a Mer-
cator fellow at the Media of Cooperation collaborative research centre
and the Locating Media research training group and graduate school.

Dr Gencel Bek, thank you so much for your time. We really
appreciate your support for this book. Shall we start with your
departure? When and why were you forced to leave Turkey?
It was 9 February 2017. We left two days after being fired. We had
already had plans to take a short-term break in Germany, to be honest.
You weren't allowed to take international trips at the time without
the permission of the chancellor's office. They set up special tables at
Istanbul airport where security officials would check these permission documents. At the time, people with green passports had to get
a stamp there declaring them 'suitable for travel' before moving into
the normal travel line. So people without that document weren't able
to enter the normal travel line.

You're one of the peace signatories. I remember that you had
requested your pension after you signed the petition.

No, not when I signed the petition. We signed in January 2016. I submitted my resignation request in early 2017. While I was resigning, I wrote that it was contingent on my pension rights when I reach the age of retirement. I want to finish this before coming to that, because it's important. We left to take a break for at least two weeks and no more than three months. Because I had requested my leave from the chancellor's office during the 15 July period, they probably thought I was going on holiday. But I didn't think that I would be able to cross the border after being dismissed. We only set out to try something, with a flight to Germany with a stopover in Istanbul. That day alone was very important for me and my family. Leaving was psychologically devastating as someone who had had little control over her life until this point. Would I return to Ankara after the flight to Istanbul or would I move on? I think they hadn't alerted the relevant units or the state bureaucracy had reduced the speed of its mechanisms. I really don't know what happened. This was incredibly traumatic for me, because I knew I wouldn't be able to return easily. I left at a time like that.

I asked about my pension. As I said, I had written a letter of resignation. The fact that our friends had been fired before us evoked a profound sorrow in me. At first, we honestly didn't understand. We thought it was a mistake. We thought they would probably rectify it. We were shocked that something like this could be done over a signature. At least on my own behalf. But the days went by, and there was no mistake, nothing was corrected. I understood later that it was intentional. So I didn't want to enter the school anymore, teach there or pass through the hallways. We had already posted the photograph of our friends on our doors, just like when we did the same for our friends who went to prison. I think we rebelled during that time, even if it was a passive action. So I wrote that I wanted to resign contingent on my pension rights. When things after 15 July grew thoroughly convoluted and legal functions were suspended, we engaged in a dialogue with the chancellor's office, thinking, as Academics for Peace, that we would be placed in the 'Gülenist bag' during the state of emergency. I went to demand that these baseless investigations be dropped at once. The chancellor said he was sick and tired of my intelligence file growing thicker each day, and I was shocked. I had no involvement in anything illegal. What association? What organisation? I wasn't even a member of a party. I had only worked actively through civilian initiatives in campaigns for the HDP to enter the assembly. He lobbed threats at me, saying, 'Not only will you be fired, everything of yours and your pension will be gone. I'm going to bring a white paper. You will sign it. Everything will be done.'

You're talking about Erkan İbiş, right?
Yes, Erkan İbiş. 'How can you take my entire life's worth of labour!' I said. I'm still angry. But I didn't accede to his request that day, and I didn't sign the paper. I told him that I had come to represent the community and that I would communicate this to my friends. But I was shattered. Officially – and we're talking about the mafia bosses – this was a mafia operation in my opinion. I spent thirty years at the same university, twenty-six years of my labour. More than being fired, the fact that all my pension rights were stolen was the point in question. This is illegal. So I thought they would block my pension. They decided to end everything for me, so we came here. Socialists who came to Germany much earlier (after the 12 September coup), people whom we came across and formed relationships with said, 'Next are your assets. They'll seize your assets now.' Now I'm scared of this. We just have a little home and nothing else. We sold the car and left with that money. What good is money from a car here anyway? It was gone in two months. So from the airport all the way here, I felt that I had probably lost everything. It was incredibly grave.

Why did you choose Germany?
One day, I wrote to about 10–15 colleagues I knew. I had friends there.

Before your dismissal, correct?

Yes, before my dismissal. People suggested this to us, saying, 'Your turn is coming. Make a plan. Things are getting serious.' We received indicators of this. People working in international academia or at human rights institutions and who were monitoring Turkey said this. I'll go at least for a little while, I thought. It wasn't me who chose Germany, actually, because I don't know German. Germany was a place where I had come every once in a while for conferences, where I had stayed in three or four cities and hotels, which I hadn't seen much of, which I wasn't too impressed by. A German colleague of mine was the fastest to respond to the message I sent and get involved from among these 10–15 people. The reason why I did that, why I wanted to stand on my own two feet was because I didn't want to apply to fellowships like Scholars at Risk or Philipp Schwartz from the BAK (Academics for Peace) correspondence list. I didn't even apply to institutions issuing risk reports at the time. But I later felt the pain of that, because they found three-month fellowships, then five-month fellowships, then eighteen-month fellowships for me in Siegen, and each time when a three-month fellowship was found, I had to go back to the Ausländer office to get a visa during the second month. But I was at peace and had a clear conscience. My CV was good in an international sense. I could have found other opportunities in different places. I could have found them if I had applied much earlier, but I didn't want to leave Turkey in any way and form another life. I had already done my PhD abroad. I had recently worked as a visiting scholar at MIT. I submitted an application at the time. And I was accepted at Bath University in England after I arrived. It was a beautiful, exciting project about diaspora and museum relations. I did the interview and was accepted immediately. But I didn't dare gather my bags from Germany again and go there. I didn't know whether I could travel around abroad. I was anxious about whether our passports and names had been given to Interpol and what had happened. I wasn't confident and didn't go to England, even though it was a place I knew better, where I at least knew the language and had friends. But friendships were slowly established here.

Was your passport voided?
Yes.

You have to form a relationship with the consulate for certain processes. Were you able to do so? What did you do? That's your homeland there, your consulate.
No, we're stateless. We ended up being stateless. We weren't able to use the consulate in any capacity, and we were treated very poorly there. We weren't paid attention to as a party, we weren't seen as citizens. Whenever we went, they tried to take back the passports in our hands. We couldn't get them to process any requests until 18 August 2020. Right on my birthday. The day I turned fifty-one, my lawyer said that the restrictions on my passport had been removed. 'Go and be persistent at the consulate,' my lawyer said. We had gone dozens of times already when the terrorism case against us was dropped and at other turning points, and we had left empty-handed. For the first time, we went decisively to have them process our request. Even there, our application was only taken after a fight. Think about it, the restrictions on my passport had been removed, I needed a birth certificate for my daughter. I've moved past myself now, I needed a birth certificate for my daughter saying that she was born in Turkey and her birthdate. The German school here wanted it. They wouldn't give it to me because they didn't know me. They wouldn't process the request for us.

The treatment we generally received at the consulate was like this: a low-ranking official greets us when we first enter. Their face changes the moment they log onto the computer. They get nervous all of a sudden and immediately grab their telephone. They call their friends. 'You wait here, don't go anywhere,' they say. 'Can we have your passports now?' they say. 'We didn't bring our passports,' we said, because we knew they would take them. The supervisor comes. 'Return the passports immediately,' they say. 'We came for this,' we say. 'No, I can't do anything for you. Hand over your passports,' they say. And we say, 'We won't give them.' Then we leave. We're left with no other choice. Even the day when I learned from the lawyer that the restriction had been removed, I told the official, 'Look, the restriction has been removed from my passport, the terrorism case against me was dropped months ago.' The official there responded, 'We are sick and tired of you.' They said this. 'You've been taking up our time for years. You come, you go, you don't understand anything. We tell you and we tell you again.' 'How can that be?' I said. 'We aren't saying "Give us a green passport again". Give us a normal passport. We want to travel.'

And then your passport continued as a green passport, no?
No, they didn't give us green passports. There was still a phrase, 'A green passport will not be provided', on the green passport.

And your pension rights?
I got my pension rights after a fight. But it was very tricky. I hadn't been able to privatise that so that no one who would be interested could do anything to it. Everyone interested in this issue, everyone from whom I requested a simple file tracking, was threatened in some way at those official bureaus. First, the chancellor's office was very slow to send my papers. Then, despite my being a professor for more than five years, the Social Security Institution sent a document saying I was an assistant professor. They said I would be fired from my position as an assistant professor. That wasn't the case. I think it was done because of my absence. People come and go between the chancellor's office and the Social Security Institution. Finally, when the Social Security Institution said 'Yes, she's a professor', they put the file right at the bottom. Our relatives who went were threatened. They were told, 'If you come once more about this file, if you bother us, it will be very bad for you, something bad will happen to you.' People were

scared to go and ask about my pension. I told the lawyer when my terrorism case was dropped, that my file was waiting. 'They have no right to do this, I'm going to call and ask,' my lawyer said. After that, they immediately initiated the transaction on the same date. I fought for a year to get that pension, even though it's my right. I finally won what I am entitled to, but the payment got stuck at a bank in Cologne. 'You need to get your first pension payment in Turkey,' they said. 'I can't go,' I told them. I would go if I could. The restriction on my passport hadn't been removed. I waited a few months. And then I went back to the bank. 'Look,' I said. 'I know that you can do this.' And then it was solved. But obstacles were placed in front of my pension at every level of government. And as I said, people were informally threatened. They had no right to do this.

While you were experiencing all this, did the German state, your German colleagues or the universities or institutions you were affiliated with at the time help? How did they act?

Not directly on this issue, no. But it happened at a point for employment to be able to remain here, to make sure I got by. My colleagues at Siegen were supportive because they liked my CV and thought that I would support them with my research and academic background. We won a big project, as they had hoped, and we recently created a research group at DFG. Starting in January I felt financially secure for the first time in about four years. I know that I can pay my rent each month, that's what that means. But for example, for nearly all of last year, I was doing all this work and was dropped to part-time at the decision of the chancellor and struggled immensely. It was impossible for my husband to find work because of Covid-19. The people I worked with were different, but the university administration was separate. They can reduce the labour force they call a human expense, saying we'll get buildings and grow. When we think about what we call Germany as different institutions and people, my colleagues at the university were willing, yes. The dean sat down between a pile of work and wrote a long and wonderful letter to request residence for me from Article 19: 'Let this person have residence, because there is no equivalent in Germany, and we need this person to develop the sciences in Germany.' They wrote an unbelievably persuasive letter, saying, 'She's not just excellent, she has academic skills that exceed excellence.' Normally, I need this letter to get my residence from Article 19. But it didn't happen. I still have a limited visa, because if you have money, if you can get by on your own, if you won't be a burden for the state, you're accepted. I'm not tired of struggling with the officials at the Ausländer office and sending hundreds of documents. Most recently, they said, 'We want all of your works in German.' I had only done my CV in German. And the official got angry with me, saying, 'Why aren't you sending me the documents I asked for?' Why should I have them translated into German? I've been an academic since 1991. I began publishing in 1993. There are thirty pages of titles on my CV. Which of my works should I have translated? They cut me off by asking for a document that would be impossible for me to submit. Of course, I could have chosen the refugee route. We had actually purchased a secondhand car once because of how far away my daughter's school was. We were berated the day we went to register it without involving the university and because it was urgent. They don't speak English. Our German is inadequate. The man shouted at us, 'You can't register this. Go to the camp now. Sign a document to be a refugee.' Or go to Turkey and get your visa there. We told him that if we go, we can't come back. 'Then go to the camp,' he said. There's nothing between his ears. I mean, we go to register a car and are invited to a refugee camp. Germany is an extremely challenging place, because the bureaucracy here doesn't like unconventional or atypical incidents. Their minds and categories are set, but our lives can't be easily categorised. They're not clear, there's a lot of uncertainty. We can't stick to any routine. I haven't received any support from the government so far. I don't think I'll receive any in the future either. I don't regret not initiating the refugee process because doing so would prolong my return to Turkey. But my daughter and I recently went to Turkey after 44 months away. It was good for our psychological state. It was good for our normalisation. I mean that 44-month exile psychology ended then. It ended, but as I said, it lasted for 44 months, and that was a very long period for us.

As far as I know, you are with your husband and child. First, what kind of solidarity and challenges did you encounter in this process? Second, there are Academics for Peace like you there, people with leftist views, Alevis and Kurds. Primarily, how are your internal relationships with your family, and how are your relationships with these groups? Semi-official estimates put the number of Turks in Germany at close to 5 million. Have the experiences of those who migrated before you helped you at all? Have they helped you?

We stayed close as a family, side by side, as much as possible, but it was difficult. It wasn't easy. My husband left a lot behind and came. He's a former journalist himself. Then he set up a real estate office [in Turkey] with his friends. He left that company and came. He left all his relationships, and he's quite a social person. If something had happened, he couldn't have gone to his mother's side. If he were to go, he couldn't come back. The fact that my passport had affected them devastated me psychologically. They paid a heavy price in this process. A child is experiencing exile in her youth. This is incredibly burdensome. We stood together but were very hurt. 'When will Turkey open up, Mum? Mum, hasn't your passport been reinstated? Mum, hasn't your terrorism case been dropped?' It's been dropped. 'So why can't we go?' We've had this talk dozens of times. 'Why can't I come?' I came so that a special team won't raid my home in the middle of the night. This was my motivation for coming. I didn't want my child to experience this. But my child has suffered worse. That's life. I mean, you can't know [what will happen]. She has friends here, she wants to stay here.

In terms of intra-group relationships, we have an Academics for Peace organisation in Berlin. They're active. While it's with a rather weak circle, I got connected, and my connection is ongoing. I was in a deep depression at first. I wasn't in a state to be able to contact anyone. But I was consciously uncomfortable at the Nuriye Semih actions. I participated in those. I came across other Academics for Peace, others in exile, other migrant women in Cologne and even at events in Berlin, and I connected with them. It was good for me.

Do you regret signing the petition after suffering this much?
No. I was given the chance to remove my signature; ironically, I'll remind you of what İbiş had said. I didn't withdraw it. Did I know that I was going to go through so much trouble – some have suffered much more than us? I didn't, to be honest.

This was also a process when some groups who wouldn't have come together if they had remained in Turkey and everything was 'normal' came together over this pain. You were able to meet with Gülenists, for example, and that doesn't appear possible, at least in Turkey. So do you have a relationship in Germany with people who are not politically in the same position as you but whom the state still drove out of Turkey?
This is one of the most difficult questions for me to answer. We came together a few times. One time, there was a journalistic project about journalists in exile, for example, at a festival. Although I'm not a journalist, I went because I'm a journalism professor and work in media. I found myself to have very conflicting feelings. The people there were mostly conservative or were close to the Gülen Movement. I resolved this in myself: I met with these people at other conferences. Some even came to our university. I said 'Welcome' to them. I asked if there was anything I could do. I said I hoped their families and children were doing well. This was an issue over which I fell to pieces when I encountered them at that journalism festival; nobody's child should have to swim across a river to emigrate. I definitely support them on that point, when their rights are violated. I support them on the point

of their rights being violated, but I don't think I stand in solidarity with them today.

What was Turkey's breaking point for you? How do you interpret Turkey, and how has this interpretation changed while you've been in Germany?

As far as I can see, analysing and understanding my own limitations, the first moment when I said 'What is going on?' started with the massacre in Suruç. I was thinking rather naively until that point. I myself was saved from the Ankara massacre. If it had taken a little bit longer for my daughter to use the bathroom, I would have been among those killed there. And when we arrived, we arrived right in the centre of the stampede a minute or two after the moment of the explosion. I was saved there, we were saved as a family, but many friends of friends and people we stood together with had died, had been slaughtered. And then the next day we were in front of the train station. I participated in a lot of street demonstrations outside academic environments, we held hands to create chains for peace and democracy. Perhaps if more people had reacted to these massacres at the time, another would not have happened, or we wouldn't have arrived where we are today.

Will you return to Turkey?

I want to go back. I signed a four-year deal for this project we started. There's a possibility that it will be extended for up to twelve years. They want me to be there. On the one hand, it's like a blessing in a precarious situation. On the other hand, I'm not sure, to be honest; will I stay for up to twelve years? I still get pleasure from conducting academic research, from teaching about issues I'm interested in, but it was at the centre of my life before, and it's not as magical a world as it used to be. On the other hand, I want my daughter to grow up somewhere where there's the rule of law, to go to university, to live somewhere where the value of her labour will be known. She has four or five years until she goes off to university. We will definitely be here for a certain period for her. I can't predict anything after that, but my wish – I mean, I could be forced to do something else – is to return.

But when you return, your child will remain for a while. You'll have a two-pronged life.

Yes. That's how it seems.

15

MURAT ÖZBANK

**Turkey's democratisation is not only a political matter for me.
It's something which is very personal. My return ticket
to Turkey is Turkey's democratisation.**

Murat Özbank (PhD Carleton University, Ottawa, 2001) is an academic, author, translator and part-time activist. He taught several courses on (contemporary) political theory at undergraduate, postgraduate and PhD levels in the International Relations Department of Istanbul Bilgi University between 2001 and 2017 and in the Diversity and Social Conflict Department of Humboldt University, Berlin, between 2017 and 2019. He has translated and authored several books on political theory, among them Neden Demokrasi, Nasıl İstikrar: Rawls–Habermas Tartışması *('Why Choose Democracy and How to Maintain*

Stability: The Rawls–Habermas Debate', Bilgi Üniversitesi Yayınları, 2009) and Gezi Ruhu ve Politik Teori *('The Spirit of Gezi and Political Theory', Kolektif Kitap, 2013). He was one of the leading organisers of the first unionisation effort in a private university in Turkey. During the Gezi Protests of 28 May–15 June 2013 he represented the Green-Left Party of Turkey, of which he was a founding member, in the meetings of the Taksim Solidarity network. Currently he is co-curating with Nil Mutluer the Library of Resistance/Divergent Roads of History exhibitions and the accompanying panels as parts of the 'Gezi: Ten Years After' events organised by the Maxim Gorki Theatre to commemorate the tenth anniversary of the Gezi protests. He thinks that hope is a scarce but luckily still available resource.*

Dr Özbank, can you tell us why you decided to leave Turkey and live abroad?

This question has two answers based on what it means to leave. First, Nil [Mutluer] came to Berlin after being fired because she had signed the Academics for Peace petition. We came to Berlin together. While she continued her work in Berlin, I would come and go between Berlin and Istanbul. And I can say with mathematical certainty that I spent half the year in Berlin and the other half in Istanbul. Because I was still working. I went to Germany on a Schengen visa during that year. But we had reached the limits of the Schengen visa. During that period, a whole lot of other political incidents took place in Turkey. If I'm not mistaken, the Büyükada cases began. The Academics for Peace case against Nil was ongoing. Nil couldn't come to Turkey, and I couldn't go to Germany because of the Schengen visa. I couldn't stay long enough in Germany. 'It can't be like this,' we said. I left my job at Bilgi in 2017, I retired, and I came to Germany full time. I settled in Berlin. It took between a year and a year and a half for me to start living full-time in Berlin.

Does that mean you did not choose Germany as your main destination but love brought you here?

I chose Germany entirely because of my wife's situation. The reason my wife Nil chose Germany was because she was unemployed and needed work. She received a job offer, an opportunity in Germany. If it had popped up in Belize or the Caribbean, we would have gone there probably. It came up in Germany, so we came to Germany to earn money. I came to Germany because Nil had come to Germany. She wasn't my wife at the time, actually, we were together. We tried to keep things going by travelling between Istanbul and Berlin for a year. There was actually a story here: I couldn't enter Germany because of the visa, and Nil couldn't come to Turkey. So we met in Montenegro one summer because I didn't need a visa and it was somewhere Nil could comfortably go. So the only criterion here was to find a job in Germany that we could feed ourselves with.

You're a prominent figure among Academics for Peace because you were right in front in that famous picture that came out in the newspapers. Your wife was also a signatory, and she was fired because of it. Did you suffer any hardships or pressure or a legal process where you worked because of this?

The institution where I was working at the time was Istanbul Bilgi University, and it was more comfortable on this issue compared to many other universities. The reason it was comfortable wasn't because it adopted a position to support us institutionally. At Bilgi University, there were sixty to seventy signatories, including those who signed later, for that petition. Most importantly, we were an organised group which spoke to one another and acted in unison. So being fired all together was something that would disrupt the function of the university. As a group, we were able to speak with the administration, because we were an organised force. And our organisation originated from the labour union movement that we had started earlier at Bilgi. We had started a labour union movement at Bilgi. It was the first union organising effort at a private university in Turkey. We had an experience coming from there, a habit. So if you ask if I saw pressure at Bilgi

University, it wasn't pressure, but we were engaged in an organised fight. But we were also lucky. Some other universities were lucky too. Although there were few signatories there, the administration chose to adopt a democratic position in favour of freedom of expression, and nothing happened. Some universities were very unlucky, and as I said, for example, the petition was signed in January and Nil was fired from Nişantaşı University in February because of her signature.

Apart from this, at least during the interim period until coming to Berlin, I said some things in the public space. One or two of my interviews were published that defended my signature. If you ask whether there was pressure, we certainly felt the pressure. It's not easy to say I didn't feel pressure, there was no pressure in a situation where there was an investigation being conducted into crimes of terrorist propaganda and a criminal case was later opened. Regarding being one of the prominent signatories of the Academics for Peace petition, I'll say that I joke with myself about being 'the positive face, the figure in the window display for the Academics for Peace petition'. They used that photograph as the follow-up picture. They Photoshopped trenches in the background of that picture and published it as the 'academics of the trenches'. I'm waiting in front of a trench dug in the south-east, folding my hands together. It's entirely a coincidence and, as a matter of fact, an embarrassment above all else. The period when we signed the petition from Academics for Peace was very difficult, very heavy. It was a time when the curfews were implemented in the south-east after the 1 November elections, when grave violence only against civilians prevailed. We talked with one another, saying, 'It can't go on like this, we have to do something.' While speaking in a group of a few academics at Bilgi University about whether to sign something calling for a dialogue of sanity, one day this petition appeared in my inbox. 'Oh look,' I said. 'Something's been written.' It was a text calling for peace and at least asking for the ongoing violence to stop. I signed my name. And to tell you the truth, I didn't consider anything when I did. This needed to happen, needed to be said. In this way, there's nowhere we can reach with these securitist policies, with this violence, the weapons need to be silenced, and we need to come together sanely and calm down. I came home that night, and Nil told me, 'I signed a petition.' 'I did too,' I said. Nil had received a warning from a group of people at the university for going to Diyarbakır. She asked me, 'I signed this petition, but will they say something at our school?' I said, 'Oh cut it out, for God's sake. What could happen because of a signature!' Anyway, we signed it. It was a Friday, if I'm not mistaken. They said on Saturday that the number of signatories had risen to 800, and we were shocked. 'On Monday, we're going to announce this petition to the press, there will be a conference somewhere,' they said. We went. 'Let's have all the signatories come on stage, we'll announce it together,' they said. The number by that point had risen to 1,128. We got up from our seats and took the stage. I went on stage. I found the place for myself that you see in that photograph. And all of a sudden I was ashamed. Because the swagger of that work was that I hadn't done anything for the press conference, I hadn't gathered signatures for the press conference, I hadn't done anything and despite that, I was in the front of that photograph that was distributed to the public, and this didn't sit well with me, being unfair to the work of others. Because I was on display for an issue that I hadn't helped with. So I looked around saying, 'Standing at the very front isn't good, maybe I should step towards the back,' and the cameras started to flash. Being the sort of person in front of the cameras running to the back is also bad. So I stood there, frozen. So the picture was taken, that image was taken. And then there was the follow-up photo. In fact I was joking that Nil was fired from Nişantaşı University. The press reported on that. Which picture did they use? They used mine. So they opened a prosecution investigation into some people. This was reported. Which picture was used? Mine.

How was it psychologically to have your picture constantly in the papers? You see that picture in the papers and head out onto the street, to Beyoğlu, Nişantaşı. What kind of feeling was that?

Funny. Ultimately, those who recognised me because the picture came out already knew me. I mean, there wasn't anyone who saw the picture and recognised me on the street. But there were people who knew me before, at my local market, for example, where I come and go each day, where I shop in the neighbourhood, who saw the photograph and said, 'Ah, I saw you, you were in the picture.' 'You did,' I said. Or my wife, close friends, students, people who already knew me in my private life in some way, people who already had a relationship with me, they noticed me when they saw the photograph. But someone who never knew me didn't see and recognise me because of the picture. The picture didn't make me famous in that sense. So I didn't get caught up in feeling like I became famous with that picture. In a way, it was good. The news, the discussions that emerged in the media after that photo and press release were so far from the reality of what happened that it was funny, truly hilarious. It made me laugh, to tell you the truth, the stories written about that photograph. If you ask whether it made me uncomfortable, the picture didn't, but being targeted, the risks of being declared a public enemy certainly did. But there was nothing to be done about that. In the conversation I had with *Evrensel*, I said, 'This is a known process, propaganda, creating an alternative reality, trying to shape public perception – a totalitarian propaganda method.' And that's being done, it's being used. You find yourself within that. But because I know that the stories explained there have no relation to my reality or the reality I know, I don't feel a personal irritation, anger, fury. But this told me something about the trajectory of politics in the country. When the Nazis first rose to power in 1933, after Hitler was elected and in the transition from the Weimar Republic to the Third Reich, there was a one-year period during the transition from a poorly functioning constitutional democracy to a totalitarian order at the hands of the regime, All the independent and semi-independent institutions of the state, civil society organisations are sought to be connected to the same revolution through executive will. What is there to do?

The promise of loyalty to universities is created. Nazi Party supporters are appointed as chancellors for universities. All the staff in labour unions, civil society organisations are changed, and Nazi Party supporters are appointed. The political parties in parliament are sought to be connected to the same revolution or are included in the Nazi Party, or are excluded, marginalised and finally pushed outside the political system. This is a period when the central administration seeks to disseminate its own will throughout all of society. And during the period when this peace petition was signed, I said, 'Has the process begun where universities are to exclude the dissidents?' And I said this during my interview with *Evrensel*.[1]

Do you feel like you're in exile right now?

I mean, no. It's complicated. It's easy to say that I'm in exile, but I can also say that I'm not. I feel like an exile, because there aren't the conditions for me to live in Turkey. I don't know where I can earn a living when I go to Turkey. Ultimately, the only job I have done throughout my life is teaching, I teach political theory courses. I write some things and publish them. I earn a living here. I also do translations. There aren't the circumstances in Turkey for me to earn a living. I'm not sure I can find work. My living here and coming to Berlin isn't a preference but a necessity. So I'm not of the spirit like, 'Oh, how wonderful. Things in Turkey are getting worse, I found the opportunity so I left, and I live abroad.' On the contrary, what I've internalised, my desire is to live in peace in my own country. If possible, to live in a coastal town on the Aegean. To read and write there, to draw. And if all this hadn't erupted, hadn't reached this point, I would be trying to establish a life between Istanbul and Palamutbükü. I had taken steps

---

[1] See Şerif Karataş, 'Barış için imza atan Murat Özbank: Korkup sustukça, korktuğumuz başımıza gelir', Evrensel, 7 February 2016, https://www.evrensel.net/haber/271929/baris-icin-imza-atan-murat-ozbank-korkup-sustukca-korktugumuz-basimiza-gelir, accessed 7 April 2023.

for that, together with Nil. If we consider it like that, then yes, I'm in exile. I live in a country I have to live in that I didn't pick myself for a reason I didn't want. This enters the definition of exile. On the other hand, I have friends who want to return to their home but cannot, who want to visit but cannot. It's such a funny thing. But this situation is not independent from Turkey. Because the fundamental reason we are here, the source is in Turkey. I saw Nil being fired for signing the petition as a great injustice, a misfortune at the time. I mean, she was fired while a number of others were not. Why was she fired? I thought about this, I experienced this. But now, looking back, I think that Nil's being fired in February 2016 was one of the best things that happened to us. If she had been fired in late July 2016, what would have happened to her? We have friends who were fired by presidential decree during the state of emergency, and they haven't been able to go to Turkey for five years because their passports were revoked. Their families are there. But what kind of stories have we lived here? The wife is here in Germany, the husband is an academic in Turkey, the children are in Turkey. The wife can't go to Turkey because she won't be able to return if she does. The husband can't leave because he can't get a passport because of the presidential decree. The family is separated. I have journalist friends here. They arrived, followed Turkey from here and produced news. They can't enter Turkey. We'll enter Turkey in a month. We'll probably go to the sea on the Aegean coast. At least I have the freedom to go to Turkey as a visitor right now. I have friends from Academics for Peace who can't do this, who were forced to apply for asylum. So if I were to call myself an exile, I don't know what I would call them. If you ask whether I feel like I'm in exile, I would say no when I'm with them. I'm in a very fortunate position, because at least I can enter and leave Turkey. And then there's the issue that being able to enter Turkey and work creates politically: this 'privilege' – being able to comfortably enter and work in Turkey and see my mother and father there – you still must be careful what you say and how you say it here to be able to retain this privilege. You can't speak freely. Yes, I'm someone who continues to talk about Turkey's public space in Turkey. I write some things, draw some things, but I think as if I'm living in Turkey while I do this. What would RTÜK say to someone directing an alternative media channel in Turkey and how would they say it? If they're calculating whether a case will be opened because of this, you're doing the same despite living abroad.

As you said, there are some who are unable to go to Turkey because their passports were revoked. Has anyone said to you 'You can go to Turkey, so you don't fit in this category', because of that? Is there such an overt or subtle debate among Turkey's new intellectual migrants?

Don't ask me this question, because I don't have the answer. There are a lot of debates raging among Turkey's new intellectual migrants. But whatever I say politically, I say for myself. As long as I can speak for myself while engaging in politics in an organised structure, I remain within that structure. So when hierarchies like this are created for this reason and I can't speak for myself, I distance myself, saying, 'Okay, I don't need you. I'll say this anywhere and in any way.' What I'm telling you is a sociological case, it's a fact. Ultimately, when victims become organised, especially in Turkey, whenever victims of something become organised, a hierarchy of victims is formed. If you work together, a hierarchy of labour is formed. Interestingly, when Turkish people work together, they can't work without forming a covert or overt hierarchy. I haven't observed this, if you're going to ask, because I don't care. Or wherever it does happen, I don't say anything and continue on my way. There's nothing to be done. The fact that I haven't observed this doesn't mean that it doesn't happen, but that's why I said don't ask me this question.

You have relationships with groups in Germany which are close to you ideologically, which you knew from Turkey or with which you formed partnerships earlier. These relationships, as

far as I understand, continue in the same way. There are also a number of groups abroad right now with which you have a slim possibility of coming together in Turkey. Do you have relationships with them? Is there a situation where you meet at a common denominator or come together? For instance, Gülenists, other Sunni Islamist groups that left the country, those coming from more conservative segments. Do you have any kind of dialogue with these?

I have interactions with them, but I haven't personally engaged in any efforts at a systematic dialogue.

What about them?

We establish a dialogue when I come across them. How do we come across each other? There are two conferences I know and have personally attended in Germany. The Gülenists have also been invited to places where there are intellectual dissident segments that came from Turkey to Germany, people like me, other leftists and leftist-liberals. We've met there and talked. I know that a language is formed and can be developed over shared victimhood. But I certainly didn't establish with them a closeness that would be enough for a relationship of trust, a will for a joint organisation to emerge. But the common denominator of 'We are all people who are forced to live far from Turkey for one reason or another' creates the opportunity for dialogue that doesn't exist in Turkey, and by opportunity for dialogue I mean the opportunity to have a conversation, to establish human communication. I haven't observed this personally regarding this issue. But when you say Sunni Islam, there were people I knew from the Sunni Islam sector while in Turkey, people I liked, people I worked with despite being neither an Islamist nor pious. I recently published a four-part article series in *Yeşil Gazete*. What you said – that all people coming from different intellectual, ideological, religious traditions can agree on a series of shared principles through different ideological and philosophical reasonings – is what I call the union of views overlapping with different thinkings.

I think that the emergence of this and, in this shared conscientious foundation, the exhibition of a will for democratisation through the coordination of different segments on such a shared conscientious foundation, is the only way for Turkey to attain democracy. If you ask whether I did something for this: no, I have not. I mean, I still write and draw. I try to share my ideas in some places. But I'm not an organiser. Forming organisations and bringing people together to do something with that community is something that requires special skills. I'm not a person who succeeds at that. That's not where my excitement lies. While being amazed at people who can do this, that's not something I have done. What should I do? The only thing that I do as much as possible is reading, writing, drawing. Producing ideas, doing something else and sharing this. I do this from Germany so that what I do can serve this purpose. But I do it for Turkey. If there are movements, organisations that attempt to make political change possible in Turkey and an invitation comes from them, I try to participate and certainly support them, but as I said, I don't have anything like an organisation. But I don't reject these opportunities for dialogue when I see them.

The picture of Academics for Peace and the fact that you're still writing in Turkey makes you a notable figure. When you encounter Turkish institutions in Germany, do you see any pressure from them because of this visibility? Most simply, you have absolutely had to go to the consulate. You encounter Turkish nationals every day in Germany. Have you encountered a reaction, not directly from a state institution but from people more adjacent to the current regime?

No, it hasn't happened at the consulate. There hasn't been a clear situation where a state official recognised me at a state bureau and refused to process my request, saying, 'You're this or that.' The fundamental reason for this is that I wasn't an academic dismissed by presidential decree. And the reason for this is that whatever happened to us happened before the coup. There's no logic for whatever reason for this, like 'With your having left the country, you're a Gülenist so you fled, that's why this is happening to you, but you're an Academic for Peace, so that's why it's not'. Fundamentally there's not really a logic like this generally, but you encounter this pressure if your name is on the presidential decree list. I have friends I know who have personally encountered this, leftist academics whom I've witnessed. People who refuse to speak with people from the Gülen Movement, refuse to engage in a dialogue even when they see the opportunity to do so because they were fired by presidential decree. I am not subjected to this, because I wasn't dismissed by presidential decree, so I think I'm lucky in that sense. As far as I understand, the state has different obsessions at different levels. They've fixated on me more lightly. For example, I won't be able to find work at any public or private university when I go to Turkey, because I know that I won't pass the security inquiry because my signature is on the petition for peace. Because almost all my friends who signed the same petition are fixated on the security inquiry when they reach the stage of new appointments. But this is a level of fixation. This tells me not to come as an academic but to come to the country if I want, and I can work in another job and to work if I find someone who will hire me. This is a level of fixation. If my name had appeared on a presidential decree, if I had been fired from my job at the university by presidential decree, I would have encountered the pressure of 'we can't process your request' at the consulate. There are people who do encounter this and can't see their children because of it.

If I'm not mistaken, you had lived abroad for this long when you did your PhD, correct?
Yes. I did my PhD in Canada and stayed there for seven years, between 1993 and 2000 or 2001. Then I returned to Turkey.

So this is your longest stay outside the country after your PhD. Has leaving Turkey, new encounters, what you experienced led you to interpret Turkey differently?

The answer I would give after returning from Canada and the answer I would give for the current situation in Germany are different. I came to Turkey in 2000, and I lived in Turkey for sixteen years, until 2016. I've been in Germany since 2016. After coming to Germany, in a sense, I never left Turkey. I mean, I follow Turkey. I follow news about Turkey. I talk about Turkey, I write about Turkey. I meet with people from Turkey. So physically, yes, I live in Germany, but it's not like I've left Turkey. So it's impossible to talk about a difference, a disengagement between my interpretation of Turkey from before I came to Germany and my interpretation now. On the other hand, yes, the period between 1993 and 2000 was a formative period for me. My thoughts about the Turkey I left in 1993 and Turkey after I returned in 2000 have combined with the things at the time. I began teaching at Bilgi University in 2001. I haven't been to Turkey in the past three years. The dissertation I wrote in Canada has nothing to do with Turkey. I wrote a dissertation on the intersection of the United Nations, international relations, comparative politics, democratic theory and the mix of human rights, international relations and political theory, and it related to the universality of human rights. And I did this because I would have done it in Turkey if I'd wanted to study in Turkey. I wanted to focus on an issue I couldn't do in Turkey, that I couldn't focus on in Turkey so that I could end up learning something new. The period when I returned to Turkey was when there was still the 2001 economic crisis, when Kemal Derviş was called from abroad. I said to myself, and I think it is still valid: the common denominator for the Turkish right and Turkish left is Turkishness, and there was no such phrase as nationalism [*ulusalcılık*] at that time. The main issue is not formed through rightism or leftism but through this state of Turkism. This is what must be overcome. I had read Gün Zileli's memoirs, which explained his days in the Enlightenment movement. I noticed at one point that we would play a game while in high school where if you consistently change the words in a sentence, the meaning changes significantly. If you write the leftist references in Gün Zileli's book in a leftist language, in a rightist language, you could interpret it as an Idealist [ultranationalist] book. You could read it as an Islamist book. The language is so similar that incidents explained in that memoir could be written as incidents that happened in a group of Turkish rightists with even the smallest word changes, and it wouldn't make the slightest difference. After returning to Turkey in 2000, I thought that something was needed so that a democracy unknown in Turkey could become known. This was one of the reasons that I returned to Turkey from Canada. I taught during the final years of my PhD. And I struggled to explain to the Canadian students that people could die or kill for political reasons, that this happened around the world, that this is why wars erupt. It was something so far removed from daily reality. I couldn't explain that 'Friends, this exists, unfortunately it exists – I mean, violence is something that exists within political language. Everything doesn't occur calmly, beautifully by speaking sweetly. It exists in the reality of life. We don't like this reality, but violence is taken seriously in politics.' Because using the language of violence is something truly ingrained in culture. I returned to Turkey. I struggled to explain to my students in Turkey that politics are something which can be conducted through intelligent debates, which don't involve violence, which can be conducted to search for joint solutions to joint problems. Because there is no other type of politics, no understanding of a different type of democratic politics here. I had said, at the time, and I still say now that the average citizen does not live by conducting significant political analyses with a superior intelligence in any country around the world. Everyone, good or bad, creates views and beliefs regarding their own memories at the level of their habits. The only difference relates to which country the memory is in. I mean – everyone lives from memory, to tell you the truth. But some people's memories are inclined to a more peaceful politics, and others' are more confrontational by nature. So I thought that a new culture needed to form for that memory to change in some way, that a different understanding needed to be prioritised regarding a new culture of democracy, a new politics of democracy in Turkey. This was the reason I returned to Turkey. I mean, I asked myself whether I wanted to spend my life explaining democracy to these people in Canada. What need is there for this? What meaning would this have? I told myself that I would go to Turkey and explain democracy to Turkey. Ultimately, the fact that I'm here meant that I wasn't able to do so.

We are conducting interviews with people from many different groups for this study, and we see that everyone has a separate Turkey, a separate breaking point. For you, what is the breaking point that caused you to be in Germany today?

The short answer to this question is Erdoğan. I joke with Nil that we owe Erdoğan for our happiness. Thanks to him, we were forced to live outside Turkey without having any plan. I saw Montenegro, for example, a country I had never thought of in forty years. We opened up to countries outside Turkey thanks to him. The direct reason I'm in Germany right now is the peace petition we both signed, and as I mentioned initially, our coming here wasn't a choice but a necessity. It was a necessity for me, in that we were forced to come to Germany because there were no longer the conditions for Nil to live and work in Turkey. And I came to Germany to live with Nil, because I didn't want to leave Nil. Was it spouse related? I mean, I wouldn't say it's spouse related. So if there hadn't been that peace petition, if Erdoğan hadn't directly targeted us at the time, if cases hadn't been filed, we wouldn't be in Germany right now. This is the personal response. If you want a more political, historical answer, the breaking point for me – more precisely, the place where this incident began – was Gezi. There are two intellectual, conscientious currents, sub-streams in Turkey. And by saying this, I'm not talking about rightism or left-ism, Islamism, Turkism, *laïcité*. These two sub-streams emerge from time to time. One is a more liberal, more egalitarian – more demo-cratic, to be concise – type of sub-stream. I'm careful not to say more Western. One is the sort of authoritarian, patriarchal, top-down political nature we're experiencing right now. The more liberal, democratic sub-stream exploded and erupted at Gezi. And the second sub-stream began at the end of Gezi to suppress that first sub-stream once again. The polarisation about which everyone complains today and which even the flanks of the regime complain about began at the end of Gezi as a conscious policy. Erdoğan shot off the first signal flare for this, saying, 'I'm forcing 50 per cent to stay at home.' In saying he'll keep 50 per cent at home, he communicated that 'if this sub-stream overflows onto the streets with a demand for freedom, I have a group opposed to this too'. This was the first indicator. Then came 17–25 December. Then came the local elections on 31 March 2014. Erdoğan – and I'm not saying the AK Party, but Erdoğan – rose up from the 31 March local elections in the fight with the Gülen Movement by increasing the game, despite the scandals, the corruption and illegality scandals that emerged, despite Gezi. I felt something there: I published a book entitled *The Gezi Spirit and Political Theory*, and it was published in November 2013. I wrote that immediately after Gezi. And somewhere in that book, I said something about a junction for Turkey. Turkey would either go down a path of more freedom, along a more democratic, more participatory path towards a democracy compatible with the spirit of Gezi, or it would head towards greater polarisation through these conflicts. Right now, as I said in November 2013, Erdoğan unfortunately appears to have adopted the belief that the second path is more favourable for Turkey. I saw that the walkways on this path embarked on in the 31 March elections were functioning. I sat down and mourned after those elections. In fact, I told a group of my friends, including political theorists and sociologists, that 'challenging times are coming, the trajectory of this issue is grave. We don't know what fascism is in Turkey, we think fascism is top-down politics, but fascism comes from the base as a populistic movement. And we have set out down this road. Very difficult times are coming, and we have to do something.' I wasn't taken seriously in the political party of which I was a member and where I was engaged in politics.

'No, no, don't be ridiculous. Nothing like that will happen,' they said. In fact, I went to a psychologist friend and asked, 'Give me a paranoiac diagnosis so I can find peace. Because terrible times are coming. Let this be my paranoia, because I don't see this trajectory as being good.' I didn't get the diagnosis. The point at which Turkey has arrived today is the point that I predicted. This is the fundamental reason why I think the critical junction you mentioned is Gezi. Because Turkish politics truly came to a junction at Gezi. These two sub-streams – the liberal and the oppressive sub-streams, and I say this independently of intellectual and religious differences. Because the doctrines that primarily comprise liberalism and egalitarianism and that comprise oppression are not ideological or things in the monopoly of belief-faith systems. I mean, I know a lot of liberal Muslims and a lot of liberal leftists. And the exact opposite. So the fault lines between these two sub-streams do not overlap with the fault lines between the intellectual groupings which we are used to in Turkey. These are differences related to a style of policymaking. I'm not talking about a difference between the ideological and intellectual content of crafted policies. So these things rose up side by side, one at first and then the other, during the multiparty era. Waves of oppression emerge during the coup eras, and then a more liberal, democratic period arrives. Then a societal movement supports more freedoms but quashes them, and so forth. Things that go with balance became no longer able to create that balance or reach a junction in one way or another in Gezi. And the conflict between those two sub-streams became visible. I'm not saying that we started down a path at that junction, and we'll go from here. I already said this in the most recent series of articles I wrote. A liberal route opened up in Gezi, and Turkey could have gone there and followed that. But the regime at the time couldn't brave this. The regime at the time is the regime of today. I'm saying that Erdoğan could have left Gezi as a hero of democracy, but he didn't have the courage for this. And more than just not having the courage, he read this from an incredibly false position. He sincerely believed that this was a conspiracy that directly targeted him and was triggered from some places. To move forward by putting that wave behind him was a political choice. He didn't do that. Instead, he tried to head down the other path. He saw that as a more certain path for himself and for Turkey. So a pathway was opened at Gezi. It seemed like Turkey was going to set off down that path, but it didn't and turned towards the oppressive path. We've been moving down this path for eight years since Gezi. I think we've reached the end of the road. I can't predict where we'll head from there, but I think the path that was opened in Gezi is still open.

Do you see yourself returning to Turkey?

I really want to return to Turkey. Being able to return to Turkey, or at least knowing that my preference is to remain in Germany if I'm going to stay in Germany is the situation I want. Ultimately, we've been living here for five years. We set up a life here, whether it's good or bad or disorderly, we set up a life. We can't decide to break up this order and return to Turkey, even if we want to. Because there aren't the conditions for this in Turkey. I want Turkey to have these conditions and for there to be a situation in which I can say, if we're staying in Turkey, that we're staying because we want to. That's my wish. Prediction . . . To be honest, I was not at all hopeful about this until the Istanbul municipal mayoral election. The precondition for our return to Turkey is that a democratic state of law reliant on human rights regains control in Turkey. And I'm saying this in the most academic sense. I know this may be possible . . . and that's because I'm a political theorist, I know the political history of Turkey. There is no example of an enthusiastic totalitarian regime being overthrown through democratic means. These regimes are crushed under their own violence, otherwise there's no departure from this state of affairs without a massive collapse, a collective collapse. So I'm very pessimistic about this. What we experienced in the Istanbul metropolitan municipal elections, if you want the truth, was actually something that could constitute an example for the history of global politics.

I mean, we're talking about a situation where the will of the people was able to impose itself directly on the regime. In an environment where any and all propaganda was banned for the opposition, where the one-sided propaganda went kicking and screaming and the opposition was demonised, the opposition won an election. One, the fact that an election was held was interesting. Two, the fact that they were able to win this election was interesting. How do we know that Turkey is governed by an oppressive regime? Elections are cancelled. This election is considered invalid, ignored in a way that defies everything legal, logical and factual. İmamoğlu isn't given the election mandate. A second election is held. İmamoğlu increases his vote in the second election. If I had lived in Turkey, if I had not been looking from outside, perhaps I would have been much less hopeful about Turkey. Because people in Turkey, people from my neighbourhood especially, people in the leftists, left-liberal neighbourhood have given up hope for the public, have given up hope for the ordinary citizen. I spoke with Turkey's liberal intellectuals. Because when democracy functions, it gives us something like this regime, so it gives us law but not democracy. I tried to explain how there can't be democracy where there is no law, but there is a hopelessness for the people, for the shared will of the people. But the 23 June elections show me that the electorate in Turkey – and, in fact, an electorate not from our own neighbourhood – can make political choices through a certain conscientious channel, can send messages saying that explicit injustices have advanced considerably. It's not that we should trust the people, but there must be a way to bring to life this consciousness, this shared consciousness. Because I believe that something that gives shape to the electorate's political choices in Turkey is, one, its pocket, and two, an intense perception operation, an operation aimed at shaping the public perception the regime is conducting. This is called ideological propaganda. It's not only manipulation. What there ultimately needs to be in democracy is 'Yes, my pocket guides my political preferences, and my conscience guides my conscientious beliefs'. We do not freely form conscientious beliefs. Perhaps it's manipulation, yes, but they form through fears within a series of intense contortions. And something else can happen with your pocket when consciousness can be mobilised. The opportunity for democratisation occurs. The answer to this question is that Turkey's democratisation is not only a political matter for me. It's something which is very personal. My return ticket to Turkey is Turkey's democratisation. And I'm not so hopeless about that. Enough, let them hold elections.

16

NAZAN ÜSTÜNDAĞ

I mourn for my people. I mourn for my people being poisoned [. . .] broken off from their own identity and from their own roots and being entirely in the grip of capitalism, racism and nationalism. My greatest feelings of mourning relate to Turkey.

Nazan Üstündağ received her PhD in 2005 from the Sociology Department at Indiana University Bloomington. Between 2005 and 2018, she worked as an assistant professor at Boğaziçi University, in the Department of Sociology. Currently, she is a fellow of the Gerda Henkel Foundation's Patrimonies programme. Her work concerns political imaginaries, gendered subjectivities and state violence in Kurdistan. Her most recent articles have appeared in the journals South Atlantic Quarterly, History of the Present *and* Differences. *She is a member of Academics for Peace and Women for Peace.*

Dr Üstündağ, thank you for agreeing to conduct an interview with us. I want to start by asking: when and how did you leave Turkey?
I was on sabbatical between 2016 and 2017. I went to CUNY as a visiting scholar, but before that, I had a court date because of an article I wrote for *Özgür Gündem* called 'Autonomy, Youth and War'. That court case was ongoing at the time. They cancelled my passport while I was in America because of the case. The notification went to [Boğaziçi] University. My lawyer at the time notified me about it. Then the police went to the department, and when my mother was getting something from the notary – she had a power of attorney on my behalf – the police surrounded her. They raided her home and detained the people who had directed my mother to the notary.

Actually, at no point was I considering not returning to Turkey, but I love my family, my mother and my father, and I didn't want to worry them. So I said I'd stay another year in the US. Then a few more criminal cases were opened against me for speeches I gave in Diyarbakır. An arrest warrant was issued. I resigned from Boğaziçi when that happened. I was in Berlin at the time. I received a six-month fellowship from the Rosa Luxemburg Foundation. After that, I received a two-year fellowship from Academy in Exile and the Scholar Rescue Fund. Now, I'm on a fellowship from the Gerda Henkel Foundation. That's how I've stayed here. They froze my application for associate professorship, which was reinitiated amid all this, but there was no conclusion. And this first criminal case was dropped, because to my surprise, a criminal case in Turkey must be initiated within six months after the article in question was published, so it was dropped because of that. Apart from that, my arrest warrant and other criminal cases are ongoing.

When you look back, what kind of Turkey did you leave behind?
Having been in Turkey between 2013 and 2015, having been in Turkey during the peace process was a great privilege. I thought I had truly tasted freedom at the time. I tasted happiness. The peace process was truly a moment of liberty and happiness, both psychologically and socially. When I first left, it was devastating enough that this process had ended. I had also lost my friends fighting ISIS in Kobane. What happened in the Sur, in the Cizre uprisings and when people were burned in the basements, I felt great resentment for Turkey. I'm ethnically Turkish, and I'll forever defend all the demands of the Kurds. I therefore received a lot of threats. I was exposed extensively. A number of articles were written about me. Being seen by my own nation as the enemy also affected me deeply. That's the kind of Turkey I left behind. I was in mourning. There was a situation I was grieving over.

Now, however, the fact that, on the one hand, what's called the people are poisoned to this extent and, on the other, Turkey is being governed by gangs drags me towards a state of hopelessness. Although, the fact that the state no longer has its former strength and is becoming a gang brings along with it some advantages, because ultimately, I oppose the state. On the other hand, I mourn for my people. I mourn for my people being poisoned this much, being broken off from their own identity and from their own roots and being entirely in the grip of capitalism, racism and nationalism. My greatest feelings of mourning relate to Turkey. I want to return, but my friends say that the country I would find when I return is no longer Turkey. But I don't want to believe this. I am inspired by my own land despite it having such an immense history of racism and colonialism.

Had you ever thought you would live abroad before your passport was revoked?
Never. I thought I wouldn't leave even if a civil war broke out. And I made a mistake. If I had gone to prison, I might have been released

by now. I think I made a huge mistake. I fell victim to family love. I couldn't break their hearts. I think I made a huge mistake. My life is like a prison right now. But there, I may have been able to leave the prison in the end. I'm fighting here; it's not that I'm not fighting here, but there is a concern for the friends we left behind and fighting there provides a sense of strength. As someone who is a writer above all else – I'm not saying that I'm an academic anymore, because I don't take part in academia – as a person who works to produce information, of course, being broken off from the arteries that nourish me, being broken off from Kurdistan and Turkey, is arresting and constricting.

The peace process made us believe that an atmosphere of democracy and liberty was possible, but this process later collapsed and a series of incidents occurred back to back. What was the breaking point for you among these?
The basements. The basements in Cizre. The bombs that exploded in Ankara and Suruç. All of these were of course very upsetting and were small breaking points, but I could say that my relationship with life truly changed after the basements in Cizre.

Did you feel helpless? Not being able to do anything to prevent what was about to come?
What I experienced wasn't a feeling for whether I could prevent it but a feeling of disbelief. I always thought there would be an exit from there, whatever happened. I thought they would be able to get out of those basements. For the first time, I experienced a resentment not towards the Turkish state but towards the Kurdish Liberation Movement. Maybe I shouldn't say the first time, as I have certainly criticised the Movement, but there's a difference between criticism and resentment. There was a feeling of resentment for both sides. I think that was very hurtful, because I'm someone who believes that the righteous party in the war is the Kurdish Liberation Movement. The fact that the group I believed was justified just stood by this upset me a lot.

Do you believe the text the Academics for Peace signed had any impact? Did it have the desired effect among the Turkish and international public in your opinion?

I don't think it had the desired effect, because the desired effect was that the war would stop, of course. Ultimately our objective was to bring attention to the war. But the petition and what happened afterwards directed attention instead to the academics. It had another impact in this sense. Of course, I'm glad to have signed that document and to have contributed to its publication, because the most important slogan for me at the time was 'We won't be a party to this crime'. I think for academics, setting themselves apart from the actions of the state was an important gesture. But in the end, the fact that it directed attention towards them reframed the terms of the initial radicalism embedded in the petition. It fitted it into the liberal framework of 'freedom of expression' to a significant degree. In that sense, I don't think it had the desired effect.

You didn't leave just because of the Academics for Peace petition. As you explained, you were targeted for other reasons as well. How do you feel now? Do you feel like you're in exile?

It depends on what you mean when you say exile. You end up being separated all your life. If you think about migration as Kristeva wrote, migration and depression are actually very similar. I mean, I feel like I'm in exile. I want to return. I hope that I will return if the situation changes. I don't have any desire or wish to adapt to this place. But I think this relates a bit to age. Ultimately, I was someone who had taught at Boğaziçi University for years. My entire social life had reached a certain point. And leaving at that point to come here made me not want to accept in any sense the feeling of starting anew. I won't accept something like starting again. But in the end, there is a mobilisation here as well. The HDP and the Kurdish women's movement have local branches here. And I can say that I feel a little bit at home by participating in those organisations and writing.

You said you want to return if the situation improves. What would it take for you for this situation to improve? When might you make this decision to return?

The fact that my mother and father will believe that I won't be arrested if I go back. That's what it means for the situation to change for me.

When was the last time you were in Turkey?

October 2016.

How is your life in Germany? How is your daily life?

I spend my daily life alone. I spend it trying to write. I have a few friends, and I meet with them. I work at Jin TV, a Kurdish women's television station. I also work for the Freedom for Abdullah Öcalan Initiative. I participate in projects for these two positions. I have friends there, and am able to make friends there. I haven't taught at all since I arrived. That's become a bit of a trauma; I have a fear about teaching. That's how my days go by.

Did you receive any support from diaspora organisations when you arrived?

I had Kurdish friends from Turkey here and friends whom I knew from when I came to Europe for conferences and so on. I met up with them. I was exhilarated when Jin TV was founded. A feminist women's television station was formed for the first time in the world. There are a lot of international people – Germans, Rojavans, Arabs and Turks. To learn new things like montages and cameras as a woman . . . I mean, it wasn't because I needed to learn these things, but the fact that we all were performing a function given to men on television with a feeling that we could do anything, that there were no men, that we made the studio ourselves – all this was very exciting for me. I dedicated myself entirely to that during that period. And that kept me afloat.

Is there an old–new distinction between the previous migration wave and the current migration wave in Germany? What have you observed on this issue?

I don't feel it, because I don't organise with either the new arrivals or the old arrivals. I have felt a bit of fear based on my experience in Turkey. That's why I didn't want to live in Kreuzberg, for example, where such organisations would be more accessible, because I was scared when I heard Turkish. But I did hear about this tension you're talking about, because Germany has given a host of opportunities to the new arrivals. If you ask whether it's good or bad that there are these opportunities, I think it puts a liberal frame around how we are received here. I see this in myself because I also took advantage of this. I'm living a more solitary, non-organised, individualistic life because of that. I don't have any concern about organising with those friends I came with. This is definitely due to liberalism.

Some people who were interviewed for this book have said that they have been invited as a 'token Turk' to various events and expected to make various speeches against Erdoğan in exchange for these fellowships and opportunities. Some have said that when you want to talk about another issue, you're asked to only talk about authoritarianism in Turkey. Have you felt something like this?

I haven't accepted this, starting with America. In America, I said, 'If I'm going to talk about authoritarianism, I'm not going to talk about Turkey. I'll talk about Trump or authoritarianism in Europe. I'll talk about the state system, about how people have fallen victim to the liberal system.' That's why I'm not called to these sorts of talks anymore. So I don't have any problems like that.

You said that universities in Europe as well as in Turkey have become more neoliberal and that there is actually no freedom

of thought anywhere. Do your experiences in Germany illustrate this?

I'm not saying this about my experiences in Germany. I wouldn't want to be at any academic institution in Germany. But in Turkey, I was at a wonderful place like Boğaziçi, where the relationship with the students is amazing. But the sort of arrogance and toxicity that comes with being an academic, what you gain from having truly valuable ideas, your own valuable actions and from how your students look at you – this all happens. I feel like I've grown politically because I've been cleansed of all this.

You said that you would work at Jin TV while you continue living in Germany after this. I also hope you'll continue to write. Do you not have any intention to return to academia?

No, I don't. I don't want to return to academia. I want to continue producing ideas. I want to collectivise idea production. I am doing this collectively as much as possible at Jin TV, but I'm writing a book right now, and I want to see what I can do collectively after finishing that book. I thought that I grew with my students. There are still a lot of students around me right now. Could I create a collective with them in which I can contribute to their ideas, in which I can think together with them? I'm pondering that. I write poetry, and I'll keep doing that.

Recently academics in diaspora studies have discussed the concept of extra-territorial authoritarianism. People in the diaspora often feel the shadow of the authoritarian state. Do you feel Turkey's breath on your neck in your life in Germany? Or do you feel like you're in danger as you walk down the street?

No, I don't feel that. Germany's own authoritarianism affects me much more, and America's authoritarianism affected me much more when I was there. Germans in Germany and the German state intervening in every aspect of life, the German identity and German nationalism disturb me much more. I get apprehensive even at the market that they'll get mad at something else. There were, though, two incidents. One was on the metro, I was chatting with a friend. I have never watched *Aşk-ı Memnu*, but when I want to cry, I watch the scene where Bihter dies. That and 'Zahit Bizi Tan Eyleme', Mustafa's death. I've never watched *Muhteşem Yüzyıl* either, but I cry during that scene. I was telling this to my friend: 'What a horrible man Sultan Selim was.' A man got up and attacked us, saying, 'You're an Alevi, only an Alevi wouldn't like Sultan Selim.' I wasn't scared, but it was very bizarre. Because I had always been perceived as a Kurd, I had never physically felt that being an Alevi was that great of a threat. And I'm not an Alevi. But when I physically experienced that, the depth of the Alevi–Sunni issue in Germany and its depth in Turkey upset me, and I was really affected. And also when Süleyman Soylu read my article on television about three or four months ago . . . He read it beautifully; 'Bravo,' I said. I was proud of myself because my own words came from the mouth of Süleyman Soylu and because I made Süleyman Soylu say the words 'guerrilla' and 'Gever'. But the fact that my words came out of his mouth also caused me to suffer a ten-minute panic attack. I was frightened, thinking, 'They're going to come. They'll find me and kill me.'

After these incidents, many academics begin to censor themselves. Are you doing anything like this, thinking about the possibility that you'll return to Turkey one day?
On the contrary, I say things I never did before, and I'm positioning myself more radically. Definitely not. Because if I return to Turkey, I will continue to fight there so that there could be and will be such a position there too. I can't describe myself without that fight, because I believe that when you start to hide yourself, when you start to censor yourself, you begin to believe what you say and position yourself through what you say to overcome the feelings of guilt and shame inside you. I have seen this in many people. I don't want to experience

that kind of life. But I'm not young. I already have a criminal history in the Republic of Turkey. That's why I don't tell anyone to follow my example. But there could be a position [where you do not censor yourself], and I want this to be known, because it has become very natural to say, 'I'll return to Turkey, so I won't do this.' I mean, look at what we all did between 2013 and 2015. We must own that, because our desire is to return not to 2011 but to 2013.

Do you see differences between the mentalities of people who have lived in the diaspora for many years and activists currently living in Turkey and Kurdistan?
I meet with organisations within the leftist or Kurdish women's movements as much as possible. I don't feel anything like that. But I think this relates to being organised. If you're not organised, of course you can consider other things, but I haven't encountered anything like that.

What do you think are the differences in the experiences of the diaspora coming in the 1980s and this generation?
Most likely, there are a lot of similarities. I don't know, and I don't want to talk about something I don't know much about.

You said the authoritarianism in Germany bothers you even more. How is Germany greeting the new arrivals?
I could say, at least from my experience, that Germany wanted to drive a wedge between us and the Kurds. They don't want to talk about the Kurdish issue. They want to see more academic pleasantries and freedom of thought – that sort of thing. I think that's why they created funds for academics, journalists and artists. These funds and disinterest in Kurds but interest in academics, however transitory, work to isolate Kurds and academics from each other. On that issue, I think a decoupling more severe than it is in Turkey is taking place financially and in terms of class.

They invest funds and end up opening a space for Turkey's intelligentsia as well as making a brand for themselves by saying 'We support their freedom of thought'. Is this the case?

Yes, it's branding, but most people don't buy this. You are the outcome of the situation in which you are forced to live. So I can't say we've become more liberal as a lifestyle. But on the other hand, everyone has very serious criticisms of this situation. This isn't just a criticism that I have articulated. I mean, they don't let you talk about the Kurdish question when you go to a meeting. They only want to talk about freedom of thought. There is also a lot of disaggregation being done in the courts and in asylum practices. They asked me whether the PKK is a terrorist organisation. I said, 'I refuse to answer such a question, this is the exact same question that Turkey asked.' I came here so that I wouldn't be asked that question. But it was asked.

Turkey and the Turkish diaspora are polarised. We have heard that members of the Gülen Movement have become very isolated and that the civil society that has convened for Turkey's democratisation doesn't want to include the Gülenists. Does this polarisation still exist, or has exile brought people together from different groups and ideologies in some way?

There are instances when it can bring people together, but regarding the Gülenists, I'll say that I can't speak for all Gülenists or the whole diaspora, but there's something that comes up when discussing among academics, which is that the Gülen Movement inflicted so much hardship on academics and Gülenism did so much that of course this wasn't forgotten. That's why there's a barrier between leftist academics and Gülenist academics, because ultimately, academics encountered so much injustice from the Gülen Movement when becoming assistant professors, entering a university and hiring an assistant that this won't be forgotten.

The fact that the Gülen Movement has adopted a victim discourse without any sort of reckoning and receives so much support from civil society and the state in Germany bothers many people, as far as we understand.

Definitely. We encountered two Gülenists at a meeting. I treated them well individually, but I said to them, 'What will you do when we show up in your court tomorrow or the next day? Have you changed?' Because we, as the leftists and Kurds in Turkey, know the religionists, nationalists and Sunnis are at war within the Turkish state, but they'll end up leaving hand in hand, as they did with Ergenekon, and we are burdened with the cost of that. And so it could have been good for us to act politically and develop a series of partnerships with the Gülenists with this in mind, but people can't accept them, I think.

You said that you regretted leaving the country at the start of this conversation. So is there anything that makes you say you're glad that you left?

Right now, I really appreciate and admire the actions of the people at Boğaziçi University, of course, but I can guess how the internal discussions there are going. One single thing is probably that I'm happy I'm not there alongside those internal discussions. I've said frequently – and I still say it – that a good thing that happened to me here is being removed from the community of academics and the university environment. Of course I love my students, but not belonging to an institution, being an academic in that academic hierarchy and being together with students who are devoted to you and being equal, losing a sort of class and status has been very beneficial for me personally. I think it has made me more mature. I think that's the best thing that has happened to me.

17

NİL MUTLUER

There were many times when I felt exiled in Turkey too.
For example, Beyoğlu has changed so much, that it was no
longer my Beyoğlu and I felt very lonely and exiled, and
moreover I didn't have any other village which I could return
to. I mean it is something very isolating. This is a feeling I
have for many places in Istanbul. Or sometimes when we fight
with each other instead of trying to understand each other in
dissenting groups, that is, when we fight each other, instead
of Erdogan, when there is a process of othering, gossiping
going on et cetera; these may seem small, but I feel exiled
at those points again.

Nil Mutluer (PhD, comparative gender studies, Central European University) is a social scientist, and occasional journalist, TV programmer and consultant for civil society and art projects. She thinks and writes on gender, sexuality, ethnicity, belief systems, migration, memory, nationalism and everyday life and is an advocate for rights and freedoms, acting in the intersectional space between academia, civil society, media and arts. Currently she is working as a senior researcher at Leipzig University's Institute for the Study of Religions on a German Research Foundation project titled 'Piety and Secularity Contested: Family and Youth Politics in post-Kemalist "New Turkey"'. She is also affiliated with EUME (Europe in the Middle East) – Forum Transregionale Studien in Berlin as a research fellow. She was a guest scholar in the Diversity and Social Conflict Department at the Humboldt University in Berlin, Germany, where she was the Einstein Foundation senior scholar between 2019 and 2021, and a Philipp Schwartz research fellow at the Alexander von Humboldt Foundation between 2016 and 2018, as well as an interim professor of public law and gender studies in 2018. She has worked as a lecturer at different universities in Istanbul, as well as at Getronogan Armenian High School in Istanbul, where she taught a course on human rights and democracy. She produced the sociopolitical discussion programme Başka Düşünce *('The Other Thinking') for fifty-two weeks at* ArtıTV *in 2021–2. She also co-produces the occasional sociological and political analysis television show* ÖteBeri Yeniden *('Paraphernalia Again') at Daktilo 1984 (with Emine Uçak), which was first broadcast on IMC TV in 2012–13. She is a consultant for various art projects including 'Me and Nuri Bala' (2009, directed by Melisa Önel), a documentary about the life story of Turkey's first feminist transvestite stand-up artist, Esmeray, which won the 46th Antalya Golden Orange Award. She is also one of the two co-curators of the Library of Resistance/Divergent Roads of History exhibition and the panels organised around it (with Murat Özbank), which is part of the 'Gezi Ten Years After' events hosted by the Maxim Gorki Theatre, Berlin, to commemorate the tenth anniversary of the Gezi uprising. Nil lives in the transnational space between Berlin and Istanbul. She calls in-between-ness home.*

When did you leave Turkey for good? Why did you leave?
We were targeted after signing the peace petition titled 'We Will Not Be a Party to This Crime'. I am one of the first signatories who was fired from the universities. Actually, in the beginning, I was not thinking of leaving the country. We had just started explaining what was going on in Turkey, the rapid progression of authoritarianism in particular, to our connections in Turkey and abroad, such as in the European Union and European Commission. In short, I was doing what I have been doing for years on democratisation. At that time, another peace academic from Humboldt University in Berlin, whom I did not know before, Professor Gökçe Yurdakul, emailed me and suggested that we apply for some funds together. I was aware that I would not be able to return to the academy in Turkey immediately, as we understood that what we were going through was the beginning of the deterioration that the universities in Turkey are suffering from now: they are being turned into centralised institutions, devoid of scientific and critical thinking. Thus, I decided to go abroad from Turkey, but of course, our transnational efforts to explain the authoritarianism and lawlessness in Turkey continue, just as we still maintain our solidarity and relations.

Actually, if such an opportunity had not come to your door, you would have continued your activism in Turkey.
Most likely I would. I mean, at some point I might have considered spending some time abroad, because I always had it in my mind to do a post-doc. We are academics with international connections. However, as a social scientist, Turkey's political and sociological dynamics and the areas that need to be studied lead one to stay in the country. Until I came to Berlin, my field work was exclusively on Turkey. Now here in Berlin, I do research discussing the transnational dimensions of my

previous work in Turkey. I carry out field work on Alevi and Kurdish groups, religious believers, women and men from Turkey and their institutions and organisations. When it comes to questions and problems of one's country, it is not emotionally easy to leave them behind, but the fact that I have a small person depending on me affected the way I made my decision, and I accepted Professor Yurdakul's offer.

How would you describe the political atmosphere in Turkey? How was the situation in Turkey when you left?

The situation in Turkey is now painfully bad. And it's getting worse and worse. By watching the videos of a mafia leader who has had links to the state for years on end, many people see the truth of what social scientists and journalists have been saying for years, at least the provable part. The political, social and economic situation in Turkey today is without doubt very, very bad. I think the period that we, Academics for Peace, were forced to leave Turkey, was the beginning of the coming big purges of academia and bureaucracy, crackdowns on media and civil society, and restrictions on all kinds of freedoms. I think the situation especially starting in the post-Gezi period was the initial phase of the increasingly oppressive policies. In that period, namely after summer 2013, there were legal amendments restricting freedoms and rights, and the state initiated heavy and violent policies in the cities where mainly Kurds live. The state's oppressive policies during the post-Gezi period had not been as visible as the post-2016 coup attempt policies, because the 2016 coup attempt affected wider segments of the population, especially Muslim groups like the Gülenists. In the moment between post-Gezi and the 2016 coup attempt, targeted by the state, Academics for Peace, which is a small group of individual academics, were left as marginalised traitors and also put into a very isolated position. We had been turned into a small group of undesirables called 'Academics for Peace'. Universities, nourished by their connections with the government, immediately started firing Academics for Peace and opening investigations against them. We predicted that it would spread. The very history of the republic suggested that such things had happened in the past and could happen again. So it was not surprising at all. The academy has always been under governmental control. Academics who worked for a democratic and pluralistic Turkey and an independent scientific working environment had experienced dismissals and exclusions before. After the 1980 coup, for example, we saw the establishment of YÖK (Council of Higher Education) as a state institution to supervise and control the universities. This said, the process which started in 2016 and which continues to this day is the largest purge ever experienced in the Turkish universities. Targeting the Academics for Peace proved to be a very useful tool for President Erdoğan. For a while, he was sending his messages to us, academics, through the speeches he gave in the regular meetings he organised to meet with village foremen. As if we, as 'aloof' academics, were elites dissociated from the day-to-day realities of Turkish society, and he was a politician in touch with the popular grassroots. Far from it. Most of us were and still are social scientists who are doing field work on the streets, with the grassroots. In addition to all this Sedat Peker, who at that time was a mafia leader supporting and supported by the government, even though they seem to have parted company nowadays – well, that Sedat Peker even threatened to take a shower in our blood. In those early days when our marginalisation and purge from the universities had just started, our isolation from the rest of the society also instilled another type of fear. We were afraid of violent attacks against our persons even in Istanbul, but we were more worried about the safety of our friends in remote Anatolian cities, especially those working in Anatolian universities with only one or two signatories. Some of them had their homes raided. The difficulties they experienced were of a different order. We who lived in big cities like Istanbul were relatively more sheltered. But we had friends who were alone, isolated. I was a single mother and even though my partner and friends used to visit me frequently, I was living alone with my baby daughter. The owner of the off-licence in our neighbourhood once said to me, 'If the police come to your house at night, let us know immediately, and we'll take the baby to safety.' In other words, there were also people who stood in solidarity with us, who supported us politically, but they were few and far between. Afterwards, the coup attempt became a pretext for the spread of authoritarianism. Lawsuits began to be filed against us on terrorism charges.

Have you ever regretted it? Do you wish you hadn't signed and never had to leave?

No. I didn't even think once. On the contrary, considering what happened in the Kurdish provinces in the summer and autumn of 2015 – the violence, children's and civilian deaths – no. On the contrary, I felt a strange relief. It was as if we were no longer passive bystanders but we too had become a part of the discrimination that they, the Kurds, have been subjected to. However, I am not talking about a state or feeling of equalisation. Losing my job is in no way comparable to the suffering of those who have lost their children and families, who experience the fear of violent death as part of their everyday existence and who have been systematically subjected to discrimination for years. No, it is not the same thing and can never be. My PhD thesis is on those who came to the Tarlabasi neighbourhood in Istanbul through forced migration. I know very well and follow very closely the socio-psychological processes that led to the events of 2015, and how the pressure on and the belonging of the Kurds have been shaped. Moreover, I have been working on and thinking about questions of democracy and democratisation for quite a while, there have been many occasions on which I have stood in solidarity with friends and democratic activists who have faced political persecution. In that sense I was not surprised by what we experienced. Being singled out, being targeted, being mobbed or harassed in academia, in the media or in civil society because of one's different political views – these were and are not exceptionally rare occurrences in Turkey. And frankly, signing an open letter criticising the government's policies was one of the lamest political acts I have ever done in in my life. For example, in January 2013 I published a three-week series of daily articles in *Milliyet* on the political plurality of the Alevis during the ruling AKP's time. The headlines and language I used in that series were much more pungent. And after the Demiroren family bought the newspaper, they hastily put an end to the second series which started in September 2013, citing the 'displeasure' of the 'higher political echelons'. Similarly, in October 2015 the government declared a state of emergency in the Kurdish southeastern regions of the country, and I went to the region, to Mardin and Cizre twice, first with a small group of peace defenders, and the second time with a larger group of public intellectuals and opinion leaders. As is usual, I informed the administration of the university I was working in at the time by filling out and submitting the form required when you leave the city. I told them that I was going there to do field work. On my return I realised that there was an intelligence unit active in the university, for I was 'informally' cautioned about our activities and public statements in the region. I did not take it seriously. Then, when I signed the peace declaration titled 'We Will Not Be a Party to This Crime', I asked Murat Özbank, who too was one of the signatories, whether he thought that there would be some consequences of our doing so, like being disciplined or fired by the universities we were working in. And then we laughed at the thought, saying we wished that our signatures were that consequential! But I had sensed that our signatures were about to be blown out of proportion from the 'informal intelligence warning' I had received from my university. So I have never regretted it, I have not been surprised by what we have experienced, but I must admit it has been difficult for me, for all of us. The dissidents in Turkey are going through very difficult times indeed.

Okay, then, when you consider the process since Gezi, do you think of any turning points? Are there any events about which you said 'After this, nothing will be the same' or 'There is no turning back from this'?

Actually, there are. My suspicions were raised for the first time in 2007–8 about a matter concerning women's issues. Gender and sexuality are areas where political and sociological trends can be sensed in advance, because family, reproductive and sexuality policies are all issues related to the capillaries of society. At that time, some regulations came to the fore that envisaged women working in home-based occupations, that is, women were positioned in a family structure focused on domestic labour and care services. However, since similar social and economic policies are also seen in neoliberal Europe, it was possible to think that there was nothing peculiar about those regulations, they were part and parcel of the global system everywhere. Yet, Erdoğan's rhetoric, which started with the statement that 'each family should have at least three kids' and continues to this day, was giving very perceptible signals of an encroaching neoliberal conservatism. In fact, after the 2011 general elections, the AKP preferred to form a government with a neoconservative and authoritarian approach. Thus for example in 2011, the AKP's provincial chairman for Istanbul, [Aziz] Babuşçu, made a public statement saying that they would no longer act together with the liberals, who actually supported them until then. He predicted that the liberals would not like the new Turkey that the AKP intended to build and that they would therefore position themselves on the side of those who were against the AKP. That statement itself was a sign, because these people were not prone to making statements like that out of the blue, without calculation. Then Gezi happened, and after Gezi everything just went south – laws were passed which restricted freedoms of expression and communication, increased the powers of the security forces, furnished intelligence agencies with impunity, and encouraged ordinary citizens to act as informants ratting on political opponents; and after that came the massacres in Suruç, at Ankara Central railway station, the killing of Diyarbakır Bar president Tahir Elçi . . . Eventually there was the attempted coup of July 2016, and with the declaration of the state of emergency and the executive decrees purging tens of thousands of public servants, here we are. The 31 March 2014 local elections were the first popular elections after the Gezi events and the corruption scandals of 17–25 December 2013 and despite the heavy flak it took, the AKP won the elections, increasing its votes. In those days, Murat Özbank, with whom we were active in democratic circles in Turkey, used to say to anyone who would listen: 'These election results suggest that the political game in Turkey has changed. We have entered deep into the realm of the irrational. There will be a period of populistic authoritarianism which takes its power from the grassroots, from an irrational yet popular majority. And for the first time in Turkey we will find out what fascism really looks like and what we will see will be ugly, very very ugly.' We thought at the time that he was worrying too much, that he was exaggerating the threat a bit. But everything he said came true step by step. In other words, I can say with reference to him, that the ability to rely on a grassroots majority despite popular protests, despite the corruption scandals, gave the AKP the opportunity to gain and maintain an authoritarian stronghold on Turkish politics and that Gezi and the 31 March 2014 local elections were, in that sense, important turning points.

Whether it is the central railway station massacre, or the Suruc massacre, every time you said 'It cannot get any worse than this', something worse happened. But that did not discourage you. You tried to remain in Turkey and tried to open up a public space of action in civil society. What types of activism were you engaged in in those days? I think you were active in the women's movement. I also remember your name from many articles and book chapters you authored on the peace process.
I think I care about the contribution of academic research to society as much as its contribution to the literature, perhaps even more. At this point I feel closer to the researcher-activist position that has been discussed more recently in the literature. Of course, in this position, I take guidance from such values as ethical concerns and being on the

side of the truth. My story started like this: my doctoral thesis is on the daily life practices of the Kurds, men and women, who came to the city through forced migrations and village evacuations in the 1990s. As a person who grew up in the western part of the country, my first encounter with the reality of the forced migrations and village evacuations was when I was a university student and that was the reason I chose that topic for my doctoral research. In those days, reports in the media about the military raids on Kurdish villages were few and far between, giving the impression that these were sporadic events not adding up to a systematic policy. But then a friend of mine brought over the photo archives of one of the Kurdish political parties which was closed down in that period, as he thought that the house I was living in with my family would be above any suspicion and hence safe to store those photos. That was when the real dimensions of the problem hit me in the face. I saw the defilement of the guerrillas' bodies by the security officers, which we are now unfortunately beginning to see again in social media. That is how I started to realise the gravity of forced migration as a social and political problem, and then, in the 2000s research revealed its real dimensions. As I researched the issue, I realised that what appeared to be an isolated village raid was in fact the continuation of the deportation policies pursued since the days of the Ottoman Empire. And as my awareness of the problem increased, I continued carrying out research and practising activism. Other topics were added to the Kurdish and gender issues. When I was fired from my position at the university, I was doing research on discrimination against the Alevis, the socio-political constellations in the AKP period, the structure of the Diyanet and plurality within the women's movement. And my activism was focused on democratisation, freedoms and gender, ethnic and religious equality. I was active in a number of NGOs working in these issue areas. Also I like this kind of dialogue and being a bridge in my work. Sometimes I think of myself as a 'cable'. That's why I did a lot of things with people from the religious sections of society in different periods. When I was dismissed from my job, I remember that people from the religious community, people I least expected, called me privately. For example Cihangir İslam. Not that he is someone I wouldn't expect to call me, but we didn't know each other very well. He called me immediately. And various students of mine who I knew were close to the AKP also called me right away. That was also a very valuable show of solidarity. So I thought that I had actually touched some people in my life in a very real sense.

How do you think academia reacted to this? Because a lot of people were also disappointed. You mentioned those who stood with you, those who stood in solidarity, but we also had fellow academics who did not stand with us. How did this make you feel? How do you view the silence of the academy?
As for academia and the frustrations with academia, this actually says something about the academia in Turkey. We opened a window in academia for a certain period. I will not be modest about it. When I say we, I mean as a group, we were first a thousand, then became two thousand. Of course I also include in this group the colleagues who are not signatories but who are honest and ethical in their work and behaviour. However, we are few. I think we should all recognise and appreciate our share in this. So a window was opened. But I remember having difficulties in the universities where I taught before, we were pushing to open that window. But when there was such a pressure, we saw how people who pretended to be critical and to defend such great democratic, secular values were actually trying to maintain their academic positions, or rather their existence in those insignificant positions. But let this not be misunderstood. I do not mean to say that people shouldn't try to make a living, should quit their jobs or leave. No. But not saying anything at all, that kind of thing makes one very sad. On the other hand, it does not surprise me. Because this country has always been like this. What I mean is, it says something about the character of the people. Sometimes, when I chat with friends, we say 'What we count on is the spinelessness of this people'. I mean when

the power holders change, so do they. But they will have their own place in history, that's for sure.

You mean, their to capacity to forget?
Of course, but what we are talking about is a very selective form of forgetting and remembering. What's important is to walk the path we are walking. That's why it is not surprising. Because I was struggling even with more serious things. For example at Nişantaşı University, where I last worked in Turkey, I was objecting to things like 'We will send you a list, and if students have not paid their tuition fees, you will not disclose their grades to them'. I cannot accept this. I was telling them, 'Don't mix monetary affairs with academic affairs. The grades are between me and my students, they to belong our academic relations and I will disclose their grades, no matter what.' When I raised such ethical issues out loud in academic meetings, there were only one or two people who openly supported my position, the rest chose to remain silent. Also, you are in a neoliberal system. So on the one hand you try to understand that fear, but on the other hand it is important to continue the struggle. As the number of those who continued the struggle diminished, we started to experience the problems we are experiencing.

I also remember the article you wrote for OpenDemocracy. At that time, when people were looking for the smallest crumb of solidarity, you wrote a very critical article about Europe's and Germany's approach to the arrivals from a decolonial perspective. Let's talk a little bit about that. What kind of environment did you find yourself in when you came to Europe?
This also feels strange. I can't help thinking, what did these Europeans suppose we were? I mean we lost our jobs, the lives we'd had, our homes, precisely because we were practising critical thinking publicly and openly in our homeland, so how could we not continue doing this in Europe too? Not seeing this, not expecting this from us is unbeliev-

able. On the one hand they applaud us because of 'our Western education', but when the criticism is directed against them they become
flabbergasted. This is sheer hypocrisy. But is anything new there? Not
really. A whole postcolonial, decolonial literature talks about this.

How exactly? Do they expect you to feel grateful?
Let me explain it with the triangular formulation that I first wrote
about in OpenDemocracy and that we then used in the article I wrote
with Seçkin Sertdemir Özdemir and Esra Özyürek: now, there is a perpetrator, there is a victim and there is a saviour. And of course in this
formula, Turkey is the perpetrator, we academics, journalists, political
migrants are the victims and Europe and the West are the saviours. But
can this relationship be explained in such a simplistic way? Of course
not. First of all, Europe has a not insignificant share in the authori-
tarianisation of Turkey and the deepening of this authoritarianism.
When I was still in Turkey, right after Gezi, the NGOs I was active
in were telling the Europeans not to turn a blind eye to the ongoing
human rights violations in Turkey. European officials seemed to trust
Erdoğan implicitly and anyone who warned about the rising tide of
human rights violations in the country was treated as some sort of
an Islamophobe. However, especially after the Gezi uprising, it was
independent democratic civil society organisations, which have been
in existence for years, that were doing the warning, and European and
other Western officials knew very well that these organisations were
fighting against all kinds of phobias and discrimination, so they could
not be Islamophobic. In short, how much of a saviour is Europe? Or
is Erdoğan alone the perpetrator? Are the victims victims, or are they
subjects in search of truth, defending peace, democracy and freedoms?
These questions deserve multiple, plural answers.

**When the Academics for Peace meetings were taking place, a few
European MPs came. They criticised, saying 'But the language
of the text is also problematic'.**

I missed the European MPs', but I remember similar criticisms in Turkey. It was a rather pointless debate. Whatever 1,000–2,000 people had written to criticise the government while authoritarianism was on the rise, the same thing would have happened. It has nothing to do with language of the text. As for the text, it may have its short-comings, but it was not a bad text. I don't think that there is such a thing as a perfect text. Besides, haven't we all signed even really bad texts just to show our solidarity in the past? We have. So in the end, it was not about the text. It was about why a thousand, two thousand people – what's more, a thousand, two thousand people with a very high level of education – came together. This was what made the text so effective, not its language. If you have heard this criticism from European MPs, we should of course look at the spirit of the period in terms of Europe, borders, migration. We know that one of the historical events that marked the period was the refugee deal which Germany struck with Turkey. Before we, the individual peace academics who came together, started to be targeted and fired, the process that led us to sign the petition was the same process that led to the refugee deal, that is, what happened between the elections of 1 June and 1 November 2015, especially in the summer of 2015. What was the main reason for the AKP to declare an election invalid, an election that was properly held at the time and that led to the HDP, a party close to the left, Kurdish and libertarians, passing the electoral threshold on its own? It was Selahattin Demirtaş's – who was one of the co-chairs of the HDP – open and direct objection to Erdoğan's bid for presidency. Moreover, the HDP's entry into parliament in June 2015 meant that the AKP lost its government-forming absolute majority in the parliament. This was also a period of human rights violations due to the state of emergency Erdoğan declared in the Kurdish provinces, a period which was marked by civilian deaths including children. At such an important time for Turkish politics and democracy, and at such a bloody time for the Kurds, Merkel's personal visit to Erdoğan was a move that directly affected internal dynamics, which meant the EU's support for Erdoğan. This visit also legitimised the policies of Erdoğan, who had already begun to become authoritarian and was escalating violence in the Kurdish provinces. Since the European Union's priority of protecting its borders took precedence over Turkish democracy, the signing of the refugee deal, which restricted people's right to seek refuge and asylum, was important. This deal was also a turning point for Europe. Europe was itself violating a human right which it had adopted as one of its fundamental principles long ago, namely the right to seek and enjoy asylum in other countries. This puts people who are in favour of transparency in an ambivalent position. On the one hand, there is a small critical circle in academia in Germany, unfortunately much less than I expected. What we mean by criticism also needs to be clarified. Whoever you ask in academia would say they are critical, but on the other hand, there are known red lines about what can be discussed. The narrow critical circle I am talking about are those who are open to questioning these red lines. This group of people easily includes those who criticise both Erdoğan and Europe at the same time, in their work. Because they themselves criticise without red lines. There are also those in academia and bureaucracy who speak with 'buts'. The 'buts' we know very well from Turkey. Answers that come in the form of 'You are right, but . . .' Most of the time these answers are little more than nationalist rhetoric, or liberal cop-outs.

I have a memory regarding the second example. When I first arrived in Germany, the then German vice chancellor and foreign affairs minister Sigmar Gabriel called a group of migrant academics to a meeting. We were academics from Syria, Turkey and Yemen. A Syrian colleague spoke before me. 'Germany has been a very good home for us,' he said in his speech. 'Even my children call older Germans here *Opa* or *Oma*, Grandad or Granny.' When I think about what the Syrians have been through I can understand this approach. They came from a war environment. But of course, our situation, the reason and the way we came to Germany was not the same. When it was my turn, I said, 'I understand very, very well my

Syrian colleague and what he is going through, and what Germany is doing is very important. Thank you very much for supporting us. Now we are in the academy, and look, we are talking with you freely. Yet, the important problem of the academy here is that it is based on established networks, and if you do not belong to one of those networks, it is very insecure and precarious. This precariousness is difficult for us, but it is also difficult for our German colleagues.' This time there was a denial and a rejection. A very well-connected professor and a bureaucrat from the Ministry of Foreign Affairs were also there, and both they and the minister simultaneously objected: 'No, academia in Germany is not precarious, everyone has a secure job.' I replied. 'No, it is precarious. Most of the jobs are project based and time limited and there are so many established networks, that it is impossible for outsiders to penetrate them. Also doing research based on the whims of funding agencies limits academic thinking and more importantly, it limits critical thinking. However, encounters in a free and independent environment can open up a rich space for knowledge production. No matter how much we and even the professors who support us want to create this space, it dissipates within the neoliberal and established channels.' Whereupon they replied that the German academy is an international one. I replied: 'I am an international academic, and I feel freer in an international environment than in Germany. Here that field is very cramped and cautious.' 'Then you must get integrated in the German academy', said the bureaucrat from the Ministry of Foreign Affairs. I couldn't stand it any longer. I replied: 'Then you should decide: is the German academy international, or am I supposed to get integrated into it? You cannot have it both ways.'

And what do they mean when they say 'get integrated'?
It is an important point. From my observations and the experiences of former migrants, I have come to the conclusion that integration in Germany is a one-way street and it is very harsh. It is not about people

creating something in common in interaction with one another. In particular, the first immigrants who arrived in the 1960s were the first to feel this harshness and started to organise. Of course the character of migration and Germany's political and social policies have changed over time, but there is still a harsh, bureaucratic aspect that involves the adoption of the local as the only basis, rather than learning from and understanding the newcomer. They say 'You will adapt to me'. I can understand this up to a certain point. Of course it is important to respect the culture of the place you are in, this is understandable. However, this one-way attitude and the fact that the door to criticism used to be closed and now is still only slightly ajar means ignoring the existing problems and in a sense sweeping them under the carpet. This leads to the perception of those who migrated once, even if they become citizens, not as citizens but as immigrants. So much so that, in some academic meetings, German academics would still position a German-Turkish family that has lived here for four generations as immigrants. It is as if the existence of dual or multiple belonging is an area that is only now beginning to be internalised . . .

Also, even if you speak German, there is no way in which you can have a foothold in German academia. Because it has its own traditions and if you have not studied there, if you are not part of it, it is difficult.
Absolutely. Moreover we are not talking about a tradition based on knowledge. What we are talking about is a structure built on the established networks I mentioned earlier, a structure that has become almost feudal with professorial chairs and cumbersome with heavy bureaucracy, and a neoliberal project-based state of competition which is obsessed with success measured not by the quality of the knowledge produced but by the size of the managed budgets. The neoliberal, project-based part is of course not specific to Germany. However, it has a great impact on diversity in academia in Germany, especially on the diversity of the knowledge-driven, intellectual

side of work. When you look from the outside, both organisations and academia appear to be attributing great value to 'diversity', but more often than not, what is meant by that is little more than a box-ticking exercise in a checklist of identities. There is not much of a methodological concern to achieve intellectual plurality, to generate such a pluralistic intellectual environment. Academics from recent wars and authoritarian regimes have now been added to that diversity checklist, and a category for 'migrant' academics was also added. What those migrants bring is, in fact, a different point of view and the encounter with that different point of view is a very nice encounter. A completely different set of ideas can come out from that encounter, but unfortunately the fact that the academy is not open to such encounters, coupled with project-driven competition, undermines the ground for producing common ideas through such encounters. In fact, although Germany has its own peculiarities, this state of the academy, the precarious working environment, project-centred thinking et cetera, is not unique to Germany.

And the question is, are you only invited as a token academic when Turkey is criticised or are they really interested in your academic work?
You are right. It seems there are two different approaches. Indeed there are people who invite me because of my former and my new work. What we went through, what I went through formed part of my academic research in recent years. There were academic events where I found the opportunity to present my work, or media where I could write about my experiences. Structures like Scholars at Risk are ready and willing to listen. There are also organisations where I thought I would never be invited again, and yet I have been invited. I shouldn't underestimate this part of the job, and I shouldn't be unfair in this respect. But there are also some who only expect me to express my gratitude. Especially the perception of Turkey and of the people from Turkey plays a big role in this. In my field work

here, I realised that being a person from Turkey in Germany is more difficult than being a person from Turkey elsewhere. Somehow you are always a *Schwarzkopf* – black-headed. At first they don't realise that you are from Turkey. Because you speak English, and the way you dress doesn't give it away. Then, there is no problem. However, when they somehow learn where you are from, his behaviour changes. Let me give you an example about the difference between being a person from Turkey in Germany and elsewhere. My daughter attends a French school in Berlin, because she is a French citizen. Some colleagues who were conducting a study on education with families from Turkey and children in Germany also conducted an in-depth interview with me. During the interview and in our conversation about the study I realised that the answers I gave were far removed from their question patterns and the problems my daughter experienced at school were different. Does my daughter experience exclusion like any other migrant child or child with a different identity? Yes, from time to time and not too frequently. However she experiences exclusion or hardship, it is not because she is from Turkey. When there is an exclusion, it is mostly among the children themselves, and not because she is from Turkey but because she is not a native French speaker, and there may be other children, from other nationalities, experiencing similar problems at the same time. The excluders and the excluded share a pluralistic identity. In fact, such instances of discrimination happened when my daughter was really young, and by the time we learned about them, the problem was already solved. However, when I talk with the children of some friends who go to German schools, I see that not a few of them experience exclusion specifically because they are from Turkey. Of course there are also many idealistic teachers who immediately intervene and the problem gets solved. Therefore being from Turkey also means being perceived in a certain way. Add let me also add this. Of course there is an important segment of German society who do not engage in such discriminative acts, who are really sensitive. On the other hand there is a pressure to learn the language and that pressure has a lot to do with coming from Turkey and the east. I know British and French people who have been living here for ten, twelve years, they have no problems or plans to learn German, whereas we constantly worry about the level of our German knowledge. That is something that is expected from us because we are from Turkey. In other words, whether you are from the East or the West makes a difference in your experience as a migrant in Germany. And of course the biggest problem is not being able to talk about certain political issues, for example about the Palestinian issue in Germany. But fortunately I have Israeli friends who are concerned about the Palestinian issue, who are concerned about the fact that it is a taboo subject in Germany, so I can talk about it with them and they've got my back. What I mean is, the culture of confrontation with the past has developed here up to a certain point. There are definitely open-minded, sensitive, democratic people around, but when I look at the system, I can see that it is permeated with a lot of hypocrisy. I have, for example, a wonderful German neighbour, who is nothing like that. The doors of our houses are open, our children come and go. The problem is not the German people, but the institutionalisation of that point of view and I find that very dangerous. Because in an environment where the far right is on the rise, it doesn't matter whether that law is amended or this government has been changed, as long as that mentality remains in place – that feeling doesn't sit well with me.

There are already stereotypes and prejudices about Turkish people. And now there is a new wave of migration from Turkey. It is not only peace academics and intellectuals, but there is also a Kurdish exodus going on as a result of the collapse of the peace process. Members of the Gülen community are also coming. How do Germans view this new wave of migration?
What people who are critical like us don't like is when people compliment us by telling us that 'we are not like other Turks'. This is

not something that anyone with a sane, pluralistic worldview would like. Since you already look at sociological issues from a critical perspective, you understand very well what sort of a categorisation that so-called compliment refers to. I usually answer them: 'Yes, Turkey has a diversified social space. We came here for different reasons, at different times, but we should not forget that if it were not for those who came here earlier, the German economy wouldn't be where it is today. Therefore they are valuable as they are, in fact every person is valuable in its own right.' Because the discriminating approach is very disturbing. Of course we all have our differences, but it is very problematic to use those differences as complimentary adjectives rather than as factual descriptions. All comers are positioned according to the needs of the specific period, and people are viewed from the perspective of their functions in the 'market' – as if they are not people, they are just workers required to do certain jobs and nothing else. This, itself, is of course very, very problematic. Because it creates a hierarchy within itself and this is a great injustice. Disposing so quickly of people who spent their lives here for so many years, who sacrificed their health, who contributed to making Germany what it is with their physical labour, and now with their intellectual power – well, that's not acceptable. And I say the following for those of us who are newcomers: If it wasn't for those who came earlier, we wouldn't have it so easy here. Some of them, especially the first comers, were very left-wing, they contributed a lot to unionisation. The organisations they established cannot be overestimated and we should thank them for those institutions.

Your new project looks at the relations between groups from Turkey and how events in Turkey are reflected here. How do the old wave and the new wave relate to each other? And now very heterogeneous groups are coming from Turkey. For example, Kurds are coming, dissident Turks are coming, a lot of people from the Gülen community are coming. Our 'fights'

in Turkey are somehow being reproduced again and again. But they are reproduced by changing their shape. What did you find in your field work about these issues?

It is very interesting actually. First, there are encounters between newcomers. Let me start here. Political changes in the transnational sphere directly affect Turkish people in Germany. For example, if we look at the Diyanet or at how the sociological composition of the DİTİB mosques has changed, previously members of the Gülen community were frequenting them, now it is mostly members of Milli Görüş. Therefore political change in Turkey affects Germany as well. Especially in terms of who will be in the administration of these community organisations. Otherwise, of course they all worship in mosques. But here we come to another peculiarity of Germany. In Germany religious communities are autonomous and places of worship are organised at the grassroots level, by the believers themselves. However, DİTİB's management is appointed by the central government of the Turkish state. With the recent changes in the legislation, DİTİB, the German branch of the Diyanet, no longer elects its own management from the grassroots. Ankara determines it. This is a double standard.

There are other encounters as well, such as the encounters between the Kurds and the members of the Gülen community. We know that the Kurds are among the groups who have suffered at the hands of the Gülen Movement. In addition to the activities of the Gülen movement in Kurdish provinces, we know that especially in KCK operations in 2009, right at the beginning of the peace process, not all Gülenists, but the Gülenist intelligence structures active within the state actually initiated the process whereby unarmed KCK members were detained and a lot of civilian cadres, political cadres, were destroyed. Kurds remember this very well, it is still alive in their memory, because it destroyed experienced actors in the democratic Kurdish movement. Encounters between these two groups in the refugee camps in Germany stir these memories. Let me give some examples that stuck in my mind. In these encounters some people first keep their distance from others, tactically so to say. Sometimes they don't speak Turkish at all. If they speak English, they communicate in English. But then, in different ways, sometimes through the solidarity of women, especially women and children, and sometimes through the solidarity of people in the restricted environment of the refugee camps, they meet one another as human persons, for the first time, so to speak. Kurds are always more open to such encounters, but of course this does not mean that they forget history. It is more complicated for the members of the Gülen Movement. The environment from which the religious people received their information was such a closed world that they did not know much about the particular truths of other people. There are some people who are just beginning to learn certain things which we already know.

Kurds are not homogeneous either. Now every Kurd who arrives finds himself directly in a single Kurdish movement. But encounters that were not possible in Turkey are probable here. This may lead to a kind of polarisation, but it may also lead to a confrontation and reconciliation. It is still too early to say, we will see in due course. But for the first time they say 'Well, the others are human beings too, and we are going through the same problems.' This, I think, is new.

Do you feel the oppression in Turkey in the diaspora as well? I mean, do you engage in some form of self-censorship or do people, especially the Gülen community, feel that Turkey is following them, spying on them? Or is there an atmosphere of trust in the diaspora?

As far as I can see, the Gülen community has had a lot of trouble on the ground. The German editions of some newspapers in Turkey have already targeted them by publishing their addresses in Germany. Plus, the Turkish state, more specifically the chief of Turkish intelligence, Hakan Fidan, gave the German government a list of the Gülenists living in Germany. The German government openly rejected accepting the list. They experience problems in this sense, but they experience this problem not so much from the German government but from the encounters they have with other people from Turkey. Or there was a time, and not only the Gülenists but also the Kurds experienced this, when there were interpreters who leaked information, especially in migration centres. Then the German government, more specifically the department of the government responsible for refugees, apologised for this. All this created an insecure environment in the early periods. In that sense, yes, there is an insecure environment.

But I didn't directly feel that transnational insecurity. I saw that what I was doing could have consequences in Turkey. But what happened here was that there were pan-Ottomanists in the neighbourhood and in the vicinity. The German government is very much after them. But for example I have a neighbour who used to be an AKP supporter but now he is very angry with the AKP members. I talk politics with him very well. I know he is looking out for me, and I am looking out for him. I feel worry in some places but not when I speak with, for example, Milli Goruş members. Coming under the radar of some more radical figure gives me a feeling of fear, and I know that some Kurdish dissidents and some journalist friends, particularly those who are rather alone, feel that way too. But it feels like the German government has done its best so far in that respect. But that does not mean that there are no racist murders in Germany. But that is another dimension. Yet still we are usually very conscious and careful of what we say when we talk about politics.

Visibility can also bring danger for you in a sense. Activism here is not safe no matter what. There are radical groups. Do you feel yourself in exile? Because exile is a very loaded concept.
It is a very strange thing; yes and no. We used the concept of 'exile' with Seçkin and Esra when we were writing the article, but there we used 'exile' to refer to everyone who was exiled. Because we actually experienced such an exile. But there were many times when I felt

exiled in Turkey too. For example, Beyoğlu has changed so much, that it was no longer my Beyoğlu and I felt very lonely and exiled, and moreover I didn't have any other village which I could return to. I mean it is something very isolating. This is a feeling I have for many places in Istanbul. Or sometimes when we fight with each other instead of trying to understand each other in dissenting groups, that is, when we fight each other instead of Erdoğan, when there is a process of othering, gossiping going on et cetera; these may seem small, but I feel exiled at those points again. Academics for Peace showed great solidarity, I don't underestimate that at all, but I experienced such things as well. Our court cases were merged and, in those cases, half of the list, me and some colleagues, were sentenced to twenty-two months' imprisonment, and some to twenty-five months. At that time someone wrote in an email group 'Nil got twenty-two months, I couldn't see her statement, did she apologise or what?' The very fact that this person could find the courage to write this shows that we are not above lynching each other even within our own group. When I see that we can do such a thing, I feel isolated. But on the other hand, we are experiencing so much solidarity with one another that I think such things are the sacrifices we need to make for that blessing. Also, the leftist tradition in Turkey is an ambivalent one. As much as it has an emancipatory potential, it is also a very formalist tradition, stuck in a form of identity politics which expects everyone to behave the same way. But on the other hand, Academics for Peace are showing an very interesting, intense solidarity and we even received an award for that. We are all actively involved in the effort, we show solidarity both in material and in moral terms. We cannot dismiss that dimension of it. We say that we are human, and we are doing all these things for human beings, for life. This issue is something like this: if we are going to build a new democracy, a new critical culture, a new form of coexistence, we will do everything openly and we will do it in solidarity and we will do it with sincerity.

I think you've explained it very well. Because exile is not just about having your passport cancelled and having to leave the country. Exile is also a very emotional thing that you feel in all your cells. You can feel it in Turkey, you can feel it in your own neighbourhood.

The state of exile within yourself affects you a lot. But of course the first two or three years were also very difficult for me. Some of our friends suffered losses in their families, they lost their mothers, loved ones, and couldn't go to their funerals. My difficulties cannot be compared to these. But precisely for this reason, if we are talking about such grand things like leftism and solidarity, we should be more sensitive, more caring and less rough in our relations with one another. But we all learn from our traumas. There is that too. As I said, many good deeds have been done. But I have to say that our leftist tradition of treating one another roughly, of identity politics, creates a feeling of exile too.

Do you think you will return to Turkey?

If there is a democratic Turkey, why not? And by democratic, I don't mean that they should prepare everything and then we will go, but if I see at least a hint that some reform process will start, it might be possible. We are not doing great here either. There are difficulties, finding a job is difficult et cetera, but at least there is an environment where I feel that my daughter is safe. Otherwise we would have returned long ago. But I can still concentrate better on my academic work here, because in Turkey I would be divided more than I am divided here. But if we see a little bit of change in Turkey, if there is something that opens up a little bit of space, then we will of course go back to support the struggle, to lend a shoulder, to hold hands. But that will take time. For now, it makes more sense to stay here and keep doing what we can from here. Because there is no such thing as being here and being saved. We are also struggling a lot here. We are struggling both for our existence and to find a job. We all have very concrete concerns. We all feel it. There is no shame in talking about it because we are all aware of it. It has nothing to do with being a good or bad academic. The system is like that. And I think it has something to do with age. We are in our most productive years. Our students still remember us fondly and miss us. So if we could go back and see that the academy can exist in the form it should exist, we would want it to exist there. I mean, there is a feeling that if there is a possibility to do something there, I can still go back. If I were twenty, however, I might think differently.

There is a feeling of being caught in the middle, you think that if things improve in Turkey, you will leave. Then, when you follow politics every day, it can feel like it will never happen. Also, you have a daughter now, you are thinking about her, as you said. So it becomes a complicated situation. When you look at the current situation, what do you think awaits Turkey?
Imagine me answering that it is up to Soylu and Peker! I am kidding of course, but in a Turkey where deep forces are polarised, it is almost impossible to predict anything for the long run. Even if the opposition wins the elections, the transition will not be easy. Besides, first the judiciary and the bureaucracy need to change. When I say change, I mean that the new nationalist and conservative pro-AKP cadres need to be cleansed of mafia ties and corruption, some of which we only heard about from figures like Peker on good evidence. This will not take place immediately and effortlessly. Even if the change in official channels is not within the framework of the desired freedoms and democracy, it is important to create a culture of confrontation and reconciliation, especially in the political sphere. Because then institutions can become more courageous. If the political environment starts to change and there is a mass response from the grassroots – even that much would be enough. And in a political and social environment where confrontation and reconciliation have not happened properly so far, it is also important to prioritise issue politics over identity politics. Although it is not easy, if we can develop common policies based

not on our identities but on our common issues, the political areas that will be developed on our common values, goals and concerns can give us hope. This will provide a pluralistic space instead of the communities and areas that are now riveted to polarisation by politics. It will open a space, but of course it needs to be worked on.

In other words, people in those communities need to show the courage to understand each other again.
Yes. And basically the Pandora's box has already been opened. With the economic crisis, there are now urgent common needs, which are also starting to be felt by those who were close to the AKP. There are serious problems in living humanely and accessing basic needs such as food, shelter, health. And these problems exist for everyone who cannot afford them. Common opposition groups have emerged in the public sphere, but are they yet practising politics in a way that fully addresses voters' problems? I hope they will, in due course.

18

RAGIP DURAN

It will take a long time to create or restore a Turkey with
freedom and independence in the short or medium term.
Turkey hasn't fallen to zero; it's in the minus-20s. We first
need to get back up to zero from the minus-20s before we
can rise into positive digits. It's a cesspool in every area:
nature, economics, education and law.

*Mehmet Ragıp Duran has been a journalist since 1978. He has worked
as a correspondent and editor with* Aydınlık, Hürriyet, Cumhuriyet,
Nokta, Özgür Gündem, *AFP,* Libération *and the BBC in Istanbul,
Ankara, Paris and London. After graduating from Galatasaray
College and the Faculty of Law at Aix-Marseille University he studied
journalism at CFPJ (Paris, 1983) and became a Nieman fellow
at Harvard in 2000. He has published three books in Turkish on*

media criticism ('Media with Epaulette', 1980; 'This Is World Police Radio', 1996'; 'Mediamorphosis', 2000) and one on Afghanistan ('With Afghan Warriors', 1980). He has received two international journalism awards (Hellmann-Hammett, New York, 1997; Noureddine Zaza, Paris Kurdish Institute, 1999) and five national ones (Human Rights Association, Istanbul 1993; Journalist Assembly, 1998; Contemporary Journalists' Association, Bursa, 1999; Publishers' Union, Istanbul, 1999; Journalists' Association, Istanbul, 2004). He taught journalism (media ethics, news writing and global media) at Galatasaray University and Marmara University (1994–2015) and conference interpreting at Bilkent University (2005–15). He also worked as a conference interpreter (1978–2016) in Turkey and Europe. He also worked as a conference interpreter (1978–2016) in Turkey and Europe. He worked with Artı TV and Artı Gerçek, based in Cologne, from 2017 to 2021. He has lived in Thessaloniki since 2016 and currently produces a weekly programme ('HistoryGeographyMedia') for Özgürüz Radio in Berlin and a weekly column for TVXS.GR, Athens.

Mr Duran, when did you leave Turkey?

We left immediately after the failed coup attempt. It was actually a bit of a coincidence. We had gone to visit a friend in Thessaloniki before the coup, and we had really loved the city. We returned to Turkey on the day of the coup. There was a project we were working on that we could not continue after the coup so we returned to Thessaloniki.

Did you leave legally? What were the motivations encouraging you to leave?

I left legally. I still don't have migrant status. I'm a journalist working abroad. The basic motivation behind my leaving the country was because I'm a journalist. When the opportunities to work as a journalist freely and independently disappeared in Turkey, we set up a website and TV channel called Artı TV and Artı Gerçek, which I work for today in Germany. I've been working there for four years.

There were no legal threats against you that compelled you to leave Turkey, but you've been abroad for four years. Do you come and go to Turkey?

I went once two years ago. I haven't been back since then. The reason I went was because I was tried as part of the Özgür Gündem solidarity trial and was sentenced to eighteen months in prison. I was found guilty at a first-degree court, and the Court of Appeals approved this. However, this ruling was reversed when it became necessary – in the minds of officials – to push for a three-pronged trial. The case is in the Court of Cassation now, and we're waiting on the outcome. Apart from this, there don't appear to be any legal obstacles for me. But there's something known as a secret investigation. And I don't have a job in Turkey. I mean, there's nothing professionally requiring me to be in Turkey. I theoretically should be there as I'm awaiting the Court of Cassation's ruling. But because there is no such thing as law anymore in Turkey, I can't know if there are a few secret investigations into me or whether those investigations will be launched when we cross the border. I choose not to go because I have no assurance of any kind on this matter. Because anything could happen at any moment. The latest example of this is Ömer Faruk Gergerlioğlu. He was punished I don't know how many years ago for a tweet he shared. We're people who write news, who read the news on TV and who evaluate the news, and it won't be difficult for the regime and the state to find an excuse to target us. I had already shut down this work when the time came. I became familiar with prison in Turkey a while back. Prison is not the place for a journalist. It is not possible to halt a profession of ideas and writing and drawing through handcuffs, the law and the court. They're trying to do this, and that's why I don't want to go. I do my own job – a job I love– abroad. We comply with German laws, of course. And we are careful about our publications, but we are exuberant that we are doing something here which we never could have done in Turkey.

Why Germany?

There are mostly logistical reasons for this. There was a television station in Cologne that was already set up but got closed by statutory decree. We took over the station. Germany was preferable for our team because of its large Turkish diaspora, and because Cologne is a relatively central European city, it made it easier for us to relocate to the east or the west. We made this decision thinking that the German government, having democratic traditions, wouldn't obstruct any activities despite its particularly close relationship with Turkey.

There has been an ongoing exodus from Turkey since 2008 composed of various waves. There are many diverse groups within this exodus. There are people like you who have become public figures, Gülenists, Kurds, young people, you name it. Do you think that you have some degree of solidarity with certain segments of the Turkish diaspora? If so, with which groups do you see the greatest level of solidarity? Are there groups with which you have worked?

Our broadcast policy is unavoidably established on the umbrella principle because we work in television broadcasting. The fundamental characteristics of this umbrella are peace and democracy. In fact, our formulation is that everyone who is not against peace or democracy may be a guest on our screens, and we are obliged to provide information about everyone's problems. And while we are in Germany, our hours, logic, style of working, colleagues, mentalities, intellects, all of it is in the Turkish style. For example, we contacted some German foundations but were unable to establish very productive relations with them, because, as Artı TV, we don't define ourselves as the media of the diaspora. We're not in Turkey, because of the current conjuncture, but we broadcast as if we were. That's why we don't see the value of something important in France, Germany or Austria unless it involves Turkey. Because there are other channels that can handle western European news. We cover Turkey, and we are inevitably in contact with various segments of Turkish society thanks to our work. That's why those who don't really understand – or perhaps even reject – our umbrella policy accuse us from time to time of being PKK members, Gülenists or CHP members based on the broadcasts. Thank God we aren't any of those three. We aren't like that because the reason we have not encountered this type of accusations is our set of broadcasts. When people were drowning in Maritsa, we reported that a group of people had been arrested or tried as PKK members despite not being PKK members or that a CHP member was unjustly arrested. There's nothing more natural than this in journalism. And it's not just because of journalism; not everyone asks about the identity of the victim. That doesn't interest us. That man may be a PKK member, or a Gülenist, or a CHP member. When assessing the situation in terms of news, we look at what happened. The fact that someone who drowned in Maritsa is a CHP member or PKK member or Gülenist is unimportant to us. Ultimately, they're people, victims. They are forced to flee the country because of the prevailing circumstances, falling into the hands of traffickers. In Europe, especially in Germany, we participated in several meetings with various representatives or segments of the diaspora. We saw that what was discussed there didn't really concern us. For example, the German state does things about integration with foreigners living in the country. We receive funds from two institutions, one in Sweden and one from the EU. Some of the applications for funding we submitted were rejected, for example. Because the issues they place greater weight on are issues that are incredibly ordinary, such as minority rights for Muslims living in that country. It didn't capture our interest. We already won't accept any stipulations, but of course, there are points that some foundations want emphasised in particular. It's an amorphous situation, of course; we're in Germany and we're thinking about Turkey.

But journalism requires this. At the axis of all I've mentioned are the professional matters I mentioned initially. We are forced to differentiate everything based on that. Because I'm at the management level in these institutions, I end up determining our position as an institution more often than my own personal views.

When we look at the relations that Turkish nationals have who have moved abroad and are from circles we can call leftist or the liberal left who are more recognised in the public sphere, we hear stories that various members of the already existing Turkish diaspora refuse to sell products to exiles and we've also heard about diaspora members who confront people on the street and say 'You are a traitor to your country'. Have you had experiences like this?

Nothing has happened to me or to us. Over the past four years, we have organised more than twenty-seven Artı meetings to get in touch with our viewers and those who read our website. Because our identities are already clear, no government supporters have come to sabotage those meetings. There are frightening things that Can Dündar, who does our daily commentary on television, has explained. But these are all binary: there's one segment that blindly views you as a traitor and another that's supportive. We were with Can one day shopping at the supermarket. Can was waiting in the car. Someone looked at him. Can had security problems. I came on like a bodyguard and said, 'Excuse me, did you call someone?' 'Isn't that Can Dündar?' he asked. 'Yes,' I said. He went, hugged him, kissed him and so on, but he could have attacked him too. It wasn't clear from anyone's faces what had happened. We were delighted, of course, I think Can has a lot more experience on this issue. Over time, racist, pro-government comments insulting our broadcasts appear on social media. These are to be expected, [but] those critics haven't assaulted us at any time throughout the past four years.

So have you encountered any sort of reaction from transnational branches of the Turkish state or consulates, the Diyanet, TİKA or civil society organisations close to the AKP, either individually or institutionally?

I haven't encountered anything individually, but there are some cases in which people who work at our television station or website have had problems with the legal system in Turkey. It's not in the form of attacks but, for example, they refuse to renew passports, don't do, extend or maintain things they're supposed to. Apart from that, we have friends who work with us who freely travel to and from Turkey. We took some precautions while first setting up the television station and website. We don't have any legal presence in Turkey; we don't have an institutional presence in Turkey. We broadcast in Germany, and we work on contract with a few production companies in Turkey; we place orders, and they send them. There are 100 people working with us at the television station and internet, the total number of workers in Germany, Istanbul, Ankara, Izmir and Diyarbakır. Weirdly, problems have emerged for some of our workers because of social media posts, but they don't number more than five. There have been people who are detained for a weekend or who have had lawsuits filed against them. An investigation was launched against Ragıp Zarakolu, one of our writers, because of a photograph published on our website. Ragıp Zarakolu writes for Evrensel, and [an] article [he wrote] was published on the same day as [the picture on] our website. Nothing happened because the picture wasn't used in the article on Evrensel. But a picture of Erdoğan alongside Menderes was published on Artı Gerçek. They launched investigations into both Evrensel and Artı Gerçek with the justification that the publications provoked the coup. We take the utmost care despite being based in Germany. It is very easy for a television station to be shut down. Although militant broadcasting is a respected action, we won't resort to that. We – and it will be somewhat assertive – try to position ourselves as the centrist media of the future because the centrist media has collapsed. Accordingly, we are equidistant from all segments, but of course, we positively discriminate against those whose voices are barely heard. The HDP, LGBTI individuals, Armenians and minorities facing all kinds of oppression are certainly included in this. It's not in the form of a special statute, but we strive to highlight news and views for segments that are underrepresented in Turkey relative to their power.

Are you happy in Germany? I ask this in the sense of whether you think the German government can protect you, your free life, work and broadcasting here in the face of potential pressure from the Turkish state or diaspora. One of the reasons you chose Germany was because of the scope of human resources there, but do you have a position of trusting or not trusting such a security justification or the bureaucracy of the German state?

I'm actually in Germany part time. My family is in Thessaloniki. I mean, I am not always in Germany. My permanent residence is in Greece.

You're able to compare Germany and Greece, so I'd like it if you could say something about that.

The Syriza administration was in power in Greece when I arrived. We had a group of about ten to fifteen academics, journalists and translators from Syriza in Thessaloniki. They conducted interviews with regional Syriza officials to request mitigation of the migrant issue. As far as I remember, Greece had an incredibly positive approach during the Syriza era regarding migrants – people like us who lived there but were not Greek citizens. In fact, they said, 'If you have friends in trouble, let us know and we'll inform the police and do what's necessary.' The situation changed a bit with Mitsotakis. One of Mitsotakis's first orders was to attack these migrant camps in Athens and empty the migrant camps elsewhere in the country. But the rise of Mitsotakis's government didn't change my situation personally in any way, because I was a foreign journalist accredited at the Greek Foreign Ministry. I appeared as a journalist working for the German press. We have not encountered Turkish repression. And there's something in Germany where we had thought it was good we arrived in the country when the pandemic began because the German government provided extraordinary financial and non-material assistance to all local and foreign companies without discrimination, a portion of which was conditional, like a low-interest loan, and portion not. Things like this were also done in Greece, but you can't really compare Germany and Greece economically. We have many friends working here as freelance musicians. They only have their trade union – independent musicians affiliated with the trade union. They received 80 per cent of their earnings from a month earlier in all of their bank accounts. If we had been in Turkey, we would have been unable to cover such a television expense under the conditions of the pandemic. But of course, we don't differentiate between states much because we come from a leftist culture; every state, without exception, can easily eliminate, lay waste to or dissolve the opposition, especially in its relations with other states. While the political powers in Germany until only just recently never interacted with dissident intellectuals, academics or journalists in Turkey, this changed with Erdoğan's recent visit to Berlin and Cologne.

Why? What has changed?
Because, as far as I know, the German government doesn't interact much with the opposition because it is wary of provoking the Turkish diaspora. It's still like that, preventing sanctions and attempting to placate Erdoğan. It was understood after Erdoğan's most recent visit to Berlin and Cologne that this isn't a very sustainable policy. Thus, the government began to listen to critiques of Erdoğan which it had previously ignored. We assessed this as a reflection of Erdoğan's policies. And they admitted to our friends who had been living in Germany for thirty or forty years, 'You were

saying this before, but we didn't really take note of it.' I'm talking about the ministerial level.

You had left the country without knowing when you would return. Do you think you interpret Turkey in a different light when you are far away?

I have actually spent a significant portion of my life abroad. I attended university abroad, worked at the BBC in London between 1983 and 1985, and was in the US in 2000, reading *Yeni Şafak* and *Akit*. I wouldn't have read these newspapers while in Turkey. As a journalist, I have to read everything, but it is gradually becoming more difficult to keep track of the country. There are predictions at the core of journalism and politics, and we need predictions while implementing publishing policies. Our predictions must be separate from our heartfelt desires. We can make predictions by following what's concrete and the direction in which the regime, opposition and society are moving. Change, fundamentally, is the uncertainty of the political situation, the societal situation and the economic situation, and that uncertainty increases every year. I feel this especially in Greece when I struggle to answer the questions of my journalist colleagues there. Because if you ask something relating to Greece, France, Britain or Germany in the short, medium or long term, a Greek, French, British or German person will, usually, be able to comfortably tell you their prediction. We, however, cannot. Of course, because we're journalists, we don't have the luxury of treading water like that. What you say must be grounded in facts, but there are so many variables and the variables change such that the amount of uncertainty is extraordinary. I always give this example: I attended university in France. France had a political map during that period in which northern Paris was communist, central Marseille was socialist, and Bordeaux and its surroundings were anti-Jacobin. It was all certain, more or less. In Turkey lately, the coasts are red, Kurdistan is red, a large portion of the central region is blue – it looks like a place we could call progressive conservative. But still, for example, ANAP comes first in Zonguldak, which is Ecevit's hometown. There's a certain uncertainty, unsettlement. This unsettlement is unavoidably and rapidly changing all the political, economic and societal parameters.

You said you aimed to be the central media of the future. It's clear that you still have plans, desires and wishes relating to Turkey. Would you ever return?
The short answer is that I won't go back. The reason for this is that it seems like it will take a long time to create or restore a Turkey with freedom and independence in the short or medium term. Turkey hasn't fallen to zero; it's in the minus-20s. We first need to get back up to zero from the minus-20s before we can rise into positive digits. It's a cesspool in every area, nature, economics, education and law. I don't want to go and work at the *Silivri Post* for the sake of journalism. I want to work as a normal journalist if I return. I say no because I don't believe that a tranquil life can exist in the near or even medium term in Turkey. Living in Thessaloniki is a huge advantage because it's an Aegean city where Erdoğan is not present. I studied at Galatasaray High School. We are really connected to one another. My friends from Galatasaray are the only ones I really miss, and thankfully they come once a month. With the advent of social media, we have more information about everyone than ever before. We do virtual meetings when necessary, so I don't really have that nostalgia. It's been a long time since Turkey has appealed to me. I mean, if we could broadcast without being investigated by the police, we would consider returning there.

19

ŞEHBAL ŞENYURT ARINLI

**While we – and I personally – continued this fight, while
we spoke about human rights or other issues, I said and did
this knowing for certain that it would have repercussions.
So if it's going to have a cost, that's the way it will be.
This shouldn't constitute an obstacle for staying
true to our positions.**

*Şehbal Şenyurt Arınlı was born in 1962. She studied political science
and journalism. She is a documentary film director/producer, journalist and writer, and she is Turkey's first female camera operator.*

*In the 1990s, she worked for the international press and broadcasters
and the news programme called* 32nd Day. *Her films were screened in
many countries around the world. She is the founder of BSB, the Documentary Filmmakers' Association. She has developed various workshops*

and training programmes at universities, especially to strengthen the presence of women in the field of cinema.

She has conducted oral history and social memory projects on issues such as exile, population exchange and genocide. She has taken active roles in political parties and congresses and on platforms for the democratic solution of the Kurdish problem. In 2011, she was elected as the Labour Freedom Democracy Bloc parliamentary candidate from the BDP (Peace and Democracy Party). She has been involved in the BDP Assembly, the DTK (Democratic Society Congress) and the HDP (Peoples' Democratic Party).

Her various articles have been published in newspapers such as Özgür Gündem *and* Azadiye Welat *and in various magazines. She contributed to the establishment of the Jinha women's news agency and to the continuation of its broadcasts. She has carried out projects with the perspective of questioning prejudices and hearing the voice of the subaltern in areas such as minority rights, the Kurdish issue, anti-militarism, the struggle for women's rights, and revealing ecological alternative life models. She was detained and had to go abroad, and she now lives and works in Germany.*

Ms Şenyurt Arınlı, we are grateful for your time. When and why did you leave Turkey? Where did you go first?

I left in July 2017. I had been detained. Of course, we couldn't even access our files because a confidentiality order had been issued, but we understood the files when our statements were taken through the Sound and Video Information System (SEGBİS). Even the lawyers couldn't access them. In that process, I saw that a series of ongoing lawsuits was starting, so I left the very next day after being released. In that year – in 2017, I mean – I had taken part in long-term battles with friends as a human rights activist, documentary filmmaker and politician. That case was opened for a single speech I had given in 2011. We had worked on a number of projects between 2011 and 2017. During the war that began after the negotiation table had been toppled over, we worked on many anti-war projects during the conflicts in Cizre, Sur and Kobane. Each had a characteristic that could have become the subject of a lawsuit for them. So I saw from that case that a series [of suits] was beginning, and indeed it did. The situation is continuing in this way. You know, in those days, one day they gave, and the next they took away. So I saw that it was going to continue like this, and I decided while the accusations were being read. 'Okay,' I said, 'I should go abroad when I leave the courtroom.' And I left the very next day. Within this work, I had always maintained a visa as a sort of political foresight. So I was keeping open the possibility of going abroad, and I left using this visa.

Are you able to return right now, or are the cases ongoing?
I can't return right now, because the cases are ongoing. Even if they hadn't begun, we're at risk because there's a certain insecurity about when and how the existing cases will conclude. I'm not risking returning to Turkey.

When you left in 2017, what kind of Turkey did you leave behind?
There was complete chaos and a profound hopelessness. While the peace conferences were ongoing, a serious hope had arisen in people. But when a grave series of attacks appeared, the disappointment hardened significantly. Turks have entirely lost trust in in the judiciary. This loss of trust has become more profound as the process continues. Friends sustain the fight and for the rest of us, whatever we tried to do, we were left with the sight of complete disarray. Every day, there was a process of waking up to a new crisis. The same thing is true today; not much has changed. But in the past few months, the issue of injustice seeping continuously from the AKP's own partnerships has aroused something different. We have been saying this for years. Starting when Turkey was founded, there have been a series of intense attacks through the Turkish-Islamic synthesis against

various segments. The implementation of Turkification and Sunni Islamisation against the Christians, the Jews and various segments of Turkish society and, of course, the seizure of property constitute the fundamental issues; economic issues are fundamental. Upon this, the Christians left the country, and these policies were maintained step by step. What remained was the Kurdish movement. The process continued over the Kurdish liberation movement rebellion. So we're not talking about a brand new political approach, actually. Since the founding of the country, there have been Turkish-Islamic – Sunni Islam, in fact – policies. And all these processes must be evaluated collectively. So a process began in the 1920s, around 1925, starting with the very first constitution, the 1924 constitution. On the other hand, there were a slew of superficial recommendations referred to as a 'revolution'. Accordingly, an ongoing marginalisation occurred in society in this country. Subsequent coups transpired. The military tutelage viciously applied pressure against these peoples. And these processes leaped into a new phase after 1980. The Kurdish liberation movement emerged and grew stronger. And all these developments brought about the Erdoğan regime as a result. I mean, it's not only the individual political decisions, the issues of elections of a Muslim as if the Erdoğan regime descended from the sky. It's the outcome of a certain process. It is the outcome of imposed, superficial processes wrapped within an oppressive quality instead of opening the door to the internal transformations of people. The oppression there appeared as a result of the discrete emergence of a Muslim segment by strengthening its own internal organising capacity. So all these processes should be considered collectively. I think the concepts of power and state must be scrutinised. Ultimately, the oppressed need to maintain their existence at a certain depth to reconcile with the system when they join a process of power. This gradually makes them elements of oppression. So when the founding ideology supporting the state unifies with issues of remaining in power, maintaining its existence, it can transform into dictatorial, autocratic regimes in countries like ours, unfortunately. And indeed it has. To oppose the injustices that occur in daily life through analyses of all these is not a very easy thing to do. So people who sustain the fight are forced to fight in a number of different aspects.

Is there a breaking point at which you said, 'This has happened, and I have lost my belief, I have fallen into hopelessness,' especially after the Gezi process?
I find the issue of hope–hopelessness to be paradoxical. There's no such concept as hope or hopelessness in my view. As long as everyone continues to do something in the context of their own principles wherever they are, a series of solutions always emerges and will emerge. I don't perceive this as hope or hopelessness. I associate hope with sitting and waiting, to be honest. As long as you make an effort, and if you don't sit and wait, you continue to contribute in this way or that way to the transformation of something. Of course, processes of inquiry are taking place; I personally have experienced this profoundly and have asked about this during every era when things are going well. And it is very important to me that while doing this work we constantly ask 'Where did we go wrong?' I'm someone who trusts questions more than answers. As long as there are questions, processes of review are taking place. So constantly asking the question 'Are we not doing something somewhere?' is important for whoever is fighting for human rights. And while chaotically running from here to there, while struggling with a new incident each day, you can't put the question on the table and do things while analysing the social psychological impacts and, later, the political repercussions. It doesn't happen like that. But I think we have to at least push this out of our minds as a problem. We must keep going, designing the historical perspective of what has happened and predictions for what the events of that moment will turn into. As I said, this isn't something we can always do easily. We inevitably make a lot of mistakes and we must face the consequences. We are emotional people. Sometimes

we explode quite suddenly. Sometimes we get angry and experience emotions like 'God damn it, let me sit, cover myself with a blanket and stop'. Despite this, some things – like a sort of impulse – like the instinctive effort to survive are revived, and you keep going. Because we don't live an isolated life alone. Look how all the damage we have caused in nature is poisoning our daily lives! We are a whole, so all this poison suffered in society impacts our lives regardless of whether we're isolated. This is why we feel the need to get back up and keep going. This is a form of existence.

We may not have the luxury of being hopeless in a country like Turkey.
This isn't a luxury. It's a bit difficult to explain. There's no such thing as hope because there's no such thing as hopelessness. Sometimes a horrible situation can be transformed into something new with a little acceleration. I can say that our problem is to look for this. We must frequently ask what kind of life we want. Most of the time, we avoid this question amid the chaos of the modern world. What kind of world do I want to live in? While this question pertains just to ourselves, questions like 'How do we want to live together?' are woven together one step further with a sort of communication between people thinking like this. I'm not talking about living a single way. I mean, I don't view this as 'me and people who think like me'. We can say this even for those dreaming of a whole other world and, in fact, for autocrats. They imagine a world in this way. But the fundamental issue of all this is where these values will coincide and what kind of harmony they will transform into. I want to avoid causing injury, avoid causing destruction, acknowledge each existence within the whole, but on the other hand, I want this too, and so do you – to be able to transform one another. But of course, the issue here is resorting to violence and persuasion. I honestly don't feel obliged to persuade anybody. I'm revealing a position. I try to put this position and what happened out in the open. But I try to

talk about these with people who are reconciling here, or not, and transform this into somewhere new. This is the lens I look through; others look through completely different lenses. But all these lenses constitute a lifestyle. So people who are fighting for human rights and other issues, fighting for nature must try and find methods that will more clearly demonstrate their perspectives and arguments. I'm not talking about persuasion. Okay, that world, that life until that point has brought this about. I cannot be a coercive element. I feel obliged to develop methodologies that will ensure their transformation. I think this is a peaceful method. When this is the case, of course the issue of copyrights clearly emerges. We experience the self-confidence of explaining and discussing, talking about our ideas and being able to say 'I thought wrong. Look, this is correct.' But on the other hand, groups that cannot observe or do not want the world to change tightly embrace certain moulds and are unable to be open to these types of issues because they could lose them. So what we are tasked with is trying to find other methods. We seem weak and gaunt in this sense. Because people thinking differently overwhelm us with bulldozers, weapons and all sorts of pressures. All we have against them is what we say and do, but we can't give up, so we think differently. And not only in the sense of ideas. All the differences that exist in nature – how should I put it – they're not like me, very different to me, but that's a value, that's a life. People with different sexual orientations, people with schizophrenia, autistic individuals, every difference is actually another life, and there is great pleasure, happiness, beauty that each of us can learn from one another, what we can contribute to one another. What do we want from the world? I think these questions are the foundation of democracy and human rights.

Do you think we realised these aims in the peace process even a little, or was there always a degree of doubt?
I honestly haven't ever been optimistic in this sense, and I'm not optimistic now, because there are many fundamental points that must be

faced in the historical perspective I just mentioned. There are political recommendations that skip over these fundamental points and are presented like superficial solutions. I saw personally that everything was a chain, that without revealing the fundamental problems, of course, things wouldn't be able to progress. I still think that, but to be clear, this doesn't mean that every step taken is a contribution. The peace process issue was a valuable series of projects. But it was a point that was reached as a result of all these battles that have been fought. So every stage is intrinsically valuable, but only when we consider it from the lacking perspective of Turkey to the same degree. More superficial processes will occur than honest reckonings on the issue of the Armenian genocide, the seizure of property, the regime's relations, and the issue of their of power. These intermediary periods only serve as respites. This is very important. What happened during the peace process? People took a breath. The atmosphere of violence that had lasted for years suddenly stopped. However, people were still dying in the Kurdistan region, but in lower numbers. In society, at least, the idea that we can coexist was quite apparent. This was incredibly valuable, but as I said a moment ago, there was always the question of the point to which the regime would sustain the peace, because there was no foundational approach, and the tables did indeed turn, and terrible days returned.

But it seems like certain developments are happening again now . . .?

I don't view these as developments. And I don't because they're only an illusion. And that is, a person who grew up within all these dirty relations and contributed to these relations rose up and uncovered the swamp.[1] This is a fact. Now, they'll either change or not change

---

[1] For more information see 'Peker videos: Gang leader's claims rattle Turkish government', BBC News, 25 May 2021, https://www.bbc.co.uk/news/world-europe-57242840, accessed 6 March 2023.

the issue of the point at which this fact is approached. But what I can see right now is that the main opposition party isn't even touching the edges or corners of the issues. Because it is one of the fundamental owners of the founding ideology, almost its owner. So when you don't consider the main issue, issues sparkle and disappear but the aggregated dirt is continually transferred to future situations. All this was revealed in Susurluk. I'll first talk about what happened before. Those who were drowned in the Black Sea, those Topal Osman slaughtered, his later massacre, the support of the state for massacres that happened in all these rebellions, the incident in Dersim; it needs to come out who was responsible for all these in order to take real, permanent steps towards solutions. Don't let there be regression. Yes, of course, we need not to make things more difficult; I'm not saying let's start from the most historical point. But I'm saying this in the sense of an approach to these fundamental issues. Things are expected right now from the judiciary. They're saying, 'Are there no honourable prosecutors?' No, not possible, because to expect something like this is like not seeing the greater picture. All this filth has become so organised that it has infected everyone else. Like whoever is explaining all this, everyone must say, 'I am guilty here, I did this and this, but they're also guilty.' But no mechanism or tradition has appeared that can do this. These types of issues require a societal tradition. We've been talking for years and years about a society that has existed by constantly covering up its crimes. A tradition of covering these things up that developed over constant deception is dominant. The finger-pointing is ever present. We – and I'm saying this in terms of people who conduct human rights work in particular; I myself am constantly trying to review – have to ask the questions 'Where did I make a mistake?' or 'Which bad incidents did I cause by doing this?' True reckoning appears from these places. And we can change. Having made a mistake isn't something that destroys us. I tell myself 'I can change this. Damn it, if only I had acted tougher there, perhaps if I had been more understanding that person would have opened themselves up to me.' But our aggressive language sometimes prevents others from changing their ways because we build walls, defensive spaces in each conflict, individually and societally, and this is natural. It seems like there's a need to emphasise understanding and explaining without needing to defend one another. So if I go back to the beginning, all this brings along with it a lifestyle and cultural battle, and unfortunately, Turkey will start to discuss this newly and more profoundly. We haven't been able to fully come to these places yet, honestly. And in this sense, I think this process will last a long time. I don't think that a regime this filthy would disappear at the ballot box. I have never thought this, it became quite clear with issues of arming the public. Moreover, the issue of distributing weapons here and there has been discussed for years. It's emerged numerous times. What is actually said is that what has appeared to us as hope, that has changed something, is issues that have been articulated in certain circles for a long time. And it only appears as hope because someone within these incidents admits this, but like I said earlier, the issue is what this will turn into. There is an imperative to continue working on, researching, exposing, uncovering these points. I think that when this uncovering truly continues through research, people may say, 'Huh, maybe.'

If the cases against you are dropped, do you want to return to Turkey and continue the fight there, or do you see yourself staying abroad for a while?
My feelings on this issue are a bit complicated because of course I want to return. But there is an issue which relates a bit to age. The limits of endurance grow weaker as you grow older, as you are burdened with fatigue, an effect of long years. While in Turkey, I fought against the existing system of values. This system of values won't change easily with a new regime. I'll put it very simply: I struggle in states where there is rubbish left at your picnic site, where there is no perception of value. Or existing as a society that

shouts without being aware of its surroundings, that listens to bang-
ing music without thinking whether people around like that music
or that lives purely within its own existence. It's complicated in that
sense. Otherwise of course, I continue my fight from here, and of
course, I'll come and go and perhaps truly go. But my feelings right
now are that it hasn't fully improved yet. My nerves haven't grown
tougher. With the teacher, the school of a society that dismisses an
autistic student for being different. Or a schizophrenic, someone
who is only different in terms of brain chemistry and who is someone
else when they take their medication. It is difficult in a place where
the perspectives of all these are angular. Ultimately, by God, nothing is perfect. It's difficult, of course, as it is everywhere. And the
world is now integrated. The decay in one place passes quite easily
to somewhere else. Or it's possible to say the exact opposite, but the
issue of how to approach it is related to the issue of whether society
is ready to take this on. Look at Russia; Putin's regime has ruled for
years, and the autocracy there is being exported around the world
as a sentiment, as psycho-social structures. Erdoğan's regime is following suit. This autocracy, these dirty relations are being exported
around the world. We can give examples of this from many other
countries. I think it is important to be wherever you need to be for
the exact opposite to be exported.

Do you feel like you're in exile? What does exile express for you?
Of course I feel like I'm in exile; I am in exile. It's very beautiful
while sitting at home here or while together with Turkish friends.
But I have come involuntarily to another society. Recognising this,
trying to understand these mechanisms and overcoming the language barrier are not easy things. Being unable to reach the people
you love, feeling insecure economically or being unable to use the
mechanisms of the system – health insurance and such. When I
think about all these, then yes, I am an exile. It's a heavy process in
my opinion, but it's different from past exiles. And that's because

channels of communication are more accessible and rapid than before. Look at how far apart we're talking. We talk with friends in Turkey. So distances have broken somewhat due to communication channels. But in terms of networks of solidarity, I don't think there's a very big difference. Because when I read about the lives of the writers and intellectuals who were in exile after the books were burned in Germany in 1933, I see that a stronger network of solidarity was formed between exiles despite the distances and broken communication, despite the fact that they communicated by post. There are very few networks of solidarity now in my opinion. Everyone is trying to advance through individual solutions in their own fields. There's a network of solidarity for academics, which is very important. The Puduhepa group that women in Berlin formed created a network of solidarity. I had initially contributed to this project. But there doesn't seem to have formed a great number of solidarity networks between journalists, writers and cartoonists, students or in a brief and general sense, between those from geographic spaces in Turkey. Maybe I don't know about them, I'm not sure. There are a number of formations that existed in the past. There are groups that formed after 12 September. But as far as I have seen, they exist by constantly linking to one another amid very narrow relationships. Who are these people who were exiled during that period? What are they doing? Under what circumstances did they come? How did they form relationships with one another? How did they rely on one another professionally or psychologically? I haven't been able to see these or much of a network of relationships that observes these, whatever the need. It is difficult to expect the new arrivals to develop these sorts of solidarity relationships, because everyone is preoccupied with their own challenging situations. Those who came during earlier periods, who came a great distance, could reach out a hand to the new arrivals. Perhaps, as I said, they have, but I haven't been able to make contact. Maybe they're in other countries. Of course, I know what it's like in Germany.

Have there been solidarity groups that have approached you? Have there been diaspora organisations that have tried to work with you or called you in for meetings?

No, maybe the German diaspora has a unique character. You're in a relationship with whichever city you live in. At least, that's been my experience. Of course, we have had serious relationships with all the structures in the city where I live. Let them not be lacking, they ask what there's a need for. Beautiful relationships have developed, but what I'm trying to say is more about the big picture. Friends in other cities probably experience similar things. Those in Cologne rely on those in Cologne, or those in Berlin rely on those in Berlin. Maybe different political, psychosocial dynamics are stepping in, I don't know. So I can say that I have seen more support from German organisations and from Germans on my behalf than from diaspora organisations. One of the fundamental issues in exile is continuing our professional work. I mean, okay, I'm still doing my work. The support I've received from PEN certainly plays a big role in this. But many writers, cartoonists, journalists and skilled people more generally have to work in completely new jobs. They are forced to do things completely different from their previous professions, meaning they have had to toss aside all the experience they had accumulated. This is truly exile. People who have done valuable work are unable to continue gaining this experience because of language barriers or for other reasons. This is an upsetting situation. I've even thought over time, 'Okay, I'm maintaining this in a way, but it's temporary.' We live with very short-term solutions. There are valuable people who came here years earlier and covered significant distances; they can engage in different efforts to create networks of solidarity. But they don't happen, perhaps this is one of our societal characteristics. Who knows?

What are your views on Germany's position on the wave of new exiles arriving to the country?

Germany approaches intellectuals in exile by conducting an analysis through the circumstances in exile for its own intellectuals. And it can see that a very grave, painful process has taken place and is expecting them to articulate this. The main note here is that I see that this exile has not appeared in memory or at a time of new and physical differences. The conditions of the exile during this period are rather different. Due to the forms of communication for this period and the diversity of communication mechanisms, we are actively engaged in work most of the time, and we want to remain above minimal living conditions by seeking to sustain our work. But when the perception develops through the states of exiles in the 1930s and 1940s, it gets stuck and remains in a rather pathetic position. And yes, the expectation is in this direction. Personally, I didn't want to get stuck at this point. Yes, what we experienced is apparent. I'm trying to convey what we've experienced in the past and understand what is currently happening in Turkey, but on the other hand, I'm trying to stamp down on the conditions to explain my own story in terms of individual areas of interest. I'm trying to understand this place and take steps to ask the question 'How can we transform these circumstances?' So personally, I'm not really hung up on that point. But we must consider this from a few different perspectives. The situation is different for intellectuals, it's different for those who came here having acquired certain things, it's different in an educational sense for those who arrived without that acquisition. Because everyone's situation is different, the approaches to everyone are also disparate. So yes, there is the issue I mentioned just now when considering, for example, writers. They expect that our stories – that is, the country's stories – will be told. You feel condescension in the form of the question 'You just arrived here, so how can you understand this?' for the articles you've written. There's a bit of a level-measuring approach. I walk around here not only with Turkish nationals by establishing relationships with exiles from other countries. So, I've contemplated the issue of assimilation. I wrote an article about this – who will assimilate to whom? What kind of world is this? An article like this is a 'stop' article, because a million studies have been conducted over the years on integration, and now someone gets up and asks questions about the issue. It's been two years since I arrived. So a kind of measuring, estimating process is taking place. This research in Germany, issues of contemplation are very meticulous fields. Taking a long, winding road is valued in these fields for statements to emerge, but I don't think this is very logical. That's why I don't get hung up on these types of issues. I try to keep going, because if I get stuck, I think I'll get locked up in a mass of complaints. Indeed, I've seen a number of friends in exile get stuck on points like that.

I think one of the main issues is trying to learn a foreign language. Right now we're in a foreign country – regardless of what country that is – and I personally can conceptualise the society I'm in by understanding the mechanics of that society's language. What is it thinking and how? I can understand this by analysing the language. Of course, it's not possible for me to learn a language very well – especially at this age – but I've got around it by trying a little bit. I can analyse various tasks right now. But when we avoid this, it becomes more possible to get hung up on the points of complaint that I mentioned just now. On the other hand, there's another point – we said a little while ago – that every field has different problems. Academics walk around like this or that, taking quite a route in their own fields. The most serious situation, in my view, is with the political exiles who have not covered much distance professionally here. That is, the issue is mostly problematic in terms of a foreign language. It's problematic in terms of adapting to the language here. How will the people who have been unable to take many steps professionally here due to the political battles while in the country be able to maintain their lives? They can also get trapped on issues of assistance there. This creates an incredibly vicious cycle. There are also family problems. Families are coming. Families have their own problems, as do the children. In this context, mechanisms that can adapt to this system cannot be developed. It becomes a truly vicious cycle, and so life continues for Turkish nationals within a certain limit. When this is the case, of course, all eyes focus on change in Turkey. People ask themselves, 'What if it changes there into something else and we go?' This is very natural. And as a result, exile is heavy in all dimensions. I have tried to settle here in a way that pushes my circumstances in this way or that way. Of course, this is the result of the battle I fought in Turkey. I entered an environment of respite because of my education, my work and what I have done. But this doesn't at all mean that this is easy for me. And that's because a journalist friend was recently attacked. It was this Turkish national I mentioned just now, but the problems to which friends who have no opportunity to adapt here . . . people with whom I want to establish communication but have been unable to . . . Of course, they embody a certain expectation and, by necessity, don't remember me, the people I think about saying 'I'm standing here in this little corner' . . . All of this frequently pulls people down as a whole. To be revived later demands quite some energy. So the issue of strengthening networks of solidarity here becomes a point on the agenda.

We know about the incident Erk Acarer suffered. And many of our interviewees have felt that they're being monitored by Turkey in some way when they participate in panels and conferences. Do you feel safe in Germany? Do you think something will happen to you in Germany because of your dissidence in Turkey?

It could happen, of course. The Turkish regime is exporting aggression. This became clear in the incident with Erk. Before that, there were threats against a number of my friends. My God, people don't feel safe, of course. But I don't know. What will happen will happen. I'm not someone who really gets caught up in this issue, because every step has a cost. While we – and I personally – continued this fight, while we spoke about human rights or other issues, I said and did this knowing for certain that it would have repercussions. So if it's going to have a cost, that's the way it is. This shouldn't constitute an obstacle for staying true to our positions. Or at least it won't for me. We must continue to do what is necessary.

Some public figures prefer to self-censor themselves, and some prefer to speak out more.

I understand very well the feeling of standing on the sidelines. People had already experienced before this exile, it comes to the point of 'Let me take a breath'. This is unavoidable. There are pressures against their families and acquaintances in Turkey, things that are being forced upon them. These are, of course, very natural and human issues. There have been times where I have felt this too. It's not possible not to. On the other hand, it's fairly normal to toughen up. Because truly, what we, the entire society, nature and even future generations have been forced to suffer is unforgivable. What did we ask for, how do we deserve this suffering? And to use our voices wherever we are, of course. I use my voice in every circumstance on my own behalf, but my God, I'm not bringing myself out into the open. I have never done anything like that.

As a strong woman, you have been part of various resistance movements in Turkey. Where do you think Turkey is heading after this? What kind of stages await you?

I said at the outset that we must question the issue of 'power relations'. Within our format of organisation, issues everywhere under any circumstances are able to become exactly what we are fighting as long as we neglect to discuss our own internal problems with power. In this sense, our struggle is a little bit like that. I constantly feel the need to ask about my organisation or, personally, 'Who am I building power over?' So the spaces of this fight must clearly discuss these fundamental issues of internal power so as not to deviate from the struggle. I really value this fight as a woman. I mean, what we do is important, but how we do it is critical. Coming to Turkey's future, I said a little bit about it in our previous conversations. I can't really see a bright future politically in the short term. I say this fundamentally – I said it just now – by considering the discourses, structures, steps which stand like opposition yet have no use other than to support the existing structure. I'm not only considering this as a political party but as the spaces of a collective struggle. So the determining factor here is the genuine lack of an opposition. Seeking societal reconciliation in a place where the fundamental values are not questioned is not easy. So because of this, I'm not expecting a profound change in the short term. Let's say now that this regime has changed. Look at the probable picture for what will replace it. Again, national values, a state and so forth. How will there be transformation? Of course, it will offer us respite, but this is completely separate. This doesn't mean lasting forever. Yes, there's a need for this, for respite, especially for the battle being fought over women and children. I had hoped for that actually; this new regressive law for these children isn't acceptable. What does it mean to prove child exploitation? What is this? Who benefits from this? This shouldn't be considered just an issue of religious sects. Child exploitation is very common in society. So violence against women is a thing, but the issue of child exploitation is truly very painful. It isn't possible for me to describe this. As such, we're talking about a transformation of a societal state. And for this, there's a need for structures that will vigorously defend, legalise a series of powerful values. There's a need for a powerful will that will, in every sense, monitor and resolve this by revealing what's inside and out. I honestly can't see these. This could shift to a trajectory with a tiny transformation. I mean, the Turkish people could be opened up to brand new places if they're saved from the grips of this propaganda. This is a reality for this social structure. But we must produce a series of decrees that can open up these talons. We're experiencing these issues globally within a massive system of relationships, but we're also experiencing a chain of relationships in which tiny sparks can quickly burst into flame. So we must push this work without saying big or little but with an interdisciplinary system by diversifying these spaces in a manner such that it will have focus and continuity. It is never the case that only a single field is in question. The field of art, the political space, women's issues, the battle for health, I think all these spaces are in a position to introduce willpower in these fundamental values. We do not consider these issues as palliative. A political party said something, I don't know what this will turn into. There's nothing like this in the flow of life. In short, the outlook doesn't seem too bright. But as I said just now, when a space is opened from the top in these talons, there is a sense that there is a potential for transformation. The fight is that of expanding on that potential and ensuring it flows directly.

20

YAVUZ BAYDAR

**I still ask myself whether I've wasted my quarter-century
[of professional life], and I'm not fully able to answer that.
I'm bitter and hurt, I'm hurt for Turkey.**

Yavuz Baydar is the editor-in-chief of Ahval, *a trilingual independent online news site, and he produces podcasts on Turkey. Since the
attempted coup on 15 July 2016, he has lived in exile in Europe. Baydar
co-founded the independent media platform P24 in 2013 to monitor
the media sector and the state of journalism in Turkey. His opinion
articles have appeared in the* Guardian, *the* Süddeutsche Zeitung, *the*
New York Times, El País, Svenska Dagbladet, Yomiuri Shimbun,
the Arab Weekly *and* Index on Censorship. *Baydar has blogged
with the* Huffington Post *and* Al Jazeera, *sharing his analysis and
views on Turkish politics, the Middle East, the Balkans, Europe,*

US–Turkish relations, human rights, free speech, press freedom and history. Turkey's first news ombudsman, beginning at the daily Milliyet *in 1999, Baydar worked in the same role as independent reader representative until 2014. His work included reader complaints on content, and commentary on media ethics. Working in a tough professional climate had its costs. He was twice forced to leave his job, after his critical columns on journalistic flaws and fabricated news stories. He served as president of the US-based Organizaton of News Ombudsmen (ONO) in 2003. In 2014, as a Shorenstein fellow at the Kennedy School of Government, Harvard University, he completed an extensive research paper on self-censorship, corruption of ownership in Turkish media, state oppression and threats over journalism in Turkey – in the wake of the Gezi Park protests. Baydar has worked as producer and news presenter at Swedish Radio & Television (SR/SVT) in Stockholm. He was the Scandinavia and Baltics correspondent for the Turkish daily* Cumhuriyet *between 1980 and 1990. He worked as editor and news producer with the BBC World Service from 1991 to 1992. Baydar studied informatics, cybernetics and journalism at the University of Stockholm.*

Baydar was given the prestigious Journalistenpreis by the Munich-based Südosteuropa-Gesellschaft in Germany in February 2018. He was awarded the European Press Prize's Special Award, for 'excellence in journalism', in 2014. In 2017, he was given the Morris B. Abram Human Rights Award by UN Watch. In Italy he was presented with the Umbria Journalism Award in March 2014, and the Caravella 'Mare Nostrum' Award, by the Journalists of the Mediterranean organisation, in Puglia in 2010.

When and how did you leave Turkey?
I left Turkey on the afternoon of 17 July 2016. Having dual nationality, I left legally with a Swedish passport. I had been travelling into and out of Turkey for years by showing my Swedish passport and Turkish ID in accordance with the official practices in Turkey. I'm someone who travels a lot. I left legally and went to Greece by road.

What was your reason for choosing to leave by road? Why 17 July? What made you suspicious?

It was both my experiences in the past and intuition that drove me to this choice, a wisdom that the dark process into which Turkey was dragged after the June 2015 elections would lead to disorder. The successive developments after the 7 June 2015 elections, Erdoğan's ending of the Kurdish peace process under opaque, blurred conditions, the subsequent wave of violence that summer, and the outcome of the 1 November 2015 elections triggered by that violent summer had been a wake-up call. I'd say my opinion that Turkey won't easily improve after this, that it entered a long, dark tunnel, became clear on the morning of 2 November 2015.

In fact, I spoke about this with my wife on that very morning of 2 November. She felt exactly the same. 'Unfortunately, the story of a reformed Turkey has ended here and now,' I said. We thought time had come to move to a more serene existence elsewhere.

You see, Erdoğan's incredibly successful 'societal and political engineering process' had succeeded, after a brief shock caused by the election defeat on 7 June 2015, which meant that eighty Kurdish deputies had entered Parliament. The pro-Kurdish HDP had become a political actor and it was a shock to the entire establishment in Ankara. It was clear to me that, in defiance of the election results, Erdoğan and his then newly adapted allies of 'the old guard', considering, designing and implementing the engineering process following the 7 June elections, would drag the country towards another series of hardline executive choices. The first option was to continue living in this country under these conditions and continue to face all sorts of risks. But, one also had to remain ready for the worst – a disruption of the constitutional order.

'As a journalist, we – myself and many of my friends – are targets. Academics will follow. Many professional groups, especially those who disseminate news and commentary and professional groups that manage public platforms, civil society activists, along with Kurds, will be targeted.' I remember saying something along those lines. At home, we agreed. Also, some close friends whose judgements and instincts I trusted did the same. It was, from then on, a constant watch of a countdown process. I remember hearing the horrible news of the assassination of Tahir Elçi in Diyarbakır, while I was at a conference in New York in autumn 2015. Elçi was a wonderful human and a staunch defender of Kurdish rights. Hearing the news sent shivers down my spine, only confirming the darker days ahead. I spent the night of 15 July, when the attempted coup took place, thinking, 'I suppose the expected, dramatic developments are happening now, and there is no doubt where it will drag the entire country.'

Actually, there were signs of a rupture days before the military uprising. Two weeks before that, at a concert in the Beykoz district during the Istanbul Jazz Festival, I met a well-informed source close to the main opposition party, the CHP. He had a sullen face. I asked what was wrong. 'Ankara,' he said. 'Ankara what?' I wondered. 'There seems to be a huge crack within the top brass, and this one seems unrepairable, and I don't know what's next,' he said. He was truly worried. Later that night, I met a CHP deputy at the concert. I sought to confirm what that source had told me, but he only told me that 'there is some tension'. They knew no more. This was maybe two weeks before the hell broke loose.

The night of 15 July was chaotic. Earlier that night I was having a nice dinner on the balcony of a colleague of mine from the CNNTurk TV channel, joyously chatting and joking. His flat is on the European side, not far from the Bosphorus (Southern) Bridge. We were some of the first who received news of 'bizarre activity' at the Asian end of the bridge.

We hastily left the table and took off. My colleague was sceptical about the nature of the event. I was certain it was 'far bigger' than the first indications. I ride scooters normally in Istanbul, so as my colleague went to the channel, I rushed to the bridge. There was havoc. Even on a scooter I could not advance more than halfway across the bridge. Pandemonium. At that moment I was sure that a military uprising was taking place.

Returning at high speed, I rushed to the FSM (Northern) Bridge. My concern was it would be shut down in any moment, and my home was on the other side. Luckily I was able to use it. That bridge was also shut down roughly one hour later.

At home, I was watching the news, talking to friends and colleagues, and giving interviews to agencies calling from abroad. At the same time, I was constantly hearing the roars of jets flying over our district and the *ezan* (call to prayer) rising off the valleys behind me.

Kandilli was an interestingly symbolic spot that night. On one side towards the Bosphorus, there lies a cadets' school, Kuleli, and on the other side a couple of valleys, which house neighbourhoods extremely loyal to Erdoğan and the AKP. I said to myself, 'Just like the late Çetin Altan, our senior colleague, said, we're stuck between a mosque and the military barracks, and here is the real showdown.' The morning after that sleepless night – 16 July – I sat down, dazed and confused, made a cup of coffee, and concluded that leaving Turkey as quickly as possible would be the healthiest decision.

To answer to your question on why I chose to leave by road, I knew that I would leave and not return to Turkey for a long time. I packed my personal belongings, filled my car, stuffed in some books and my laptop, and drove off.

Not for security reasons?
It was clear what was about to happen, in terms of security, freedom and life in general. It became clear after some months already who and which groups would be targeted. The post-coup situation snowballed decisively into a round-up of the opposition and a massive purge of dissidents – regardless of their identity. The attempted coup was a given, but the circumstances that gave a birth to it and its consequences took an extremely long time for many intellectual circles to decode. Years, in fact.

What was the journey after Thessaloniki like? I call these 'trampoline countries'. Gülenists generally choose North Macedonia, and the 'white liberals' go via Thessaloniki. Why Thessaloniki? Why France afterwards? What was this process like?

Greece is the closest to Istanbul and easiest way to leave. It's that simple. If you're asking why an anarcho-liberal – by this I mean a devotion to journalism on the principle of its anti-authoritarian nature – like me chose such a path, it's entirely related to the geographic conditions.

I was in an advantageous position relative to many of my journalist friends and other dissidents thanks to my dual citizenship. I stayed a few days in Western Thrace – in Rodopi. I needed to understand the situation. I needed to pin down personal and family circumstances. There are a few people I know there; my family is rooted there. I watched the situation unfold in Turkey there with my friends in the minority among whom were also former PASOK MPs. Everyone was aware of the gravity of the situation. As the days passed by, the picture became more and more clear.

I must mention also that, just minutes after I crossed the border into Greece, relaxing by the river Evros over a cup of coffee, I received a call from Munich. It was my colleagues from the *Süddeutsche Zeitung* who were not only concerned about my situation but also proposed that I should chronicle the ordeal developing in Turkey. I accepted, and from that day on I wrote daily and – later – weekly articles recording what took place in the country. My column continued for over a year. I am proud to have put many details on record via *SDZ*.

After some days I moved on to Italy. I have a lot of friends, mainly from academia, in Italy. They said, 'Don't mess around too much there in Greece. Come this way quickly.' That was already my intention anyhow.

Erdoğan declared the state of emergency while I was crossing through the Epirus area on my way to the western Greek port of Igoumenitsa. It must have been 20 July. When I heard that the state of emergency had been declared while I was driving, I thought, 'Okay, this is it. Everything's developing as I guessed it would. Hell will break loose . . .' I was shocked when I noticed on social media that so few intellectuals had realised what that decision meant for their existence.

I published an article – my final column – in Turkish in the *Bugün* newspaper, for which I was a columnist. Its headline was 'Hey people! Are you aware that the counter-coup has started?' The article predicted also what would happen afterwards. Only days afterward *Bugün*, as well as many other news outlets, was shut down, a massive crackdown was launched. My point in that article was that a counter-coup against the failed coup, using the latter as a justification, had emerged. The counter-coup began with the state of emergency. And the repercussions of its 'success' have lasted for years.

Going onboard on the ferry, I had mixed feelings. While greatly relieved for myself, I was profoundly concerned for my Turkish and Kurdish colleagues and my news sources who were one way or another part of the reform process that clearly had failed – for good.

How was your passage from Italy to France? Why not Sweden? How was the process with Ahval?
In Turkey, I had grown weary of the working conditions . . . Because we all were scattered throughout our sector, here and there – more or less like serfs. Corrupt media bosses by their nature don't like honest journalists who are loyal to their jobs. They always have them messed about, knock them from pillar to post.

The media in Turkey as I experienced it was a stage of ugly ideological battles, polarisation, enmity, submission to powers, self-censorship, deep nationalism, and no job security. I had become a first-hand witness of the media culture and how it was entangled in widespread corruption in society when I served as an independent news ombudsman between 1999 and 2014. Most of the work I and a few colleagues did for ethics and public service led nowhere; nothing seemed to change for the better. These conditions really wore me out. So, at the time I left Turkey, or even some months before, I had the notion of leaving journalism too. I thought to myself that I'd write a book and work in another job.

But the most important issue on a personal level, I suppose, was that I didn't want to be far from the Mediterranean. The Mediterranean Sea is really important to me. People tend to care more about the climate when they grow older. I love Sweden very much; it is my second home. It contributed hugely to my personal formation, and it's a country to which I'm very thankful and grateful: I'd say it is where I was reborn. It's a country that offers wonderful opportunities for individualisation, but it's not a very attractive country in terms of its climate. It has some negative aspects, and it makes its people constantly long for other geographies, geographies which we belong to. So I was intent on being close to the Mediterranean. It is 'Mare Nostrum' – a pool that brings us all together. Italy and France are countries that I love very much, that are very close to my heart, and whose cultures I'm familiar with, through literature, cinema, the arts. So I stayed in Italy for a while. And two months later I left for France.

As far as I understand, this impacted your individual preferences and networks in transit. Did your networks help at all during these transitions?
Certainly – this applies to everyone. You're leaving a country, witnessing the bridges behind you collapsing. You enter a new environment, passing into a new space, and are forced to advance by feeling out the surroundings. This is a very common pattern.

No matter how mature a person is, he or she needs a support network. So former acquaintances, new friends, provide important sources of connection. One of these is, of course, family bonds. I also have friendships that had become distant but that I rekindled in Italy and France. Their support is significant – that relationship of mutual trust is important. For a while, my dear friends in the Puglia region opened up their summer home and hosted me there. They did this happily without expecting anything in return.

These are my friends from progressive circles. 'Our memory is very strong. We easily understand what is happening in Turkey and can predict the outcomes,' one of them told me. And they were as pessimistic as I was – as I still am.

Those in France are the same; they're people who know Turkey's history and have a past of their own. So, the networks and acquaintances produce a feeling of solidarity and trust that automatically transcends into friendship.

What about networks of Turkish nationals? Turkey already has its own diaspora, and within this diaspora are dissidents. And then there are the new arrivals – there's you, Cengiz Çandar, Cengiz Aktar, Celal Başlangıç . . . So is there any solidarity among you? And apart from that, you had close relations with Alevis, liberals, Kurds; with the Gülen Movement, and Armenians in Turkey, as far as I know. Did your relationships with these networks continue here?

Yes they did. The names you mention, and many others, know what exile means. Because they had the taste of it, like I did, in earlier times – in the 1970s and '80s. We keep contacts, we communicate, we share information and sentiments. In contrast to some colleagues of mine, I don't distinguish or discriminate against certain groups and alienate myself from them. I judge each and every person on a personal basis and that's why I maintain contacts from all the segments, as long as they are based on mutual respect and trust.

But, mind you, I left Turkey in a state of bitterness, and even rage, from which I tried hard to restrain myself – that's important, I suppose. I mentioned this in my book, titled 'Hope Dies at the Bosphorus: How Turkey Wasted Freedom and Democracy' (Droemer), which was published in German in 2018. It's a pessimistic book but it's realistic and its theses are still valid as things develop. Because pessimism is, unfortunately, an efficient method of prediction in Turkey. False hopes about Turkey always tend to lead to many optical illusions and deep disappointments among those who cling to them.

But, yes, I was truly exasperated, furious, I was blaming everybody.

And blaming yourself?
For my professional life being wasted, I'd say yes. I failed to help bring change for the better in society. But, do I feel duped, lured, abused? It is far too complicated to say yes to this often-debated question.

This is how I was thinking: a new party had assumed power through democratic elections and had become a single majority force in parliament, a party and government composed of many different identities. This AKP government originated from Islamist roots, and most of us – from liberal to leftist, Kurdish and non-Muslim flanks – gave them a blank cheque. Because it had promised an EU-led reform. Its programme looked progressive, and its finance minister had fully adopted an economic reform programme by a social democratic expert, Kemal Derviş, whose reformist and egalitarian views had made him famous worldwide.

I looked at it this way: a new company called the Justice and Development Party is founded and listed on the political stock exchange and you're not a staff member but an external shareholder of that company. You own those shares with the hope that the company will deliver profits for all the shareholders. My criterion, as a journalist and commentator, was simple: to monitor the company on the basis of its policy, which in this case was its pursuit of EU membership for Turkey, and its adoption of the Copenhagen Criteria. Support started and ended with that performance.

Giving the benefit of the doubt, many people in Turkey made that investment, saying, 'We want to believe in their promises, in their statements.' Minorities, Kurds, Armenians, a portion of the Alevis, liberals, even a segment of the Social Democrats despite their party affiliations . . . At the end of the day, as the story progressed poorly, everyone was forced to tear up that cheque at a certain point and throw it away or cross it through. It happened gradually, and each and every shareholder, depending on their level of insight and wisdom, had to drop that support. Some dropped out already in 2005 or 2006. Some later . . .

I tore up my shares in trust and journalistic support for the AKP's reform process when I saw the news of Erdoğan calling a statue being erected at the Turkish–Armenian border in the name of reconciliation a 'freak structure to be torn down immediately', which happened. That did it for me.

Back to what I was saying, as I said, you make an investment. Buying shares is gambling, and we lost here. They won – the embezzlers and the crooks. That company ended up being a company of frauds and they exposed all of us in some way. We had to pay the price. One of its staunch believers, for example, was Osman Kavala, who gave his soul for strengthening civil society, for democratic reform. It is clear how he had been forced to pay a price – by having to spend years in jail.

Anyway, those were the conditions of the era. There was a party out there that formed an amazing majority government with 34 per cent of the vote, well over the 10 per cent threshold under the election system created by the 12 September military regime. There was a party elected legitimately, on dubious grounds which the military should be blamed for in the first place. But they were full of promises.

It needed to be seen what they would do. As the English say, 'The proof of the pudding is in the eating' . . . I thought that was a spot-on saying.

So if I later criticised myself on this issue – and I did – I did so exactly as I said I would. A cheque was cut to the fraudulent company, which started well but grew rotten.

In fact, after going to Greece, I sat for an hour on the bank of the river Evros by the border post, and tried to think about all this as clearly as possible, and this was the bitter conclusion I reached: all of this needed to happen. This would be a lesson for the whole of society, perhaps. The citizenry had been cheated by the political classes for decades and had lost faith in them. The ground was ripe for Islamists, because of massive mismanagement at the top level.

The Islamists won. Everyone would remain suspicious, wondering whether the Islamists were truly sincere, if they would provide for us a democratic format of governance. We know now. Sometimes these lessons are costly and painful; they waste a generation or two, but they need to happen.

My disappointment and resentment towards all segments in Turkey remain, though. We are all in this and much blame should go to the opposition and the obstinacy of those parts of society who refused to see that the notion of equality was a sine qua non if Turkey was to change. We buried all this hope in some way together.

There's disappointment in this regard. Now there are those who are on the rise, saying, 'You see, we were right.' This is an extremely conformist position. In many ways, it symbolises a victory for a country in which nothing needs to change, with all the issues – topped by the Kurdish issue – piled up, ignored, denied and postponed. Resisting change for the sheer obstinacy of it was a phenomenon that was exposed fully in Turkey, and its immorality showed me how hard it was to peel that element off from its culture.

Everyone and every segment contributed to this in its own way. Take the Gülenists, for example. For a brief period, they seemed to push for democratic values, but when it came to dealing with Kurdish reforms, recognition of rights and deconstructing the injustices regarding the Alevis' status, they proved to be fully on the authoritarians' and establishment's side. This criticism can be applied in a similar way to all the other segments as well. Large swathes of the Turkish left, for example, are in denial of the permanent existence of a dominant Sunni segment in Turkey and do nothing to come to terms with them on seeking a common future with peaceful coexistence. Et cetera, et cetera . . .

So, together, in false hopes and calculations, they dug their own graves. Look at Turkey now, and the result is clear. All those segments, except a very tiny happy and corrupt minority in the top echelons, are convulsing and still unaware of what they had done to deserve this.

If there are any takeaways from this interview, it is these two lessons. First, it is impossible for any one social group in Turkey to annihilate another. For over a century after the Armenian Genocide of 1915, this primitive killer instinct has remained dominant and any social group that grabs power in Ankara sets about demonising and destroying the ones it sees as redundant. But this collective drift has only led to further anger and deeper vendettas.

Second, each and every social and political group in Turkey continues to impose its own impotent formulas for ruling the country, excluding others and ignoring their expectations. As long as this primitive pattern continues, and sadly even so many years after the botched coup and misery this goes on, Turkey's ordeal will continue. Unless wisdom is reached for a social contract, the battle between these impotent formulas, isolated to their groups, will lead to jumping from one vicious circle to another. This is Turkey's predicament, which at home is not recognised.

Not only your recent observations like this, but also your memories from the past must have helped . . .
Another dimension is that this is my second time in exile. This is an important part, yes, since I have experiences and recollections regarding this. I'm also someone who has learned three and a half foreign languages.

I know the operating system and cultural codes of the democratic world I returned from. I have the memory, the experience, the skills to be able to orient myself wherever I go. I am self-confident on this issue. And of course, the experiences of exile in Sweden were truly beneficial.

If you use it well, exile can be a very fertile space. You acquire quite a network. It has a great benefit if you open yourself up to foreign individuals, identities, spaces. I had seen that benefit from the start.

I can't say I struggled much. As soon as I crossed into Italy, I established a routine: I used Reporters without Borders, the Committee to Protect Journalists, Freedom House and some smaller European professional organisations to map out which intellectuals and journalists in difficult positions had crossed the border legally or illegally. Some fleeing colleagues had crossed into Germany, others were in Greece, and others were in camps. A few had crossed over to America; some were in Africa. I tried to help them. The only thing I tried to do to the best of my abilities was that kind of professional solidarity.

Are there cases against you in Turkey?

Certainly. In late August 2016, while I was still in Italy, I learned that there was a probe, a file against a group of people, including me and Ali Yurttagül, a columnist and former advisor to the German Greens, and 20–25 various liberal journalists. I think Murat Aksoy (a social democratic commentator) and Eyüp Can (ex-editor of the daily *Radikal*) were in the same dossier, but I can't confirm this for certain. Neither I nor Ali to this day understand what the content (accusations) and common denominator of the 'suspects' are for this file. This remains a mystery. Anyhow, on that early August morning, the police raided our homes. There was a list of 20–25 'suspects' who had no relation to one another, who had not been in contact with one another and so all were a bit of a mixed bag.

It was understood that morning that there were warrants out for our arrest. I was notified of one, through a neighbour. This later became clear through my lawyer. Although years have passed since then, we still have no information about the content of this dossier. We need to surrender to be notified of the accusations, my lawyer was told. The prosecutors say they'll announce the reason at that point. Of course, this is an absurd situation for universal law. My arrest warrant is still active, I understand. As a consequence, my Turkish passport is annulled.

So were there any actions like seizing your property in Turkey?
I don't have any property in Turkey.

If I'm not mistaken, you also have a son. Are your wife and son together with you? Were they able to leave or were measures implemented against their passports?
My son already didn't want to live in Turkey under these circumstances. He's a strongly perceptive child. 'I want to grow up abroad,' he said. He joined me soon after I left. Now, he's studying at a university in Europe.

Was your wife able to leave?
She stayed, saying, 'I'll clear things up, sort out the mess here. You go.' My son immediately decided to come with me. He finished high school in France having studied at St Joseph in Istanbul before we left the country.

There was a passport ban on my wife a short while later – I think around September 2016. She was shocked, of course. No reason was given. She was forced to leave our rental apartment for financial reasons. The passport ban lasted eight or nine months. It was ridiculous. We later applied with the help of a lawyer, and the ban was removed. There was already no reason that it shouldn't have been removed, but the state of emergency conditions were harsh and unpredictable.

Turkey quite successfully implements something we call 'extraterritorial authoritarianism' in the literature. But there are measures taken for your Turkish passport right now, and you use your Swedish passport. As far as I understand, you have no relationship with any Turkish legal institution.
No, I don't want one whatsoever. My feeling is that, unfortunately, an ignorant, disqualified, rather foolish and hostile segment has taken over the state, gradually since 2014–15. Now, folly merged with political barbarism rules, and is taking hold as a source of oppression in

Turkey against the interior. The arteries of the government and the judiciary are filled with such cadres determined to crack down on any dissent with full force. Numbers of absurd indictments and trials like the ones against Osman Kavala and Selahattin Demirtaş are examples of how far it has gone.

It is essential never to interact or come into contact with these segments in any way. To interact with irrationality is a total waste of time. Responding to the authorities' calls and demands doesn't befit the honour of an intellectual. You should ignore it, because you know you haven't committed a crime. What we have suffered for more than five years already has demonstrated this fact to us. I mean, holding humanity in a constant state of oppression, subjecting everyone, any people from every segment, day in and day out to a witch hunt has already demonstrated this ugly reality to us.

The state has certain practices such as not performing certain actions at the consulate and profiling individuals at Diyanet mosques. Apart from this, there are Turkish nationals abroad – especially in Germany – who voluntarily feel very close to the current regime. As far as I know, public figures like you with recognisable faces and voices can suffer attacks or harassment on the street. Have you had any experiences like this?
No, never. Maybe because I have always been a supporter of conducting pure journalism. I am for disseminating factual news and publishing opinions as pluralistically as possible. This is, I suppose, what distinguishes me from some other colleagues whom I respect anyway.

A portion of them in exile have preferred to engage in – let's not say the propaganda – the conveyance of a certain political identity and its messages. For many of them, journalism and reporting are interwoven with standing for a certain political position, identity. A portion do this by heavily emphasising Kurdish identity, another portion through a leftist identity, another portion through Gülenist identity, et cetera, et cetera. This is a specific journalistic choice, a sort of mission journalism. However popular, acceptable and justifiable under the current circumstances, I have never supported that attitude.

There are journalists who constantly shout and yell on social media or in commentaries, for example. I have colleagues who adopt an anti-Erdoğan stand and speak out as if they're representatives of a political party, who value agitprop with a classical, formerly leftist parlance. I have never been convinced that this was correct, that it is our real mission. Our job is to convey to the public news that has been prepared in as accurate, balanced and honest a way as possible. The most prominent 'ism' in our sphere should remain 'journalism', full stop.

I'm focused on my job. I don't engage with environments where there are Turkish nationals – and I'm not saying Turks. Covid helps too.

My disappointment – my thoroughly deepened suspicions about the future of Turkey – is solid. And it doesn't seem like it's going to pass by easily. That's why I keep my distance as much as possible. I am inspired by history when it comes to this. I always think about the voluntary detachment of intellectuals who were forced to leave Turkey in the 1940s and 1950s. This left a profound mark on me. Professor Muzaffer Sherif, Professor Pertev Naili Boratav – they're academics, scientists. I don't want to compare myself with them, but they always stood in the same position in terms of demeanour, of 'staying away' from the national communities, in the US or France, for example. Artists and painters – they focused on their work as much as possible. They didn't get overinvolved with intra-diaspora activities and engage with political matters. They always preferred to observe the country from afar, from a certain distance, raising their voices only when they must.

Maybe this was by necessity. With time, though, if I'm invited, I'll participate in the Kurdish dialogue processes. I'll participate in journalism networks, conferences, meetings, seminars, like Academics for Peace. Or regional dialogue platforms with colleagues from Greece, Egypt and Armenia.

You said you understood on 1 November 2015 where Turkey would go. We see that the Kurds' critical junction is different, the Gülenists' critical junction is different. Everyone has a different Turkey. What is your Turkey? What broke you?

I have no political sense of belonging. I never have been part of any 'tribe'. I detest political tribalism, and this doesn't work to my advantage in Turkey's tribalist, patriarchal culture. But of course I have a political perspective. I said 'anarcho-liberal' before, half jokingly. I have an anti-authoritarian perspective – which I believe is very helpful in my journalism – and I describe myself as a democrat. I believe in the rule of law and liberal democracy. These are my prisms.

I mentioned earlier that 2 November 2015 was a definitive breaking point, but let me go back even further, because for me, a steady observer of the AKP and Turkey, there were a series of incidents, as symbolic breaking points. The first trauma for me was in 2007: Hrant [Dink]'s murder and the subsequent reaction of the government and the public discourse that formed following that. I mentioned the shareholder issue; what actually happened in 2007 and 2008 heightened my suspicions over my shares and my hopes about EU membership for Turkey. The so-called Malatya murders (Christian missionaries brutally slain), the so-called e-memorandum by the top brass, the rise of pressure on the AKP leadership following those military threats, and the closure case against the AKP led me to view the issue from a different perspective. I had stood up strongly against the closure case during that period. I thought it would hinder the normalisation of politics, damage the accession process and lead to a serious tension and lethal polarisation.

The second wave of suspicion came after the end of the lawsuit. When the AKP narrowly escaped being shut down, one could observe a different, emboldened and arrogant Erdoğan. He seemed happy that Abdullah Gül had become a (symbolic) president and the internal 'checks and balances' mechanism in the AKP was broken down. Erdoğan may have seen a free ride from that point on.

The so-called protocol process had begun with Armenia at that time. This was a key development, which was a win–win scenario for both countries. For Turkey, it would have worked as a gate opener into the EU. For Armenia, a new avenue away from Russian influence. Gül had a lot to do with the rapprochement, but Erdoğan, at the last minute, interfered, to the shock of even his diplomats, and threw the process into a garbage can by trying to insert the Karabakh issue into the framework.

The new direction was already clear. And the *Blue Marmara* incident with Israel, the so-called Roboski massacre of thirty-four Kurdish villagers, the turbidity behind that incident and the ugly power-sharing fight that gradually got swollen between the 'National Visionists' and Gülenists, and, of course, the Gezi protests . . .

Gezi was a crucially important episode for me professionally. I had written two critical articles as news ombudsman for the *Daily Sabah* but was brutally censored by the chief editor. The censorship of an independent news ombudsman was globally unprecedented and sent shockwaves throughout the international community. What I wrote was a straightforward critique of the paper which its readers believed was marred by pro-government bias in the coverage of events. In other words, the famous penguins incident attributed to CNNTurk during the protests was not a singular event;[1] it applied to the large parts of the Turkish media.

Censorship had left me with a single choice. I wrote an article in the *New York Times*, describing the ordeal, lashing out at media moguls and censors. Two weeks later, I was fired. I wasn't alone; there were many more decent journalists who were sacked at that time. Soon after our sacking, with a small group of colleagues we launched *P24*, an independent platform to monitor the state of journalism in Turkey.

---

[1] CNNTurk showed a documentary about penguins when people were taking to the streets as part of the Gezi protests.

Gezi had become a test case for Erdoğan on how he sees media freedom. The response was clear: slaughter had begun for real.

And at the end of the same year, 2013, two large-scale corruption probes featured on the agenda, implicating Erdoğan, his family and some ministers. Despite the government getting exposed, both the opposition's and the media's skewed response to this caused me even greater disappointment. Both probes had a considerable amount of substance and proof, some of which was even based on FBI inquiries, and they both had great news value. But both the opposition and the mainstream media approached it with a 'dog eat dog' mindset – meaning Erdoğan saw the law enforcement as led by Gülenists, his new enemies – the deliberate neglect of news coverage had only helped embolden him even more strongly than ever before. He felt free because the secular main opposition party chose not to make a big fuss out of it, thus indirectly approving of his alleged corruption on a mass scale. It was de facto on his side. He therefore rapidly set about curbing media freedoms and started penetrating the judiciary to serve his political interests. His path forward had become completely clear. His ultimate destination would be autocracy. I had no doubts at that point.

In February 2014 I wrote an article in the German edition of *Le Monde Diplomatique*, titled 'Putsch in Zeitlupe' ('Slow motion coup'). It was an article predicting what would happen next. I argued that Erdoğan had begun to shape a new alliance with his former sworn enemies, parts of the military structures and ultra-nationalists, and he would produce a series of civilian coups that would progress sequentially in slow motion. In a nutshell, what Latin Americans call an *autogolpe* (self-coup) began. Everything after that indeed began to snowball to this direction.

My disappointment was caused by various sectors of the opposition besides the media. In the Gezi protests for example, the Kurdish Political Movement did not come out to fully support the Gezi protestors, it instead tried to defend itself with various excuses and justifications due to the ongoing peace process at that time. Its absence was a cheap tactic. At the end of the day, the Kurds were also duped when Erdoğan in the summer of 2015 turned down the negotiations, on the pretext of a murky murder story of two police officers. He acted the same way he acted when trying to destroy the Armenian reconciliation process. For the Kurdish politicians, Gezi was a failed test case.

For the Gülenists, the record is far worse. For years they seemed to support the reform process, but, as it turned out, they had unduly interfered in judicial cases and blew a lot of opportunities for Turkey to remain on track to reform. Like Erdoğan, they had become intoxicated with power, and raised false illusions that with a state apparatus under control, Sunni segments would rule the country, ignoring the plights of Alevis and Kurds and moderate seculars.

The Turkish left never realised that it should create a dialogue with the lower echelons of the electorate, regardless of its inclinations to have a say in Turkish politics.

My answer to your question is a bit long. There isn't a single breaking point, but many. These are like domino pieces or a series of events that helped me see the big picture when the pieces of the puzzle all came together.

I had completely forgotten about that freak statue incident. So much is happening every day!
It was horrible. It was a shock for me. It happened soon after the murder of my friend and colleague Hrant Dink. His family and the entire Armenian community suffered a terrible trauma.

Second, I had already told my friends after the third hearing of the murder trial that the case would be left to rot. Some alarm bells were ringing in my head. I thought that things had taken a wrong turn, but I had to wait and see what happened next. And then Erdoğan declared the statue as a 'freak' one to be demolished. There you go, I thought. Many of my friends thought 'Well, maybe this is a passing trend', and went on in their support, but for me, at that time, that was it. Pessimism is a crucial virtue when analysing Turkey. Pessimism is the appropriate lens through which one can view Turkey. The less illusioned you are, the better.

What we're experiencing today is the inevitable result of all the things we experienced earlier. I hope I'm able to articulate my disappointment. With Turkey, I tried. I gave a quarter of a century to Turkey. Turkey was the land of opportunity in the early 1990s. And many people – with my contributions – returned, saying, 'Let's contribute to something, let's create a new Turkey together.'

Twenty-five years may have gone to waste. I'm sorrowful because of that. Had I struggled pointlessly for a quarter of a century? Did I waste a significant portion of my life? I think that's as important as the self-scrutiny with regard to other aspects, but in this context, it dominates my thinking. I think many people – and my background may have been different – question themselves like this; or I hope they do so.

You mentioned on the podcast you did with Ahval that a new Turkish diaspora has formed. How would you define this diaspora? Why now? What are the differences between this new diaspora and older ones, in your view?
To put it simply, what has happened in the past 40–50 years is the expulsion of different identities from Turkey.

When I left Turkey in the mid-1970s in my first exile, I witnessed an Assyrian exodus, like many painful incidents preceding it. A significant portion of them came to Germany, another not-so-insignificant portion – as many as 10,000 – migrated to Sweden and formed a diaspora. They are prominent in current politics because they are hard-working people. After the military coup on 12 September 1980, a Kurdish diaspora also spread throughout Europe. Before this there was a Turkish leftist and Alevi diaspora after the 12 March 1971 military putsch, but the latest failed coup shows us two things.

First, there had never been a Sunni group among Turkey's social segments that had been demonised, vilified and brutalised at any point in the history of the modern Turkish republic. As such, we see that a group of individuals with a Sunni identity – the Gülenists – were demonised and subjected to persecution from 2014 on, fully brutalised after 2016. The dominant identity of most of these individuals is Turkish – they are Anatolian Turks. They have been heaped together in some places in North America and Europe.

And there is another segment. This is a group of intellectuals, forced to leave the country after 15 July 2016. A significant proportion of them are academics, journalists, military officers and members of the judiciary. I consider them more as vocational groups. Of course, there are also a few politicians among them, especially those with roots in the HDP. A major portion of this segment are in Germany, Belgium, the Netherlands and Scandinavia. I think this formation is destined to be a permanent part of the diaspora.

Why?
Because a regime change took place in Turkey on a massive scale. The regime changed in all its foundational areas and institutions. This is the result of a range of slow-motion coups that have been imposed in Turkey since 2013 and are ongoing. The critical point was the 2017 referendum. That was a referendum that more profoundly than ever before amplified the legal codes, political mechanisms and security functions of the 12 September regime in Turkey. It was the transition to a presidential system.

There is an ideological outline, framework and vision for this. The vision is to produce a standardised, monistic, autocratic republic, designed after the central Asian republic model. This is a format in which there will be no 'jarring voices', the opposition will be under severe pressure, the 'official sadism' that the hardliner circles of Turkey are known for will be intact and an Orwellian sphere will take root. As long as this vision continues to materialise, it will be impossible for any of these segments living outside of Turkey to return to the country and maintain a comfortable and peaceful life, unless, of course, they agree to abide by the new formats that such a regime imposes on groups or individuals.

Considering that this regime will not change, I believe that the degree of its permanence is one to take very seriously.

Mind you, the answer to the question of why it won't change is simple. Turkey has been unable to free itself from the 12 September 1980 regime for forty years. Four decades!.. The militarist-nationalist spirit of the current constitution is still solid. Its roots are buried deep, and get fed by the political culture. If it has already been so difficult to adopt a democratic constitution, it will be even more so to change the April 2017 regime.

If the balance is like this, we need to understand that we are obliged to exist as a diaspora. I am realistic about this prospect. In some recent meetings with exiles, I told them, 'This is a very long run. We should be realists and establish a way of life, a collective, interactive format of relationships based on this. Everyone should come together regardless of the common denominator of the diaspora.' I think this is the answer to the question. Returning to Turkey is impossible, unless a radical change takes place. Would anyone return if another brutal coup toppling Erdoğan occurs? Do we approve of coups as legitimate paths for our society to come to closure? Nobody asks this question openly.

So would you return?
I have no intention to return.

A short while ago, you said people could return if an exceptional situation unfolds. Would you not return even if that exceptional situation occurred?
Democracy is not to be taken granted. Let's face it, Turkey is known for its several coups and for disrupting politics. Its political culture

is primitive and the ground is delicate. The way power is handled in Turkey doesn't make me optimistic about the future. Would anyone in exile circles cheer if a new rupture takes place? It is not impossible. I definitely wouldn't. I watch, observe and report. What I know is, currently, as before, the fight in Turkey is not, as some believe, a battle for democracy, but a battle for who is next to grab power.

Therefore, the risks are high that the country will remain in limbo, it will brew up false hopes, people will be thrown into hypocrisy . . . I don't have the stomach for these things anymore.

I still ask myself whether I've wasted my quarter-century, and I'm not fully able to answer that. I'm bitter and hurt, I'm hurt for Turkey. I've witnessed so much folly . . . so much fatalism and conformism. I watched an elite keener on not losing its privileges than engaging in defending rights and equality. A significant majority is fond of its comfort and content with the patriarchal form of governance – religious or secular. That's the kind of society it is.

I have to trust a government or a state that it won't stab me in the back for no reason. That it respects my rights and my dignity. I'm a person who loves freedom. I'm someone who likes civilised relationships. I love environments that are civilised, gentle and distanced, in which people do not raise their tempers or speak behind each other's backs or rat one another out, in which friendships live and breathe and grow in the context of a certain security, even if they are distant. It's crucial that one is not judged by one's beliefs or stances but by who one is. Civilised forms and codes of living are important for me. Wherever there are intelligent life forms is where I intend to be.

REFERENCES

Foreword

Baser Bahar, Samim Akgönül and Ahmet Erdi Öztürk (2017), '"Academics for Peace" in Turkey: a Case of Criminalising Dissent and Critical Thought via Counterterrorism Policy', *Critical Studies on Terrorism* 10(2): 274–96.

Carrier, Anne-Laure and Sophie Ebermeyer (2014), 'La Promotion de l'égalité requiert une convergence des luttes', *Cahiers du développement social urbain* 60: 34.

Chambers, Richard L. (1973), 'The Education of a Nineteenth-Century Ottoman *Âlim*, Ahmed Cevdet Paşa', *International Journal of Middle East Studies* 4(4): 440–64.

Cohen, Robin (1997), *Global Diasporas: An Introduction*, Seattle: University of Washington Press.

Eldem, Edhem (2012), 'Making Sense of Osman Hamdi Bey Paintings', *Muqarnas Online* 29(1): 339–83.

Erdoğan, Aslı (2017), 'Il doit y avoir une erreur!', *Ballast* 1(6): 140–9.

Liversage, Anika and Gretty Mizrahi Mirdal (2017), 'Growing Old in Exile: A Longitudinal Study of Migrant Women from Turkey', *Journal of Ethnic and Migration Studies* 43(2): 287–302.

Mung, Emmanuel Ma (2004), 'Dispersal as a Resource', *Diaspora* 13(2–3): 211–25.

Paugam, Serge (ed.) (1996), *L'Exclusion, l'état des savoirs*, Paris: La Découverte.

Safran, William (1991), 'Diasporas in Modern Societies: Myths of Homeland and Return', *Diaspora* 1(1): 83–99.

Schiffauer, Werner (2008), 'From Exile to Diaspora: the Development of Transnational Islam in Europe', in Aziz al-Azmeh and Effie Fokas (eds), *Islam in Europe: Diversity, Identity and Influence*, Cambridge: Cambridge University Press, pp. 68–95.

Selek, Pınar (2010), 'Travailler avec ceux qui sont en marge?', *Socio-logos* 5, https://doi.org/10.4000/socio-logos.2505, accessed 22 February 2023.

Simet, Georg F. (2012), 'Possibilities and Risks of Influencing Public Knowledge: The Case of Hrant Dink', in Nikita Basov and Oleksandra Nenko (eds), *Understanding Knowledge Creation: Intellectuals in Academia, the Public Sphere and the Arts*, Leiden: Brill, pp. 83–107.

Zilfi, Madeline C. (1983), 'Elite Circulation in the Ottoman Empire: Great Mollas of the Eighteenth Century', *Journal of the Economic and Social History of the Orient*, 26(3): 318–64.

Introduction

Abrahams, Hilary (2017), 'Listen to Me: A Reflection on Practice in Qualitative Interviewing', *Journal of Gender-Based Violence* 1(2): 253–9.

Adamson, Fiona B. (2020), 'Non-state Authoritarianism and Diaspora Politics', *Global Networks* 20(1): 150–69.

Ahval (2018), 'Number of Turks granted protection status in Europe up by 300 percent', 1 November, https://ahvalnews.com/europe-turkey/number-turks-granted-protection-status-europe-300-percent, accessed 22 February 2023.

Aksel, Damla B. (2019), *Home States and Homeland Politics: Interactions between the Turkish State and Its Emigrants in France and the United States*, Abingdon and New York: Routledge.

Aktar, Ayhan (2009), '"Turkification" Policies in the Early Republican Era', in Catharina Dufft (ed.), *Turkish Literature and Cultural Memory: 'Multiculturalism' as a Literary Theme after 1980*, Wiesbaden: Harrassowitz, pp. 29–62.

Amnesty International UK (2020), 'Turkey's crackdown on human rights', 18 May, https://www.amnesty.org.uk/turkey-coup-crackdown-human-rights, accessed 23 February 2023.

Aydın-Düzgit, Senem (2008), 'The AKP in Turkey: Off the Hook This Time', *International Spectator* 43(4): 25–9.

Aydın-Düzgit, Senem (2012), 'No Crisis, No Change: The Third AKP Victory in the June 2011 Parliamentary Elections in Turkey', *South European Society and Politics* 17(2): 329–46.

Baser, Bahar (2015), 'Gezi Spirit in the Diaspora: Diffusion of Turkish Politics to Europe', in Isabel David and Kumru Toktamis (eds), *'Everywhere Taksim': Sowing the Seeds for a New Turkey at Gezi*, Amsterdam: Amsterdam University Press, pp. 251–66.

Baser, Bahar and Emre Eren Korkmaz (2018), 'Is Turkey really facing an "exodus"? It's not that simple', *The Conversation*, 6 February, https://theconversation.com/is-turkey-really-facing-an-exodus-its-not-that-simple-90197, accessed 3 April 2023.

Baser, Bahar and Alpaslan Özerdem (2021), 'Conflict Transformation and Asymmetric Conflicts: A Critique of the Failed Turkish–Kurdish Peace Process', *Terrorism and Political Violence* 33(8): 1775–96.

Baser, Bahar and Ahmet Erdi Öztürk (2017), *Authoritarian Politics in Turkey: Elections, Resistance and the AKP*, London: I. B. Tauris.

Baser, Baher and Ahmed Erdi Öztürk (2019), 'Turkey's Diaspora Governance Policies and Diasporas from Turkey in Germany: A Critical Reading of the Changing Dynamics', in Mete Hatay and Tziarras Zenonas (eds), *Kinship and Diasporas in Turkish Foreign Policy: Examples from Europe, the Middle East and the Eastern Mediterranean*, Nicosia: PRIO Cyprus Centre, pp. 29–45.

Baser, Bahar, Samim Akgönül and Ahmet Erdi Öztürk (2017), '"Academics for Peace" in Turkey: A Case of Criminalising Dissent and Critical Thought via Counterterrorism Policy', *Critical Studies on Terrorism* 10(2): 274–96.

Ben-Porat, Guy, Dani Filc, Ahmet Erdi Ozturk and Luca Ozzano (2021), 'Populism, Religion and Family Values Policies in Israel, Italy and Turkey', *Mediterranean Politics*, https://doi.org/10.1080/13629395.2021.1901484, accessed 23 February 2023.

Biner, Zerrin Öslem (2019), 'Precarious Solidarities: "Poisonous Knowledge" and the Academics for Peace in Times of Authoritarianism', *Social Anthropology* 27(S2): 15–32.

Brayda, Winsome Chunnu and Travis D. Boyce (2014), 'So You Really Want to Interview Me? Navigating "Sensitive" Qualitative Research Interviewing', *International Journal of Qualitative Methods* 13(1): 318–34.

Çelik, Ayşe Betül, Rezarta Bilali and Yeshim Iqbal (2017), 'Patterns of "Othering" in Turkey: A Study of Ethnic, Ideological, and Sectarian Polarisation', *South European Society and Politics* 22(2): 217–38.

DW (2016), 'Exodus from Turkey', 8 November, https://www.dw.com/en/exodus-from-turkey/av-19464542, accessed 22 February 2023.

Economist Intelligence Unit (2022), *Democracy Index 2021: The China Challenge*, Economist Intelligence Unit, https://www.eiu.com/n/campaigns/democracy-index-2021/, accessed 23 February 2023.

Ergil, Doğu (2010), 'Constitutional Referendum: Farewell to the "Old Turkey"', *Insight Turkey* 12(4): 15–22.

Ersoy, Duygu (2012), 'The Relationship between Liberal Intellectuals and Power in the Search for a New Hegemony during AKP Period in Turkey', PhD thesis, Middle East Technical University.

Ersoy, Duygu and Fahriye Üstüner (2016), '"Liberal Intellectuals'" Narration of the Justice and Development Party in Turkey', *Turkish Studies* 17(3): 406–28.

Esen, Berk and Sebnem Gumuscu (2016), 'Rising Competitive Authoritarianism in Turkey', *Third World Quarterly* 37(9): 1581–606.

Gall, Carlotta (2019), 'Spurning Erdogan's vision, Turks leave in droves, draining money and talent', *New York Times*, 2 January, https://www.nytimes.com/2019/01/02/world/europe/turkey-emigration-erdogan.html, accessed 22 February 2023.

Göçek, Fatma Müge (2011), *The Transformation of Turkey: Redefining State and Society from the Ottoman Empire to the Modern Era*, London: I. B. Tauris.

Göknar, Erdağ (2020), 'The AKP's Rhetoric of Rule in Turkey: Political Melodramas of Conspiracy from "Ergenekon" to "Mastermind"', in Güneş Murat Tezcür (ed.), *The Oxford Handbook of Turkish Politics*, Oxford: Oxford University Press.

Goßner, Christina (2020), 'Growing number of Turkish citizens apply for asylum in Germany', *Euractiv*, 8 May, https://www.euractiv.com/section/justice-home-affairs/news/an-increasing-number-of-turkish-citizens-apply-for-asylum-in-germany/, accessed 22 February 2023.

Gümüş, Pınar (2017), 'Negotiating "the Political": A Closer Look at the Components of Young People's Politics Emerging from the Gezi Protests', *Turkish Studies* 18(1): 77–101.

Gurses, Mehmet (2020), 'The Evolving Kurdish Question in Turkey', *Middle East Critique* 29(3): 307–18.

Haas, Hein de (2021), 'A Theory of Migration: The Aspirations–Capabilities Framework', *Comparative Migration Studies* 9, article 8.

Haynes, Jeffrey (2010), 'Politics, Identity and Religious Nationalism in Turkey: From Atatürk to the AKP', *Australian Journal of International Affairs* 64(3): 312–27.

Heper, Metin (2000), 'The Ottoman Legacy and Turkish Politics', *Journal of International Affairs* 54(1): 63–82.

Insel, Ahmet (2003), 'The AKP and Normalizing Democracy in Turkey', *South Atlantic Quarterly* 102(2–3): 293–308.

Irak, Dağhan (2018), '"Shoot Some Pepper Gas at Me!" Football Fans vs. Erdoğan: Organized Politicization or Reactive Politics?' *Soccer & Society*, 19(3): 400–17.

Kalaycıoğlu, Ersin (2012), '*Kulturkampf* in Turkey: The Constitutional Referendum of 12 September 2010', *South European Society and Politics* 17(1): 1–22.

Kaygusuz, Özlem (2018), 'Authoritarian Neoliberalism and Regime Security in Turkey: Moving to an "Exceptional State" under AKP', *South European Society and Politics* 23(2): 281–302.

Kuru, Ahmet T. (2017), 'Islam and Democracy in Turkey: Analyzing the Failure', *Montréal Review*, December.

Lampas, Nikolaos (2018), 'The Unknown Turkish Refugee Crisis', Perspectives Paper No. 993, BESA Center, 1 November, https://besacenter.org/turkey-refugee-crisis/, accessed 3 April 2023.

Larrabee, Stephen F. (2010), 'Turkey's New Geopolitics', *Survival* 52(2): 157–80.

Onar, Nora (2007), 'Kemalists, Islamists, and Liberals: Shifting Patterns of Confrontation and Consensus 2002–06', *Turkish Studies* 8(2): 273–88.

Özbudun, Ergun (2006), 'From Political Islam to Conservative Democracy: The Case of the Justice and Development Party in Turkey', *South European Society and Politics* 11(3–4): 543–57.

Öztürk, Ahmet Erdi (2016), 'Turkey's Diyanet under AKP Rule: From Protector to Imposer of State Ideology?' *Southeast European and Black Sea Studies* 16(4): 619–35.

Öztürk, Ahmet Erdi and Bahar Baser (2021), 'New Turkey's New Diasporic Constellations: The Gezi Generation and Beyond', ELIAMEP, 8 October, https://www.eliamep.gr/en/publication/%cf%83%cf%8d%ce%b3%cf%87%cf%81%ce%bf%ce%bd%ce%b1-%ce%bc%ce%bf%cf%84%ce%af%ce%b2%ce%b1-%ce%b4%ce%b9%ce%b1%cf%83%cf%80%ce%bf%cf%81%ce%ac%cf%82-%cf%84%ce%b7%cf%82-%ce%bd-%ce%ad%ce%b1%cf%82-%cf%84%ce%bf/, accessed 22 February 2023.

Öztürk, Ahmet Erdi and İştar Gözaydın (2017), 'Turkey's Constitutional Amendments: A Critical Perspective', *Research and Policy on Turkey* 2(2): 210–24.

Seyben, Burcu Yasemin (2019), '"My Life Has Become More Absurd than My Play": *Mi Minör* and the Crackdown on Artistic Freedom in Turkey', *TDR* 63(3): 36–49.

Sznajder, Mario and Luis Roniger (2009), *The Politics of Exile in Latin America*, Cambridge and New York: Cambridge University Press.

Tapan, Berivan (2010), '"Yetmez ama evet" diyenler gerekçelerini anlatıyor', Bianet, 10 August, https://bianet.org/bianet/siyaset/124030-yetmez-ama-evet-diyenler-gerekcelerini-anlatiyor, accessed 23 February 2023.

Taş, Hakkı (2018), 'A History of Turkey's AKP-Gülen Conflict', *Mediterranean Politics* 23(3): 395–402.

Taşpınar, Ömer (2012), 'Turkey: The New Model?' Brookings, 25 April, https://www.brookings.edu/research/turkey-the-new-model/, accessed 22 February 2023.

Tekdemir, Omer, Mari Toivanen and Bahar Baser (2018), 'Peace Profile: Academics for Peace in Turkey', *Peace Review* 30(1): 103–11.

Tepe, Sultan (2005), 'Turkey's AKP: A Model "Muslim-Democratic" Party?' *Journal of Democracy* 16(3): 69–82.

Tuğal, Cihan (2009), *Passive Revolution: Absorbing the Islamic Challenge to Capitalism*, Stanford, CA: Stanford University Press.

Tuğal, Cihan (2013), '"Resistance Everywhere": The Gezi Revolt in Global Perspective', *New Perspectives on Turkey* 49: 157–72.

TÜİK (2020), 'Uluslararası Göç İstatistikleri, 2019', 17 July, https://data. tuik.gov.tr/Bulten/Index?p=Uluslararasi-Goc-Istatistikleri-2019-33709, accessed 22 February 2023.

Turkut, Emre (2020), 'Osman Kavala v Turkey: Unravelling the Matryoshka Dolls', *European Human Rights Law Review* 2020(3): 289–97.

Watmough, Simon P. and Ahmet Erdi Öztürk (2018), 'From "Diaspora by Design" to Transnational Political Exile: The Gülen Movement in Transition', *Politics, Religion & Ideology* 19(1): 33–52.

Weise, Zia (2017), 'Turkey loses its brains', *Politico*, 17 January, https://www. politico.eu/article/turkey-failed-coup-purge-scholars-loses-its-brains/, accessed 22 February 2023.

Wrigley, Patrick (2008), 'Turkey's Ergenekon case raises Kurdish hopes and fears', *World Politics Review*, 24 October, https://www.worldpoliticsreview. com/articles/2816/turkeys-ergenekon-case-raises-kurdish-hopes-and-fears, accessed 22 February 2023.

Yavuz, M. Hakan (2018), 'A Framework for Understanding the Intra-Islamist Conflict between the AK Party and the Gülen Movement', *Politics, Religion & Ideology* 19(1): 11–32.

Yavuz, M. Hakan (2019), 'Understanding Turkish Secularism in the 21st Century: A Contextual Roadmap', *Southeast European and Black Sea Studies* 19(1): 55–78.

Yavuz, M. Hakan and Ahmet Erdi Öztürk (2019), 'Turkish Secularism and Islam under the Reign of Erdoğan', *Southeast European and Black Sea Studies* 19(1): 1–9.

INDEX